I Want My Life Back

I Want My Life Back

STEVE HAMILTON

■ HAZELDEN®

Hazelden
Center City, Minnesota 55012-0176

1-800-328-0094
1-651-213-4590 (Fax)
www.hazelden.org

ISBN: 1-59285-083-9

Library of Congress Cataloging-in-Publication Data
Hamilton, Steve,
    I want my life back / Steve Hamilton.
        p. cm
    "First published by Penguin Books (South Africa) (Pty) Ltd 2002.
  Reprinted for U.S. distribution by Hazelden Foundation 2004"—T.p. verso.
    ISBN 1-59285-083-9 (softcover)
       1. Hamilton, Steve. 2. Narcotic addicts—South Africa—Biography.
    3. Recovering addicts—South Africa—Biography. 4. Alcoholics—
    South Africa—Biography. 5. Recovering alcoholics—South Africa—
    Biography. I. Title.

    HV5805.H36 A3
    362.29'092—dc22
    [B]   2003056937

08 07 06 05 04   6 5 4 3 2 1

Typeset by CJH Design in 11/15 point Melior
Cover photograph by David Goldblatt

Names have been changed to protect both the living and the dead. While
the clinics and institutions named are real, events described as taking place
there are a synthesis of various times and various groups in which Steve
Hamilton participated, and are not in any chronological order.

Mom, Claydie and Candy

Just for today

BITTERSWEET

They don't smack them on their bottoms anymore, not like you see them do in the movies. They massage their stomachs, gentle but firm, and then you hear it – that first sound, the one that says Life! Oh, man. That's a sound that will live with me forever. I cried like a baby. I cried *with* my baby.

My son. Claydon.

And then the panic closed in again. What had we done, me and Candy? How irresponsible were we, how arrogant, daring to risk bringing a child into the world? Into *our* world? There would be something wrong with him, something physical. You don't do your bodies such damage over so long a period and expect to get away with it. And the punishment would be there, waiting in the wings, ready to sling that curve ball, just when you were beginning to relax and think you'd got away with it. Was this child to be my final punishment?

But no. Claydon was perfect in every respect. The toes, the fingers, the milky, unfocused eyes, the warm heart that beat in a steady, constant rhythm, the little soul that snuggled into my neck and said Hey, man – guess what? I chose you.

ONE

I can't write this book.

I've been staring at this sheet of paper for half an hour.

As blank as my mind. As white as a line of cocaine.

I'm qualified to write it all right, but I don't have the skills or the words. The only spellcheck I have is my sister's old school dictionary. Even if I knew how to use a computer, I can't afford to buy one. My education kind of got interrupted. I never got a matric and I've never even had a proper job, not one that I've kept for very long anyway. Some jobs, yes – but not proper ones with pension schemes and corporate ladders to climb.

My mother got me a job at Pelindaba once, you know the place – where we used to make atom bombs or something before we signed that treaty? I got to wear a sort of space suit thing and I had this appie guy, Reuben, who was black and he wore one too. It used to make us piss ourselves laughing just to look at ourselves, we looked so weird. We worked a kind of assembly line shift where we had to stick labels with arrows on them onto these components of god knows what. If the arrow pointed left it meant something significant. If it pointed right it meant something else. Either way you had to get it right or the world would blow up or something. I can't really remember. We were so high most of that time you could have stuck the arrows on my forehead and I wouldn't have known the difference.

I didn't last there very long.

But I should start at the beginning. The trouble is I've had so many beginnings it's hard to pinpoint the one that led me here, to this moment. Was it before I was born, when two families on continents seas apart, who couldn't have been more different in class or culture, threw up the two children who were to be my parents? Or was it when I died for the third time? Or maybe the day that Candy's life collided with mine and changed my view of the world forever?

Well, whatever the beginning is it's all tied up with birth and death. That's not very profound, I guess, but it's the only truth I know.

The predictable way to start this book would be simple and comfortable. You'll recognise it – the pattern and the shape. It will either turn you off immediately or you will read on, but distanced, knowing that you are reading someone else's story which has nothing to do with you, never will. This is how it goes.

Hi. My name is Steve.

I am a drug addict.

There. You see? Been there. Seen the T-shirt. Done the rehab tour. We all know where this is going and, admit it, it's one big yawn.

The trouble is the paths we take to get where we're going are so deceptive we hardly know we're on them until it's too late. Take my path, for instance. What are we looking at – broken home, alcoholic father, getting in with the 'wrong' crowd at school (hell, I was the wrong crowd at school), rebellious teenager, awkward with the opposite sex. A bit of petty theft, mom's small change, that kind of thing. It's not so unusual, probably more like the norm these days. Who hasn't got a dysfunctional family, I'd like to know?

But not everyone from a difficult home becomes a drug addict. Kids from perfectly wonderful environments, well, on the surface at least – stable two-parent, two-sibling homes, private schools, everything that opens and shuts, timeshares overseas and satellite TV – hey, they get just as wasted. You may not trip over them in the gutters first time around, but they're certainly underfoot in the rehab centres that stretch their parents' medical aid resources to the limit.

So that's the first thing.

It could be you.

No matter who you are, where you come from

and where you imagine life may take you, believe this if you believe nothing else:

It could be you.

It could be you filling in Drug Addict in the Occupation slot on your application form for a housing loan one day. If you get that far, that is. And even if you do, I can guarantee you right now that your application will not be successful. Bureaucracy is not enormously understanding when it comes to jailbirds and junkies.

So. Where does it start? I'll tell you where.

In a shopping centre. In your girlfriend's bedroom. In the park across the road. It's dead easy.

As you take that first joint from your friend across the table in the coffee shop, before your fingers touch momentarily and you share that look which says What the hell – just pause for a minute before you pull the smoke into your lungs. Just pause and remember this: there are no rules. Your friend could smoke weed for ten years and be fine. So could you. You could both be telling your kids one day that Sure you smoked a bit when you were their age. Everyone did. It was no big deal. It never did you any harm. Every kid has to experiment.

On the other hand, you could be writing this book.

The point is – when you take that first step, you don't know which story you'll be writing.

Some people say that there is a certain predisposition to addiction, that it's all in the genes. That's all very well, but how do you know exactly? And if you do know, will it stop you anyway?

What I do know is this: there isn't a high that doesn't turn on you. Not one. Not one time did the good feeling last long enough or stay clear in my memory for long enough to make me say I didn't need to feel it again.

You're not going to do it just once. Trust me. You're not.

The interesting thing about weed – which, after cigarettes and alcohol, is the next step you'll take – is that it really does feel so harmless. It doesn't matter what or where the circumstances are – and actually peer pressure doesn't come into it that much these days, no matter how fondly parents and teachers might like to bang that old drum. Let's get one thing out of the way right now: smoking weed, drinking alcohol, or going that extra bit of the way onto something more interesting – doing this stuff is not even daring. Everyone's doing it. It's that simple. Sure, you have to be a bit careful and keep an eye out, depending on where you are (the hockey field's not the best plan, and probably your boyfriend's bedroom could be chancing it) but it's pretty matter of course.

The curious thing, though, is that your first time is going to be boring. Nothing happens. Let's face it, it's a let down. Maybe you think you're not doing it right, not inhaling deep enough or something. You're unsure for a start about what's supposed to happen, and they say everyone's experience is different. Ask any thirteen year old – they're the experts.

Alcohol's different. More measurable than weed. And most people start there anyway. For the novice alcoholic it's pretty certain that, because your tolerance level is probably low, if you keep drinking long enough you'll feel dizzy, slightly uncoordinated, words'll get tangled up in your mouth, and eventually you'll vomit. You'll also feel terrible the next day. You may have a bad headache and feel nauseous. Nauseous but kind of proud. There's something of the rite of passage about getting drunk. And when you start young it's such a comfortably predictable topic of conversation. (Actually, it's extraordinary the number of people who still talk about it when they're forty-five and the note of pride is still there ... I see it every time I talk to a group of business people.) You'll talk a lot about how *vrot* you got with your friends. There'll be a sort of nonchalant 'how many Smirnoff Ices I drank before I threw up' competition. If you're a guy, girls will generally be impressed by this sort of information. At least that's what you imagine. It's information that's casually shared – that's the trick of it – with a mixture of bravado and regret and insincere protestations about how you really are going to stop drinking (as if you've been doing it since you were three and, at fifteen, it's finally time to take stock of your concerning alcohol intake). But the next time, when the headache and the nausea have worn off, and you're with your mates, you'll do it all over again. It's what you do, after all, and it's fun. You'll remember the feeling. You'll have a great time. Your confidence swells. You're funny and cool and everyone likes you. And oh no, you're pissed again – how many of those things did you say you downed tonight? Jesus, you can really put it away! Said with admiration, not disgust.

Disgust comes later.

That's alcohol.

With weed there's a subtle difference. It's not like getting drunk, when your head spins and you can't walk straight and sooner or later you deposit your supper of mealies and peas on your shoes. The effect of alcohol is definable. You can tell pretty easily when you're drunk. The effect of weed is less so. The first time, the second, even the third – not a lot happens. It's quite boring really, disappointing even. Lots of theories go through your head: you think to yourself that you're probably immune. You've heard that weed actually doesn't affect some people at all. Perhaps you're one of those. Alternatively, it may feel hell of a nice. You might find everything's funny, you might feel pleasantly weird, but it's all so gentle and mild compared to the scare stories the drug talk people tell you and the incredibly dreary lectures you get from your parents and the recovering junkies they parade during Drug Awareness week in high school. The exaggeration is ridiculous. They do it to scare you, the hand on the hot stove routine. Give you a big enough fright and you'll steer clear, although who on earth came up with that idea as a deterrent for the average curious kid? Rather believe what the rastas say: it's a herb, it's natural, it grows in the ground. God made it. Ganja makes everything peaceful. How bad is that for a philosophy? And besides, you know you can do this and not get burned.

Don't you?

Of course you do. Just like you know you can stop.

Any time you want.

TWO

My father taught me many things, but the most important thing he taught me was how to lie. He was good at it, but hell, I became the master. I was his alibi, the security he'd put down on the kitchen table when we'd taken two hours to buy a newspaper.

We bumped into Pete, didn't we, Steve? Boy, that guy can talk. We just couldn't get away. Could we, Steve?

My mother used me too, by trying to turn me into a safety net. Early on in the evening, when my father came home from work, she would use me to try and stop him from going back out again, back to the hotel. First we would go through the family charade. My father would start us off. It went like this.

I'm out of cigarettes. Just going to the café. Back in a minute.

Wait. Take Steve with you.

A moment's hesitation. But I'm just –

Take Steve.

A sigh. A small frown of impatience. I would play the role of spectator at this stage, my head turning from one parent to the other.

Then, Oh all right. Come on, Steve. Let's go for a drive.

And don't take too long. Supper's almost ready.

Sometimes my father would stop at the corner café and actually buy cigarettes. He'd bring me a packet of chips, maybe a comic, and I'd feel special, singled out. Out with my dad. Just me and my old man. Then he'd pull up outside the hotel – Got to have a quick word with someone – wait here – and my heart would drop like a stone to the pit of my stomach. What was I thinking? Did I really believe we'd go home in time for supper with twenty Peter Stuyvesant and a loaf of fresh bread? When would I get it through my thick head that I wasn't the companion I thought my father wanted? I was the excuse, that's all. The excuse. Take the boy along and we'll all buy into the pretence.

Well, that was how I came to understand it later, I guess. At first I must have believed what my dad told me. He was my dad, my hero, and I listened to everything he said. And when he told me what to say if my mother asked if we'd stopped off at the hotel, I obeyed him to the letter. We never went near the place.

At four or five years old I got used to instructions and I learnt quickly because it kept me out of trouble. Stay in the car. Lock yourself in. Don't touch the radio, you'll run the battery down. I'll only be a minute. Read your comic.

I think I learnt to drive in all those long 'minutes' I waited outside the hotel for my dad to have his conversation with a work colleague. I'd play with the gears, moving through them smoothly the way I'd seen him do – first, second, third, then lean down and get the tricky reverse gear working. I kept my eyes on the side mirrors and checked out everyone who passed by the car. I read comic after comic. I listened to every station on the radio, flipping from one to the other. I kept the windows up and watched the hotel doorway.

On average we'd be gone for an hour, but sometimes it stretched to two or even three. Some nights there'd be a plate for me on the kitchen table when we got home, covered with a saucepan lid. My sister would be asleep and my mother would have gone to my parents' bedroom and turned the radio on loud. Other nights my mother would be waiting in the lounge and, desperately avoiding confrontation, I would sneak past her, sick with guilt, and run to my room and jam a pillow over my head to keep out all sound.

My earliest memories. I *think* these are my earliest memories. I've got brain damage, though, so I can't be sure.

Anyway, what I do know is that to this day I cannot bear to be sitting still in a closed up car for too long. I have to have the windows open. I have to be moving. I have to have a cigarette in my hand. I need to watch that hotel doorway.

✳

My father was a Scot, born and bred in Glasgow. He grew up working class, where money and food were in short supply and an education meant getting out there and trying to earn a living by the time you were fifteen. His family was dirt poor and they lived in the filthy, overcrowded conditions that are typical of an innercity slumland, where running water was a luxury and one toilet was shared by several families. Alcohol and violence were part and parcel of their lives, as inseparable as a pair of Siamese twins.

My sister went to Scotland for the first time not so long ago and she visited my father's birthplace. It was a bleak and dismal pilgrimage and the place she described, it seemed to me, would be the kind of place anyone would want to make an escape from. Together we tried to find a slot in that scene for the picture we had of our father and come up with something that might make us feel better about him. It seems that he must have got halfway there in coming to Africa, to a place where the sun shone a lot of the year and opportunities were there for the taking. But something wouldn't let go of him – fear, maybe, or the prospect of not making it and having to return to the slums. Whatever it was that put the bottle in his hand and kept it there for so long, I'll never know. I can't ask him now. My father died when I was sixteen and the time I might have asked him about it or tried to understand is long gone. No father and son heart to hearts for us.

He was too busy wiping out brain cells with alcohol. I was doing the same thing with mandrax and dagga.

When my father emigrated in search of a better life, he had big hopes and romantic dreams. Once, before the booze took its place, I like to imagine that he had music running through his veins, for my father was a singer, and a good one. He had a beautiful light tenor voice and when he sang the ballads that would bring tears to my mother's eyes (they still do) – Moon River, Love Letters in the Sand – he sounded just like Matt Monroe. We thought he was *better* than Matt Monroe, and on the few occasions I remember him doing it, when he got up on a makeshift stage in a hotel bar, or once or twice at Christmas time, he could hold a room captive with a microphone in his hand.

My mother fell in love with that man.

She fell out of love with the man who replaced him when alcohol became his mistress, and the music in our house gradually disappeared down the neck of a beer bottle, along with my father's dreams.

The first job I remember my father having was about as far removed from a stage career that you could get. He worked in a supermarket. Later he got a better job, with a company that sold dog food, and quickly worked his way up to area manager. He was a hard-working man, who took the role of breadwinner seriously at eight o'clock in the morning but forgot all about it by the end of the day when the sun was going down and his mistress was calling. Miraculously, I never knew him to miss a day's work. He was late sometimes, yes, but he never missed a day. He would set off in the morning in his safari suit, pressed to within an inch of its cotton life, his dark hair slicked back with Brylcreem into smooth stiff lines, and smelling of Old Spice aftershave. I used to love that smell.

It's odd to think of it now, how fastidious he was about hygiene, cleanliness and good manners, when the overriding image of him that I carry everywhere with me in my head is my father buck naked, pissed out of his tree, lying on the lounge floor with saliva dribbling out of the corner of his mouth. Not very Matt Monroe really, when you think about it.

The dog shows were cool. He would take me along with him when he had to set up the sponsor's branding material. I loved that. I loved the whole atmosphere, the noise and the smell, kids with mutts of all kinds, serious middle-aged women with dogs who looked like them, right down to their perfectly groomed hairstyles. I nearly burst with importance. I was an insider. I worked there, with my dad. On a good day I'd be allowed to help him set up the banners and the flags and hang out with him and his buddies in the sponsor's caravan at the showgrounds. While they cracked open the beers from the small bar fridge at the back I'd wander around and watch the people with their dogs and dream of owning a champion myself one day, of putting him through his paces with my dad watching.

I, too, had my dreams.

✳

One night – I couldn't have been more than six or seven years old – we'd overstayed our welcome at the hotel. It was quite late and dark already. My father was so drunk he had to walk up and down the pavement a few times before he spotted our car, or maybe he saw my face pressed up against the window where I'd been breathing on it and drawing pictures. Whatever. I knew we were going to be in trouble with my mother this time. Deep trouble. This was much later than normal *and* it was a school night. It was dark so my father was having difficulty finding the key and fitting it into the ignition. When he dropped the whole bunch onto the floor for the second time I picked them up for him and held out the right one. He took it without saying thank you and we pulled off, gears grinding. Just before we hit the highway he dragged me onto his lap.

Hold the wheel for me, Steve. Just for a minute. I'm not feeling too good.

This wasn't the same as steering my Ferrari round the bends at the Grand Prix while the car was stationary alongside a pavement. I went rigid with fear. I urgently needed to pee.

I can't, I said, knowing as I said it that I was risking a *klap* on the side of the head. You didn't say no to my father when he wasn't feeling too good. You stayed out of his way.

Yes, you can, Steve. He put my hands on the steering wheel and I felt his left arm jerk through gears and the car bump forward, up the onramp and onto the highway. I clutched at the steering wheel. It was slippery beneath my hands. I could feel my heart in my chest beating like a hammer.

Dad –?

. . . nearly home . . . doing great . . .

In spite of my terror, I couldn't help feeling a small thump of pride at the approval in the fuzzy words. Steve was doing something right for a change.

I tried to ignore the strong smell of alcohol on my dad's breath and fixed my attention on keeping us going in a reasonably straight line. At least I knew the way home and it wasn't very far – which was just as well. My father seemed to have forgotten that there was another shift after third gear and the car made a high pitched straining sound as we drove. I couldn't look round, of course, but I think he may have been asleep. Cars zoomed up behind us and whizzed past so fast they made me feel sick and dizzy. Some of them flashed their lights. I was scared but shit, I concentrated every fibre of my small body on keeping that wheel straight and staying on the road.

Until we hit the trailer and the boat.

Dad? Dad! Slow down. Slow down! We're going to – There's a – I can't . . .

What I couldn't do, of course, was reach the pedals. The distance between the driver's seat and the pedals is not calculated with a six year old's legs in mind. All I could do was steer. Either into the oncoming traffic or into the trailer and the boat. Both choices sucked.

The driver of the car that was pulling the boat

was not impressed. I can't remember exactly what he said to my dad, but when he pulled his jaw off the tarmac at the sight of a kid driving his drunk father home, he yanked him out of the driver's seat by his shirt and laid into him, physically and verbally. I was frantic. We were in enough trouble with my mother as it was. Now we were going to be even later. She was going to *kill* me for letting this happen. I tried to get between them but I could have been invisible for all the notice they took.

Worse was to come. Swearing viciously, the boat-trailer driver reached into our car, snatched the keys from the ignition and tossed them, with a Get your fucken mind right, man, into the bushes at the side of the road.

I couldn't believe it. I nearly had a heart attack. It was pitch dark. I was six years old, on a highway, with a man who couldn't stand up straight, not only on account of the seventy-nine brandies he'd poured down his throat during the course of the evening, but because he'd mistimed his duck and now had the beginnings of a shiner on his cheekbone into the bargain. Just *how* was I going to explain this one to my mother? *And* I still had to colour in my Bible picture for school to-morrow: Abraham sacrificing his only son Isaac, with the goat standing by, just in case God changed His mind.

I searched desperately among the bushes for the keys while my father swore at me and cursed the boat and the trailer and peered stupidly at the front bumper, in between pointing me to the keys in completely the wrong direction. Cars whooshed by us, sending dust into my already watering eyes.

There – what's that? There, no, *there*, Steve. Are you blind, for chrissake? Hurry up. Stupid bloody thug, who does he think he is? What's he doing on a highway with a boat anyway? It's irresponsible. Bloody irresponsible.

I took no notice of him, intent only on finding the keys and getting us home before all hell broke loose. Although it was probably too late for that already. Fortunately, this time we were in luck. I saw a dull gleam just off the road a couple of metres back. The keys!

My father drove home. I think he was sobering up by then. We didn't speak at all. I was concentrating on holding in my bladder.

The front door was open and all the lights in the house were on – usually a dreadful sin in my father's eyes, wasting electricity, but I didn't think he'd have a go at my mother for it tonight somehow, judging from the expression on her face. I went straight to the bathroom and ran both taps in the basin, wasting water too, but I didn't care. I needed to block out the shouting that went on, that night, for a very long time.

※

It was always the same.

My father would come home late after work. My mother would see immediately that he'd been drinking and she would start in on him. We never had Hullo, honey, how was your day in our house.

Look at you. I'm sick of this. I can't go on with you like this. Look what it's doing to your son. Don't you care what your drinking is doing to – If you don't stop drinking I'll –

On and on she went. I hated it. We all did. But she couldn't help herself. And then my father would get angry. It was as predictable as the sun rising in the east in the morning.

Your bloody voice. You're like a stuck record. All I've had was – It goes with the job – Clients – I'm not bloody drunk but I should be. Living with you is enough to drive any man to drink. Oh, I'm not listening to this anymore. I can't take your endless nagging. Don't you ever change the tune, woman! I can't listen to this. And then the inevitable, now justified in his mind, next step.

I'd hear the car keys rattle, the kitchen chair scrape back, the front door open and slam back on its hinges against the wall. The door had been slammed back so many times the edge of it had made a deep scar in the wall behind it. I used to run my finger in it sometimes.

I can't stand this. I need some fresh air. I have to get out of here.

Not much fresh air in the pub, I wouldn't have thought, but he'd found the justification he needed to leave the house again and off he would go. What was a man to do, with a wife who just never let up?

My mother would cry or shout at us, or both. My

sister would tell me to leave her alone. The dog would lie farting on the kitchen floor.

Just a normal school night at the Hamiltons.

Later on, when my father came home, we were all alert, in our own way, to the signals. We could gauge, from the time we heard the family car take the turn at the end of our road, how the rest of the evening – and sometimes into the early hours – would play itself out. My sisters and I became experts at this game. If he was fighting drunk he would have difficulty negotiating the gate and the driveway. We'd hear the crunches and scrapes and the cursing. So would the neighbours, but we were beyond caring about that. Mostly he wouldn't manage the garage door so the car would stand out all night. Sometimes he would forget we *had* a garage door, or at least forget that it was closed.

Guilt would make him aggressive the minute he walked into the lounge. A single dog hair on the carpet would cause him to fly into a rage and he would have us all lined up at midnight, in our pyjamas, picking hairs – imaginary or real, who argued? – out of the carpet pile while he shouted at us all, a demented sergeant major with a beer in his fist like a weapon. My sister's hands would shake and she would cry and look at my mother, who kept her eyes on the floor. It was a patterned carpet and dog hairs were hard to spot.

One time, during a very bad patch, when the cycle was about to repeat itself yet again – my parents arguing about my father's drinking, my father about to turn his back on the relentlessly nagging wife and depart for the hotel, same old, same old – my mother followed him out to the driveway and grabbed the car keys from him and said You're not going. I've had enough. You are *not* going.

I was about ten years old, I think, but it's hazy. A lot of that time is hazy actually.

That's what you think, my father said. You think I'm going to stay here and listen to you all bloody day? Give me the keys. Give me the goddamn keys.

No, said my mother. Over my dead body.

Give me the keys, NOW, or I'll –

He took a step towards her and we both flinched. It was Saturday, late afternoon, and we were outside in the driveway for all the world to watch the show, if anyone cared to, that is. Whether it was a reflex action, I don't know, but as my father reached for my mother's arm she threw the bunch of keys high into the air. They landed with a clatter on the flat garage roof.

Both my parents turned immediately to me.

Get the keys, Steve, said my dad.

Leave them there, Steve, said my mom.

Get up there this minute.

Leave him alone. Steve – don't listen to him.

I'd been on the garage roof lots of times. It was quite nice up there. You could see all the way to Brian's house almost. In summer it was too hot to sit on though. The corrugated iron would burn blisters on your bum. I climbed up slowly, picked up the keys and looped the keyring through my little finger. There were house keys on there, car keys, my dad's office key. The keyring itself was from the bottlestore. A small gift for a valued customer.

My parents had stopped shouting at each other for a minute. They stood below and stared up at me.

Good lad, Steve, said my dad. Toss them down.

His hand was stretched towards me, ready to catch.

Steve. My mother's tone was one of warning, but there was uncertainty in it too.

I gazed over the rooftops. In a street a couple of blocks from us I could see some kids skateboarding. A man without a shirt on was mowing grass on his pavement on the other side of our road. The sun was setting and everything had gone a sort of apricot colour. A bunch of starlings in a tree in our neighbours' garden were quarrelling noisily, jabbing at each other with stiff black beaks.

Did I even think about it? I don't know. Consciously, subconsciously, what did it matter? All I remember is that I threw the keys as far as I could throw them. Backwards. Over my head without looking. Never to be found again. Just a small, symbolic act: defiance, bravery, desperation – I don't know. I must have realised, though, even then, young as I was, that my father's drinking was destroying my mother and threatening to blow our fragile family apart.

What I didn't know, at age ten, was that Steve would take up the baton and set out to finish what my father had started.

A Day in the Life ...

I cut myself shaving the other day. Just a small nick. Didn't even need the obligatory little piece of loo paper to stop the bleeding. For the whole of the day I felt jumpy and distracted. I couldn't sit still, I couldn't concentrate on anything. I felt sick. I felt angry. I was uncomfortable in my body. Candy kept looking at me. I could see she was disturbed. It made me even more irritable. When Claydon wanted me to play a game with him I told him I didn't feel like it. It took a whole day for us to work it out.

Aftershave.

There's alcohol in aftershave.

I was craving.

And I've been clean of street drugs (just for today) for about twelve years.

THREE

I've got an exercise for you. Stop reading. Think about the last sentence you've just read.

And I've been clean of street drugs (just for today) for about twelve years.

Now don't lose your place – stick your thumb in this page or use a bookmark or whatever, and close the book. Now look at my photograph on the cover. Look hard.

Look at my eyes.

I'm thirty-nine years old in that picture.

My publishers were worried that it might be too tough, that it might put people off taking the book from the shelf in a bookstore. Imagine. I'm the topic of a marketing meeting, commercial decision making.

Let's look at this cover design. How do we sell this? Would you feel comfortable with this guy? God, he looks like someone you wouldn't want to meet in a dark alley . . . Pass the coffee, please. Who wants to order pizza? Maybe we should use some little design element, something to brighten it up, you know, give a bit of lightness to the subject. A butterfly, something symbolic? Something hopeful. Who'd want to have that face staring up at them from their bedside table?

Not me.

But I don't have a choice. I have to look at that face in the mirror every day and live with the accusation in those eyes. I use makeup in my shows, but there's no makeup on my face in this picture. It's all real. Behind every shadow and deep-etched line there's a story and I know each one off by heart. Put them together and it's Steve's story, and although I don't know exactly how it ends yet, I'm guessing it's not with happily ever after.

And let me tell you, it's not cool. It's not cool to be Steve.

What would I do differently if I could close my eyes and time travel back to the kid who, while waiting for his father to love him, smoked his first cigarette and downed his first shot of vodka? Truthfully? I don't know.

It's tempting to look for someone to blame and on dark days – and I have many of them – I do. I look around (addicts are very good at this) and there are plenty of circumstances and people to choose from. Pick a family member. Pick a persuasive friend. Pick a teacher who chose discipline instead of counselling.

But that's the easy option, blaming someone else for taking away my life. I can shout at them all until my lungs burst – Hey, you! Come back here. I want my life back! But they will turn their hands up, empty – I don't have your life, man – and shrug their shoulders. And there's only me left, standing alone, outside of the magic circle. Only Steve. Looking into the mirror.

That photograph was taken in a disused prison, the old Johannesburg fort on the fringes of Hillbrow, in a cell looking onto an exercise yard that was designed so that the sun's rays would never reach down inside its high concrete walls. It was about three o'clock in the afternoon, freezing and windy, and I was conscious of where I was. The irony wasn't lost on me either. Prison. Within a stone's throw's access to any mind altering, illegal substance I wanted. Hillbrow. I could walk right out of there, turn left and be stoned in a heartbeat. I thought about it too. The time it took the photographer to get that shot I would say at least a couple of dozen deals were going down less than a block away. Perhaps someone just like me was busy dying in a toilet with a syringe in the back of his neck while his buddies were passed out in the room next door. And a mother just like Candy's was going from filthy apartment to filthy apartment, fighting down the fear and revulsion, searching for her nineteen year old child with a crack cocaine habit.

One thing to remember about addiction is that it's a progressive disease. It will ravage you physically as well as mentally and it won't simply stop when you stop drugging. That's partly what you can see in that photograph. Even if you stop drugging, you still have the disease. You're still an addict. Remember this when you're seventeen and immortal. You're doing damage and right now you might not care (We all gotta die of something. I could get run over by a bus on my way home tonight. Cancer cells might be brewing inside my stomach anyway. Hey, there's only one road to my lungs so I might as well tar it) but later, trust me, you will. And regret is a desperate emotion. It eats away at you as relentlessly as any cancer cell.

And don't let anyone kid you: a drug death is never a good death. For one thing you die with your eyes open. Try avoiding that gaze while you're pulling a needle out of someone's arm in the hope that there might be something left in it for you. It's a gaze that will pull you back from beyond the grave time and time again.

When you drug, your body and especially your brain gets used to chemicals. They get to depend on them to have a good time, to relax, to feel OK about yourself, to deal with stressful situations, to function in a demanding job, to cope with looming exams – you name it. If you look to a drug to help you function, in the end you will come to depend on that drug just to get you through a day. Drugs can make you feel good, better than you could ever imagine. You will want to feel that way again, you'll see it as an almost intellectual desire, not a physical need. However you want to lie to yourself, you are going to want to satisfy this feeling, to reach for it again, just one more time. Sometimes this need is stronger than at other times. Even when you stop and don't start again, it still doesn't go away. Start on drugs and you will always crave *something*. You may choose to continue to feed that craving with drugs until they kill you – which they will – or not. But even if you walk away from drugs, there's still damage there and your body will constantly look for something to replace them. With me it's cigarettes. Candy too. We can't stop smoking. I've tried but I can't. I might go a day without weed, pinks, mandrax, acid or crack cocaine, but there's no way I can get through an hour without tobacco. Coffee. Coke – the kind that comes in cans – certain headache tablets. This is the pattern I set in motion when I took my first drag of my first cigarette and hurled up my school sandwiches, and it's a pattern that will stay with me till I die.

I've known addicts straight out of rehab, and I mean *straight* out of rehab, actually, even while they're still *in* rehab, who, before they've tossed the Get Well Soon cards in the rubbish bin have tried to make contact with their regular dealer. I know some who have stopped off at Pick 'n Pay on their way home to buy shampoo, and not because they have an urgent need to wash their hair. There used to be a brand with beer in it, a minute amount, that's supposed to make your hair shine. I'm not sure that you can get it anymore. I think they took it off the market, but fuck, when you're craving, anything will do . . . I've seen someone OD on a mixture of heroin and mayonnaise, the promise being that mayonnaise, being thick, will move more slowly in the bloodstream and prolong the high. Yeah, right. I knew a girl who used to stave off withdrawal by drinking the perfume testers in Stuttafords, and another whose drink of choice for the same reason was Brasso. Talk about what's your poison! One smelt good, the other didn't, but who cares – they're both dead now. A couple less junkies off the street, missed by no one.

Two kids I met in a Joburg rehab clinic one year – they weren't more than thirteen years old or so, I remember, when I was there for my second or third time. Hell, they were funny. They were always up to something, like naughty schoolkids (well, they were naughty schoolkids, I suppose). At a certain stage of 'recovery' addicts are allowed to go out on outings, in the safety of a group, to try to feel like normal, regular people, doing normal, regular things. One time we went tenpin bowling, up in Northcliff. I had been elected 'chairperson', which was a kind of supervisory, senior prefect sort of role, and it was my job to see that no one went AWOL. God – you'd think I'd be the *last* person to be chosen in any kind of supervisor's position. Remind me to tell you about the time I got a security job at a *casino*, for goodness' sake. Anyway, I watched these two out of the corner of my eye. They weren't much into bowling and stood apart from the others against the wall with their hands behind their backs, talking softly to each other, eyes darting everywhere like bad actors in a spy movie. I couldn't work out what they were doing but they were obviously up to something. I left them to it but made a note to check them out later on.

Back at the clinic I found them down at the bottom of the garden just as it was getting dark. I stepped out from behind a tree and shouted Drug squad! and they nearly shat themselves. It was quite hard not to laugh. When I demanded that they hand their stuff over, a makeshift pipe with something very evil smelling smouldering in it, I couldn't believe my eyes. They were smoking moss. Ordinary common or garden moss that grows in damp places between bricks and paving stones. What I'd observed earlier in the afternoon was their patient removal, using their fingernails, of bits of moss that had grown into the brickwork of the bowling alley potplants. They hadn't a clue what, if anything, it might do for them, but they were desperate. All they knew was that they needed to get high and hey, drugs is all about experimenting, isn't it?

But back to the other weed and what it does to your brain. (Harder drugs do much the same thing, but they do it more thoroughly and more dramatically.) I want to go with the herb first. It's easier to lay your hands on than moss these days anyway. I'm not an edu-cated man and I don't have all of the technical psycho-babble so if I put things simplistically, it's the only way I know how. The way I can best explain it is this: what weed does is mess with the way your brain is wired up. Not hugely at first, just a bit of tinkering, but significant nevertheless. I like to use the analogy of your brain as a maze with a whole lot of closed doors in it laid out in a certain design. Like your fingerprints, the design is your own. It's unique. It's different from anyone else's. And your reaction to one drug will be different from the reaction of your buddy's to the same one, or to whatever combination you might be experimenting with. What you probably don't realise and might not believe is that any dormant psychotic disorder, however mild or manageable or contained it might be on its own, can be unmasked when you do drugs, even the harmless herb. This is true as much for a simple quick temper as undiagnosed schizophrenia. Drug taking will always aggravate a condition. So, for example, if you're a person who is easily irritated, one of the effects that doing drugs may have in your case might be turning that temper, which under normal circumstances you may know how to control, into major aggression.

If you're going through some emotional issues, perhaps, and are feeling down and a bit depressed, weed may make you feel better in the short term and take you away for a while from whatever's causing your pain, but don't let anyone kid you: sooner or later it's going to backhand you bigtime with exaggerated mood swings that are completely out of step with reality. Maybe not right away. But maybe a couple of days later when you have an argument with your mother or a disagreement with a work colleague. Your reaction could be extreme, but you probably won't make the connection with what you breathed into your lungs two days before when you were passing a joint around with your mates.

Each individual has different trigger mechanisms and combination locks to the doors in their brains. When you do drugs you won't recognise the triggers, and the combination sequence that your brain has stored so precisely is going to surprise you and you won't even know it.

Not immediately anyway.

So you roll a joint and pull the smoke into your lungs and you're on your way to the good feeling. You open a door and go through it. The door closes behind you and you see that on the other side there's another door and, perhaps slightly to the left or the right of that one, yet another. As you move through the doors, they all close behind you and the combination numbers on the locks all change. Just a digit or two, that's all. Not like anyone would notice. But by the time you're coming down and you need to retrace your steps, you can't. No trail of breadcrumbs for Hansel and Gretel in this story. You want to go back the same way you came, through the same doors, but you can't because the combination on the lock of the door before the last one you went through is now the number on another door, to the left of that one, just slightly, so you go through there instead, and then back through another door you don't recognise but that's the only one your combination now unlocks. You'll find your way back, don't panic, and you'll feel like the same person you were before.

But here's the thing.

You're not the same as you were before. You have

been altered. The wiring in your brain has been tampered with, and it's been changed forever. How much tampering you want to do is up to you but don't ever let anyone tell you that you won't be affected, physically or mentally, by drugging. Too late. You're already there. So tamper away but don't ever pretend that you didn't know what you were risking. And if you trigger the wrong wire, look out. You could cause a painful short circuit.

You could even kill someone.

✳

My parents both smoked cigarettes and of course my father drank himself into oblivion most nights. Ashtrays and empties were the ornaments in our house. We never had a lot of money, but we were OK, I guess. If we didn't have the extras, it was because my dad didn't believe in spoiling his children, which meant that we seldom had treats or surprises. At Christmas and for birthdays we got presents, good ones too, although not necessarily what we wanted exactly. Now that I come to think of it, although my father was the dominant person in my young life and I loved him almost fanatically, I don't think he ever knew me at all. He would give me things he thought a boy would want, not the things he knew that Steve would want.

I remember one time I was desperate for a fishing rod. It cost R5. I knew exactly the one I wanted, I'd seen it in the shop, and it was the same as Brian's dad had given him. But this was mid year, a long way from a birthday or Christmas, and my father said no. No was no. I didn't get my R5 fishing rod. I think about it sometimes and the cynical part of me believes that it would have cut into his drinking budget and god help us, but that came first.

He did promise to take me fishing though, once, me and my buddies. I was so excited. I told my friends to pitch up at my house and bring sarmies. We'd be gone all day. My dad was taking us fishing! Then the day before he changed his mind.

I'm taking you guys to the racetrack instead. Kyalami. *Be ready.*

My status shot up at school and the anticipation was sky high. Steve's dad is taking us to Kyalami on Saturday. Do you know the *speed* those okes drive! It's all I can do to get *my* dad to take us to *movies*, but Kyalami –!

Be ready, Steve, he'd said.

Hey, I was ready. So were my mates. We were ready all day, while the edges of the sarmies slowly curled up in the sun.

And if you're listening somewhere, dad – I'm still waiting.

I think that was the last time I ever invited any-one over to my house. Perhaps once or twice I risked it, but it really wasn't a good idea. There's a terrible shame and embarrassment in leading the way to your bedroom over the obstacle course of your passed out father's legs on the lounge carpet. The slack, open mouth, the drool sliding unwiped onto his chin, the soft white belly spilling over his underpants, and your friends looking fixedly in the other direction, as if the wallpaper in the passage was the most fascinating thing they'd ever seen.

No – better to keep them away.

And better yet: keep away myself.

I began to spend most of my afternoons after school with my buddies at their houses or roaming the streets or climbing trees where we would sit, unnoticed, smoking cigarettes and feeling cool. Brian and me were close. His parents both worked during the week and partied at weekends. They had a well stocked bar, with shiny mirrors at the back of it, just like a real pub, and tall glasses with transfers of naked girls on them. Brian was hell of a proud of those glasses. His parents were always having people over. There was a lot of laughing, a lot of loud, teasing voices, music and goodnatured arguments. Sometimes they would dance. And they drank a hell of a lot of alcohol. It was one of Brian's chores to help clear up after his parents' Saturday night sessions and now and again, when I stayed over, I would help him. The empty bottles often filled the whole outside rubbish bin. Once a week the van from the bottlestore would arrive with fresh supplies.

I didn't say anything but I was curious about the alcohol at Brian's house. My father drank alcohol all the time but ours was not a happy home, full of friends and good times. Privately I decided that my dad must have been drinking the wrong kind of alcohol. It was the logical conclusion and Brian confirmed it. The booze his parents kept, unlocked, in the cupboards above and below their varnished knotty pine bar counter was definitely the feel-good kind. He'd already tried it. Lots of times. It was cool fun.

We sampled a bit of everything. Not one at a time, but all mixed in together. I vomited for an hour solidly and couldn't eat any supper when I got home. I told my mother that the cheap fishpaste she insisted on putting on my school sandwiches was off. I had a stomach ache and a headache. Food poisoning. I stayed a day off school and she threw the fishpaste away and brought me dry toast on a tray.

When Brian and I met up later I couldn't even have a cigarette. I still felt sweaty. He didn't look too good either.

I'm not doing that again, I told him emphatically. You've got to be crazy. That stuff will kill a bull. And don't bring that cigarette anywhere near me or I'll hurl.

Brian was made of sterner stuff. He made clucking noises and laughed at me. You chicken, he said. You just chicken. I threw a halfhearted punch at him and he kept clucking until I laughed too.

Don't, I warned him. My head's bloody sore, man. You fucken tried to poison me.

He ignored me. I've worked it out, Steve. We just did it wrong, that's all. We shouldn't have mixed those drinks. *That* was the problem. You got to stick to one type, like vodka or wine. It's only when you mix them that it makes you sick. Come over to my house to-morrow and you'll see. My folks won't be back till late.

No, thanks.

Ah, come on, Steve. What's the matter with you?

It became our routine. I hardly ever went home after school anymore. Rugby practice, Mom. I'm trying out for the surfing team. And Brian was right. I got to know how much I could drink before I'd begin to feel dizzy and throw up and how much I had to drink once I'd reached that milestone to start feeling *lekker*. After a while I didn't throw up much at all anymore. I was smoking a pack of cigarettes a day and drinking every afternoon, mostly with Brian, but James would pull in too sometimes and one or two other guys until there was a small group of us who hung out together regularly. We had secret signs and codes as we passed each other in the school corridors. We were so laid back. We were so cool. By Grade 7 we had vodka mixed in with the orange juice in our plastic school cooldrink bottles.

There was us – and there were the others, on the outside, looking in. They would generally steer clear of me and my buddies, stand against the walls as we swept past, avoiding the eye contact that might result in a shove or a jeer. The chicks would cluster together and shoot glances at us, scared and admiring at the same time. What did we represent to them? Danger, daring, that fuck the system attitude that is so alluring to all kids who long to test the boundaries but are too afraid to do it themselves.

Whatever it was, we were invincible.

We were fourteen years old.

Years later I met one of the kids who'd been in my class, one of the outsiders. The circumstances were perhaps a little unusual. I was standing in the shadows late at night near a set of traffic lights on the main drag through town, stoned, drunk, or both – I can't remember. I was the guy who appears out of nowhere at your window while you're waiting for the lights to change. In those days people were a little more trusting than they are now and would drive with their windows down sometimes, especially on the humid Natal coast, or they would open them if you gestured and adopted the right expression. Then they'd see the knife in my hand and before the lights had turned green I'd have wallet, credit cards, watch and wedding ring deep in the pocket of my denim jacket and be three streets away.

This guy drove a Porsche. It was a beautiful car, black, music blaring – OK, it was the Bee Gees, but you can't have everything. My lucky night, though, or so I thought. I was jittery, jumpy, adrenalin pumping. I needed money, quickly. I was coming down. I needed to make a plan. I needed to score.

Before I could show him I was armed, he rolled down the window and stared up at me, frowning in a puzzled sort of way.

Steve? Steve *Hamilton*?

Fuuuuck. What the hell was this? I kept the knife in my pocket.

I peered down at him. I'm Steve, I acknowledged,

but I took a step backwards. Guarded.

God, I hate you, he said. Then he told me his name – Ronan. It rang a vague bell. We were at school together, he said. You don't remember me?

I stared at him blankly.

He shook his head in disbelief. Jesus, he said, you made my life a living hell and you don't even *remember* me? He kept shaking his head.

The lights had changed but it was late and there were no other cars around and he didn't move. I had a strong urge to run but something kept me standing there.

You guys were so – you guys –

Even then, god knows how many years later, he struggled to say what he wanted to say. Then it came out: apparently there had been a girl he'd liked at school and he was too shy to approach. Me and my buddies had got wind of his crush and had made it our mission to ridicule and humiliate him in front of this girl until he'd begged his parents to take him out of the school. They hadn't so he'd made another plan. Every time he saw us coming, he told me, he would duck and take refuge in the school library. No way Steve and his buddies would be found dead in the library. He was safe there. He spent hours among the books, reading, reading, reading . . .

He tried to laugh it off now, still seeking a kind of camaraderie. Old boy to old boy.

Then he seemed to realise the unusualness of the location of our conversation.

And you, Steve, he asked. What – he gestured

vaguely at me, standing beside his car on a deserted road in the middle of the night – so what are you up to these days?

I'm unemployed, I muttered. I've had a bit of a run of bad luck lately . . . I left the sentence hanging there, but still I couldn't move.

I own seven companies, said Ronan from the leather seats of his Porsche. He didn't even sound condescending. He sounded concerned. I felt the edge of the knife in my pocket.

I own seven companies, Steve, he repeated. I can give you a job.

I hesitated for perhaps a second more. Then, Fuck you, I told him, the words vicious and bitter in my mouth, and I took off into the shadows without looking back once.

❋

The safety I found in my buddies and in alcohol would eventually not be enough for me. I still had to go home reasonably regularly and endure the sight of my mother cowering before the vicious daily battering that came out of my drunk father's mouth. When I reflect on those days now, I sometimes wonder about the difference between physical and verbal abuse. Domestic abuse is rampant everywhere, I know, and none of it is acceptable. While my father never actually landed a blow to my mother's face or body, although he certainly threatened enough times and swung at her now and then, the emotional beatings she took every day must have left her soul and self-esteem as bruised and broken as any bone. Neither option, physical or verbal, is acceptable, but a split lip can be stitched and a fractured wrist will eventually heal. It's the inside damage, the damage that you can't see I think must hurt just as much as the physical pain, perhaps even more. And, god help me but I was about to embark on a path that would cause more pain and more damage to my mother than my father's drinking ever could.

To this day my mother's blood runs cold every time the phone rings after six in the evening. What will it be this time? Your son's been arrested again. Your son's been picked up off a street near the docks in Durban, drunk, stoned and aggressive. Your son's been shot, you'd better come. A kid's OD'd – found in a gutter bleeding from the eyeballs. We believe it could be your son.

Your son is dead.

Fear and worry became a habit with my mother, like the cigarettes she smokes. It's her lifestyle now, and I have to live with the fact that I'm the one who shaped it. When she hears my voice on the phone, I never hear relief or tenderness or even simple pleasure. She'll never say Hullo, Steve. It's good to hear your voice. Her first words to me are always questions, sharp and direct as darts to a dartboard: Where are you? What have you done? What's wrong?

What's wrong?

The darts find their mark, every time. Bullseye. Straight in the heart.

INSTITUTIONS

So they take down all the usual details and walk me through the place.

Orientation time. Here's the dining room. Down there's your section. Mealtimes – pay attention, I'm only telling you once. This is where you are. You're sharing with Robbie.

Yeah, yeah, yeah. I know. I've been here before. Just once or twice. I know the routine.

Robbie. Garth. David. Whoever.

There's a smell here. It's vague, non-specific, but I recognise it like an old acquaintance. Still it makes me uneasy. It's the smell of insanity and, like stale cigarette smoke, it seeps into your skin, into your clothes, into some dark place at the back of your head. It never quite goes away, not altogether anyway.

So I'm sharing with Robbie.

I look across the room and at first I don't see anyone. Just a small shape beneath the bedcover. I look away. This room is like the rest of them – linoleum on the floor, grubby windowpanes. Good old nurturing, caring environment. I don't care. I probably barely notice. All I can feel is a despair that's as relentless as a physical ache and there's a refrain going through my head, over and over.

Not again, not again, not *again*.

God! I can't fucking *believe* it. I've screwed up *again*. I can't *believe* I'm here. I'm back where I started. *This thing will not let me go.*

I sit shaking my head, just shaking it, slowly, back and forth, and there's a kind of comfort in the rhythm of it so I keep doing it for a while.

Someone has brought my bag in. It's on the floor next to the steel locker beside the bed. I flick open the locker door. Empty.

Empty.

I'm cold, although it's thirty degrees outside apparently today. The floor is cold and I draw my feet up onto the bed and wrap my arms tightly round my knees. I start to rock a bit, just to warm myself up.

I'm suddenly conscious of being watched. My roommate is the smallest adult I've ever seen. Small bony fingers, as thin as a child's, grip the top of the bedspread, which is pulled up high, practically covering his whole face. Only his eyes are visible and they're staring at me. I feel a mild flutter in my chest, somewhere between panic and hysteria. Great. I'm stuck in here with a mute lunatic and there are bars on the window. What am I doing here, for fucksake? I feel compelled to say something but before I can there's the clang and clatter of metal trays and trolleys and voices, and then the door slams open.

I lie back and look at the slowmotion blades of the ceiling fan in the passage, while a nurse rolls up my sleeve, simultaneously talking over her shoulder in Zulu to someone just out of my line of vision. This time I'm too weary to care. I just lie there. I'm through fighting. Inject me.

The trolley moves on. The door closes and subconsciously I register the turning of the key. This is King George V Hospital – KG Five – in Durban. It's five o'clock and the sun is still high in the sky outside.

Bedtime for addicts.

❋

I don't know what the treatment is going to be this time – and who am I to be consulted, after all? I'm just the junkie, wasting good taxpayers' money. And I don't mean that in a bitter sense at all. I agree wholeheartedly. I *am* a waste of money. My life is not *worth* saving. I try to explain this but no one takes any notice. So are we going the sleep therapy route or some other zombie trail? Whatever cocktail of street and pharmacy drugs is now moving sluggishly through my tired veins, I couldn't give a stuff today. I just lie there and take it.

I'm buzzing along, in between sleeping and waking, when Robbie, in a blur of beige municipal blankets, has cleared the space between his bed and mine in one monkey-like leap and is crouching down beside my bed, with his face inches from my nose.

What the fuck – !

What are you on?

I don't know. Everything. Anything. You?

He tells me but I forget almost immediately and feel my eyes drooping.

He tugs at my sleeve. I know where the dispensary is, he whispers.

Everyone knows where the dispensary is, I say with the disparaging tone of one who's seen it all before, but my lips feel thick and clumsy and I'm not sure that he's heard me. I'm not even sure that I've spoken the words out loud.

Maybe it's the next day, maybe a few days after that, I don't know, but we talk again. I study Robbie curiously. He is as slight as a ten year old and has tiny pale hands with long fingers like a girl. He's quite ugly but has an angelic smile. Butter wouldn't melt in that mouth. He has a one-track mind though.

Listen – Steve! The dispensary.

So what, Robbie? It's *locked* for crying out loud. They give us our sweets and they *lock* it. You got brain damage or something? There's a fucking steel Trellidor across the counter even. Will you forget about the bloody dispensary for five minutes?

He grins at me, black button eyes shining.

I'm a locksmith, Steve. Didn't I mention that?

We get away with it for a few days before, like any thieves, we get too greedy and desire takes over from reason. How we don't kill ourselves and take everyone down with us into the bargain, I don't know, but word spreads like a bush fire on the addict grapevine. In no time at all Robbie and I have a nightly system going and we're handing out coloured capsules all over the place like Smarties and everyone's humming.

Every night is a midnight feast. The nurses know that something's going down but they don't know what. They look at the rest of us suspiciously and make notes on their clipboards, but Robbie's their favourite. He smiles at everyone and flirts with the night staff, leaning over their workstation and asking for hot chocolate like a little boy.

On the last night Robbie and I are in the dispensary together and we're so high we don't know what the fuck we're doing. This strikes us as hell of a funny and we're clutching at each other and alternately whispering – at least we *think* we're whispering – and snorting with laughter and Robbie's on my shoulders reaching for a tub of something or other on a top shelf when everything comes crashing down around us, literally and figuratively.

Fluorescent lights go on with a snap! and we're instantly blinded, shading our eyes and staring round us like rabbits frozen in headlights. Shoplifters, caught red handed with our fingers deep in the cookie jar. Many cookie jars. And they're spilling all around us from the shelves we've somehow managed to overturn in our eagerness. We're in deep shit and we know it. We've been bad. Very bad. And we know what's coming.

Detention – at the very least, and all privileges withdrawn.

Privileges, whispers Robbie as he's taken away from Steve's bad influence. We got *privileges*?

FOUR

In the early days of doing my show I was invited to a school out on the Cape Flats, near Cape Town. The principal was becoming increasingly concerned about drugs in the school and he told me that gang activity was getting to be a big problem too.

The community was a poor one, a mix of cloned council housing and informal makeshift squatter homes all jumbled in together, and bad potholed dirt roads that would turn to mud in the rainy season. I'd been there before and I knew that the dealers would do whatever they could to keep me out. They didn't want me winning any hearts and minds on their turf, that's for sure. The last time I'd come I'd had a gun pulled on me at the garage when I went to fill up with petrol and now I never went in without someone to watch my back.

Domestic violence and abuse was on the increase in this community and there were a lot of traumatised children falling in between the cracks, struggling to get somewhere against often awesome odds.

That day the southeaster was howling, sending the fine grey sand into your eyes and flattening the litter against the wire fence that separated the houses from the highway. I was doing the show outdoors and it was hell trying to get any sense out of my sound system. The school didn't have a hall and a couple of hundred restless kids, squinting into the sun, had been assembled on the concrete recreation area alongside the school buildings. On the other side of the road a group of rastas with a ghetto blaster had set themselves up in competition with me. Me and Bob Marley, head to head. Not much of a contest for a whitey out of his comfort zone, especially with the wind direction in their favour.

Most of the kids at that school, like others in the area, would have had gang and drug related connections – fathers, uncles, older brothers – and, in family tradition, their life paths were pretty much mapped out for them already. They'd be members of one gang or another long before their education was complete. Some of them would die violent deaths, some would be in prison, and others would kill themselves with drugs.

Nobody could hear me. The wind screamed feedback into my microphone, my props kept blowing over and the rastas' music came across loud and clear.

It was far more seductive than the show I was desperately trying to salvage. Kids were alternately dancing and being yelled at by various teachers stationed at the edges of the concrete slab of space. And just when I thought things couldn't get any worse, I discovered that that particular school was in the direct flight path of planes coming in to land at the airport down the road. I think the apartheid government picked out locations for Coloured schools very carefully. How any child could even *hear* a teacher let alone concentrate on learning anything as the six times or whatever a day Joburg-Cape Town flights came in to land, I don't know. All I know is it gave me a headache in five minutes flat.

Then two things happened. Firstly, without any warning the wind dropped completely, and any Capetonian will tell you how unusual that is when the Cape doctor has got his grip on the mother city. The southeaster can blow for days on end without letting up. It may ease off gradually or blow itself out overnight, but it never just stops. The second thing that happened was that the rastas' ghetto blaster packed in. Just packed in, in mid song, without warning. There was a complete hush. It was as if someone had taken a big gentle blanket and laid it over us, and there I was on my makeshift stage with a sea of brown faces looking up at me expectantly.

I did the show and when I was done and was putting my stuff together, getting ready to leave, I felt the familiar tug of the wind starting up again. In no time it was grabbing briskly at my cap, and from across the road, where the rastas had been fiddling with knobs and wires for the past sixty minutes, the music started up again too – only not so loud this time.

I hummed along. I like Bob Marley actually.

Before I hit the road I looked for a sheltered spot to light a cigarette and finish the half can of Coke I'd been saving. It was gritty with sand and quite warm. While I was standing there a kid of about fifteen came up to me. He had a serious, almost worried look to him. He was thin and gangly and there were a couple of buttons missing from his school shirt. He reminded me a bit of myself at that age.

I liked your show, he said. Thanks.

We got to talking and he told me his name. I'll call him Paul September. He told me that his unemployed father had just come out of prison – armed robbery – and that his mother had left home. She'd already done this a couple of times before when things got too rough. Even the times when his father did have a job there was never very much money coming in. Paul was not doing so well at school. He was thinking of dropping out and trying to find a job. Someone had to get an income going. He had three sisters, all younger than him, and a brother whose drug habit kept him one step ahead of prison, so far, it seemed, by sheer luck and the skin of his teeth. There had been some close calls. At the moment they were all staying at his auntie's place, in the two-roomed council house she'd waited fourteen years to get, and one of his sisters hadn't come home in a week. He'd heard she was hanging out with some guys who were members of a gang that was in direct conflict with his father's gang, the one he'd be initiated into shortly. He could see there would be trouble and he'd have to get involved.

No wonder the kid looked worried. I knew his story, though. Paul's situation was the same as every second young boy's at that school and all the other schools like it in that sprawling, overcrowded place. The patterns had been set. There were hundreds of Pauls.

What's your dream, I asked him softly.

I could see he didn't understand the question.

Your dream, I repeated. If you could be anything you wanted to be? Come on – everybody has a dream.

He gave me a suspicious look from under his cap. Then he said something, almost shyly, with his eyes on his shoes, and as I bent to catch the words the roar of a 747 over our heads swallowed them up. We both looked up to watch it pass and for a moment I was lost in the strength and power and magic of such an impossible machine. The ground vibrated beneath our feet.

A pilot, Paul said. *Dis my droom.*

It made perfect sense to me. Every day this kid sat in a classroom and looked out of the window as the planes came low over the roofs of the school buildings, and what better breeding ground for daydreams than double maths on a Tuesday morning.

It was a weird moment for me. I had had dreams

of being a pilot too once. I had always loved the idea of flying – birds, planes, same thing. Anything with wings, I guess. To me flying symbolised the two things I could never have: freedom and simplicity. Probably escape as well. I discovered in prison that prisoners have a thing about birds, too. It's well documented apparently. I heard someone even made a movie about it once. Something about this lifer who kept a sparrow in his cell. When I was about ten I made a cart out of a tomato box. I put wheels on it from an old doll's pram and I would trudge around the streets of our suburb pulling it behind me, looking for broken birds to rescue and bring home to fix.

Candy says I'm still bringing broken birds home and trying to fix them.

A pilot, I said. A pilot. You know what, hey?

Paul looked at me with the old, cynical eyes of someone who knows that dreams are for other people.

You can be a pilot, if you want to be, I said. You *can* get out of here. You don't have to be like everyone else. If you hang onto that dream and believe in yourself and stay in school – you can do it. I *know* you can.

His friends were hanging around, watching us. I could see that he was beginning to feel uncomfortable. Not advisable to spend too long talking to the enemy.

As Paul September sauntered off and I watched him throwing mock punches at his mates, I reckoned there was a different kind of cockiness in his walk that hadn't been there before. I was probably just imagining it, though, willing it, even. My eyes stung as I ground my cigarette butt into the sand at my feet.

Bloody southeaster.

✳

Last year I was invited to speak at a function in Port Elizabeth. It was quite late notice and, although I usually drive, with my stage manager, equipment and stuff, this time I was being flown up for the day. I didn't really want to go. Claydon wasn't well and I hated to leave him. I'd been doing a lot of work deep in gangland in the townships again and I was exhausted. I'd been shot at twice, with bulletholes in the bodywork of my car to prove it, and two guys in a red BMW with smoky windows had followed me home late one night, almost all the way to where I was living at the time, before racing off with screaming tyres. I was worried about leaving my family unprotected.

There was some delay before takeoff. They never tell you what it is, and probably just as well. Uninformed, we sat in the sun on the tarmac for an extra twenty minutes until I was beginning to get really twitchy. Me and confined spaces are not the best combination. I'd already been through the in-flight magazine twice and it was a long while to my next cigarette. That horrible, distorted tinny music was playing out of a speaker that seemed to be directly above my head. I recognised the tune – No Woman No Cry – played on *panpipes*, for heaven's sake! Bob would be turning in his grave. Even I felt insulted. I gazed out of the window at what I could see of the mountain, which that day was covered in black southeaster cloud, and I thought of that day on the Cape Flats some twelve or so years back now and the rastas and their ghetto blaster. If you were a stranger to Cape Town you'd think thick dark cloud like that, which all but obscures the mountain all the way down its flanks, can only mean rain and not what it does indicate – a howling gale, that whips at your clothes and can pull an open car door off its hinges if you're not careful.

The static sound of the intercom system broke into my thoughts.

Would Mr Steve Hamilton please identify himself to a member of the crew?

There's a certain sort of blow to the stomach, rather like when a lift drops too suddenly and you're not ready for it. For a moment I couldn't breathe. I felt winded. As I stood up, conscious of curious eyes on me, all I could think was candyclaydoncandyclaydon. *Please, no.*

There's a message for you. Could you come this way?

I was right at the back of the plane. As I followed the flight attendant down the aisle, with everyone's eyes on me, my heart was thumping. Through the Business Class curtains. First. When we couldn't go any further he opened a door and gestured for me to go past him.

A young man in captain's uniform turned and smiled at me.

Mr Hamilton. He held out his hand. Paul September. It'll be my pleasure to fly you to Port Elizabeth today.

*

Paul September and Steve Hamilton, both aged fifteen. Time to make some serious life choices.

Actually, I was younger than fifteen when I made mine. One of the questions I get asked regularly is How old were you when you got into drugs? I tell them primary school.

Primary school? They look shocked.

I nod.

No, but I mean . . . you know, *real* drugs?

Primary school.

I can see scepticism in their eyes. I know what they're thinking and they're beginning – with relief almost, because it means they don't have to take what I say too seriously – to believe that I'm going to spin them a few bullshit stories. Primary school – oh, sure. Dropping acid while learning the cat sat on the mat? No way. It doesn't make sense. But then I explain.

My first dealer was my best friend in Grade 1.

High up in the branches of a tree in Brian's garden, at the moment that my fingers reached out and took the cigarette he was offering me, at no charge of course – *Your first time is free . . .* – I was on my way.

I know what you're thinking now, too, reading this. Every kid experiments with smoking sooner or later. They just do. The progression from cigarette smoker to crackhead is not an automatic one. That's stretching credibility too far. Most kids are not going to be like me just because they smoke cigarettes. A twenty Camel plain a day habit might mean that they won't be running the Boston marathon anytime soon, but it doesn't mean they're going to end up like Steve, strapped down and raving in a psychiatric unit, either. Get real, man.

That's true. I know that. Most of them won't. And they're the lucky ones, the ones who simply risk emphysema or lung or throat cancer. Or heart disease. Or whatever. The fact, though, is this (and I know I've said it before, but I've got brain damage so bear with me): you don't *know* which person you'll be when you start smoking: Paul September, who probably smokes and has a glass of wine with a meal and that's where it ends, or Steve, who longs to be able to have that glass of wine but knows now, from bitter experience, that he won't stop there?

Social smoker to crackhead? It may look like a ten year journey to you, but for me, it's a nanosecond. But hey – you choose. Flip the coin and watch it spiral down, head-tails-heads-tails, before you slap it on the counter of the corner café and say Gauloises Light, please.

Most of the drug talk people who do the parent evening and school circuit thing will tell you that weed is the one they call the gateway drug. Start there and the chances get stronger of you moving on to other, harder drugs. They're right and they're wrong.

Personally, I'd identify tobacco as the first gateway drug and learning to smoke as nothing more than training.

A simple cigarette – gate 1.

Nine times out of ten that simple cigarette will take you to alcohol – gate 2.

A large chunk of the world's population will go in and out of those two gates for much of their lives and be perfectly fine. But then, in the right company, alcohol will take you to weed – gate 3.

Will you stop at gate 3 and turn back? That depends. Lots of people do. But if you *do* go through gate 3, do me a favour and do this one thing: arm yourself with knowledge.

I didn't.

Nobody told me just how much I was risking and because I'm an all or nothing type of person, I charged right through that gate – hell, I probably vaulted over it – without a backward glance. And when I realised that I wanted to go back, to reverse it all, I couldn't. It was too late. I was in.

Fall in love with your first high, man, and *you are in*.

I never met an addict who wasn't planning to be clean. I don't think I've met a smoker either who doesn't want to stop. I was introduced to someone a couple of days ago who told me, rather shamefacedly admittedly, that she'd given herself two years to stop smoking. Who is she kidding? I call those people the Christmas addicts. After Christmas, I'll stop. No, wait, New Year – that's a reasonable time. New Year's resolution. But hang on – I'm twenty years old now so I'll give it to my twenty-first birthday. That's a solid sort of milestone. That's when I'll stop. I'm going to give up. No, honestly. I am.

Tomorrow.

﹡

For quite a long time smokes and beers and the company of my buddies were enough for me. They took me out of myself. With my friends I could be someone. I was fun to be with. They liked me. They listened to my opinions – and when I was drunk I had a *lot* of opinions, all of them cleverer and wittier than anyone else's. I felt safe and accepted and understood.

I got none of that at home. Things were getting worse. My father was drinking more heavily than ever and quite often he would still be drunk in the morning from the night before. My sister and I stayed out of his way as much as we could and it was my mother who bore the brunt of his evil temper. The worst was when he had made a stopover at the hotel on his way home from work. On these occasions he would walk in the front door, calling out for us in this hearty, false voice. He'd have the evening newspaper under his arm and two chocolates, one for me and one for my sister, and we'd know immediately that he was drunk already. We'd have to say thank you and my sister would duck my father's sloppy, wet-lipped kiss and the whisky breath and go immediately to her room. I would wolf down my chocolate in one go and hang around, trying to tell him about my day as if he'd actually asked me.

There would be patches, although these were increasingly rare, where we would try to be an ordinary family and do an ordinary activity together, like go out for supper. I grew to dread these occasions. My father would come home early from work, only mildly drunk, not so most people would notice. He'd had a good week. His boss had praised him for implementing some minor cost-saving procedure. He was feeling generous.

Come on – let's go out for a steak. Let's go to the Spur.

My sister would mumble something about home-work, while I'd try to suppress the lurch of hope that sprang up whenever my father behaved like a normal dad. My mother would look apprehensive, but she'd get her bag and put on some lipstick and persuade my sister to come along.

Moths. We were nothing more than big helpless moths, unable to resist the lure of the flame we knew would singe our wings before we'd got to dessert. I hated myself for believing it would be different this time. I hated my mother for letting me believe. I hated my sister for the way she locked everyone out and sat on the fringes of the family pretending she wasn't part of us.

It was always the same. My father would be bad-mouthing the waiter within the first five minutes of sitting down and my armpits would start to sweat.

Where *is* the guy? What do you have to do to get service round here? A man needs a cold beer at the end of the day.

My mother would do her best. He's coming. He'll be here in a minute. Have a look at the menu.

I don't need to look at the menu. I already know what I'm having. Steak. We've come out for a *steak*, goddammit. Now I want a *beer*.

My father would twist and turn in his seat, trying to catch someone's eye. He'd put his hand in the air and click his fingers – Chief! Chief! – and my sister would slide lower and lower in her seat. I'd play with the sugar packets until my mother slapped my hand. Then I'd sit with both hands underneath my thighs, reading the labels on the ketchup bottles, rigid with embarrassment.

On one of these ghastly occasions I saw a girl from my class at school having dinner with her parents a couple of tables away. She smiled at me and I pretended I didn't know her. I remembered her name. I remember it now – Grace. She was a solemn girl with glasses and curly brown hair. In her first year in high school she would play first team tennis and get straight As. By the end of that year she'd give up playing any sport at all and I would have her coming to me every Friday for her supply of weed, some of which she sold on to her own friends for a small profit.

I heard she died in a rehab clinic when she was about eighteen. Way to go, Steve.

At least two, sometimes three beers would go down my father's gullet before our food would arrive. Well before then my mother would start.

Don't you think you should wait until the main course before – Please keep your voice down – The people behind us are – Remember who's driving home – Steve's tired. He was at rugby practice all afternoon. Give the boy a break – I think you've had enough – She doesn't have to finish it if she doesn't – You've had enough –

You've had enough –

You've had enough.

And if we didn't clean our plates, it would only make things worse because my father would launch into his ungrateful family speech. He'd start with the exorbitant cost of the meal and how hard he worked to put food on the table and look how we'd barely eaten anything. Then he'd tell us how he was simply trying to hold this family together and give us all a treat and nobody appreciated it and all he got for his efforts was

–

On the bright side I suppose we probably kept the restaurant entertained, and we never actually got thrown out, which was especially amazing given the noise level my parents' conversation would reach sometimes. The volume could go in the other direction, getting lower the angrier they got with each other, until I could *feel* the whole restaurant straining towards our table to hear. I don't know which was worse.

We seldom made it to dessert or coffee. My

mother, my sister and I would already be wanting to leave halfway through the meal but my father wouldn't let us move. He'd deliberately order another beer and make us wait while he drank it. And when he eventually called for the bill (which, by that time, the waiter would bring in a great enthusiastic rush) he would painstakingly go through every item, querying what they charged for a Coke (daylight robbery) and asking for a refund for the extra onion rings we'd ordered on the side but hadn't touched (bloody fraud).

It was awful.

I still don't like eating out in restaurants although, ironically, Candy and I take Claydon to one of the steakhouses in the Spur chain now and again, and Spur were one of my sponsors in the early days of doing my show. They're good with kids there. You can spill and mess and be a bit noisy without feeling self-conscious. Claydon can make outrageous demands of the waiters and they'll just smile and give him two balloons instead of one.

He can leave his onion rings anytime.

After my last time in rehab, in the late 80s, I got in with a group of young amateur actors who were putting together a stage play called *Drug!* which they planned to take to schools to teach kids about the dangers of drugs and what they can do to you. They made me welcome and listened hard to what I had to offer. I was the addiction expert, after all. We got closer and I began to think that maybe I even had a bit of a talent for this stage show stuff. They tried out some of my suggestions and they worked. I like to think a couple of my ideas gave the show impact and power that it had lacked when they'd started workshopping it.

After a while they formally invited me to join the group. Although I was reluctant (groups led to all sorts of trouble in my experience), I was also hell of a flattered. It was a step, and a good one for me, because my own plan was in fact to go out there – wherever *there* was – and do much the same thing. Warn people, especially kids. Arm them with the weapon that is knowledge. I didn't know how the hell I was going to do this. I just knew I had to and that somehow something would come along that I would recognise, some sign or signal to point me in the right direction. Maybe *Drug!* and my new buddies was what I'd been waiting for.

They were delighted when I said yes.

This calls for a celebration. Come on, Steve, we're going out for dinner. It's OK – this one's on us. There's this great restaurant down near the beachfront. Ah, come on, Steve – why not? This is a big moment. Even Shakespeare had to eat, you know! If it's the money – no problem. When you find your feet you can treat us. But we're family now, hey, family. And this is a family outing, a treat. Come on. Please?

No, thanks. I'm busy.

A Day in the Life . . .

I talk to a lot of people about drugs. I do shows in schools – a dramatised version of my life, mostly – and talks to parents, and presentations at corporate functions.

I tell my 'story' over and over again. This episode, that episode, the rough ride I had in the army, events in my childhood where painful memories of my parents fighting over my father's drinking feature quite largely. My buddies and me getting busted the first time. The second time. Me and a mate stealing his dad's car and cruising the streets looking for trouble when we could barely see over the steering wheel, false moustaches painted on our faces with koki pen to make us look older.

How this buddy died. How that one died. Damn it – how and why did we all die?

You'll read about these things in here. Forgive me, though, if I repeat myself. It's not a printing error if the same story appears three times in three different time frames and the buddy who died in the first story was James and the next version has him as Brian.

I'm not bullshitting you or making these things up.

The truth is I have brain damage. Drugs will do that to you. It's one of the small, irreversible side effects of prolonged abuse most of the turnaround users will forget to mention when they're telling you their happy ending, I-turned-my-life-around-and-became-a-super-

star stories.

There's different kinds of brain damage. In my case it's my memory that has been most affected, but in a perverse, cruel way. I remember everything, that's the cruel part. It's all in there – the cheating, the lies, the stealing, the callous using of friends and family without a prick of conscience. I remember it all. It's as vivid to me as any technicolour trip. And it catches me un-awares. I can be walking on a beach on a summer's evening and, without warning, I'm back in the hellhole of a flat in Durban watching my buddy die and the only thing I'm thinking is Hurry up and die! so that I can go through his pockets and get my hands on the rest of his drugs before someone else does.

Another way my memory plays tricks on me is in the ordering of things. I don't have a clear sequence of events at all. Times and places and people get all confused. There are whole blocks of time I just can't put in the right order. So I'm not sure which institution or rehab clinic came after which, or what age I was exactly when I went to prison for the first or second time, or even how long I was there. It's all in my head, yes, but the way I see it the filing system's fucked.

So if you're hoping for a neat chronological story here, stop reading. There's nothing neat or chrono-logical about me, probably never was. If you're ex-pecting to track how an ordinary kid from a middle class family threw his life away and ended up foaming at the mouth in some gutter somewhere, then turned it all around and became a model citizen, go back to the bookstore and swop this book for a book of fairy stories. That's not how it happens. This model citizen may relapse tomorrow and be back in the gutter by Tuesday.

So I can't take you with me each step of the way. You'll have to piece it together for yourself, if that's what you need from this book. I jump around, I go off at tangents. If I'm telling you about me and Brian smoking weed on the beach before school and in the next sentence I've dragged you with me into Addington psych ward twelve years later, bear with me, OK? You see, if I remember something important or significant I have to put it down right away or I might lose it and it will go back into the filing system (in a different place, of course) and not easily be found again.

That's the short term memory damage. The HTT (hold that thought) syndrome.

❊

In between working the schools and companies, I take crisis calls and, sometimes against my better judgement, meet with the sons and daughters of desperate families who have somehow heard of me. Steve is usually the last resort for these frantic parents. They've gone through the school drug policy's disciplinary action process, which might have involved suspension or counselling or both. They've had the shame and frustration of expulsion and of trying to find a new school that will take Peter, now well into the second term of Grade 11. Peter's history of spliff smoking on the golf course in his school uniform is not going to work in his favour and he's not exactly cooperating either. They've done rehab twice, three times. They've banned his bad-influence friends from communicating with him. He's only allowed out one night a week and then only to a safe environment like a shopping centre. No clubs, no parties. But still he's drugging. Where's he getting the stuff? They're at their wits' end. What more can they do?

Angela is one of those parents. She's a nutritionist on the West Rand, with a practice that's doing fabulously well and her son Daniel has been busted three times for heroin. He's seventeen and gave up on school long before his school gave up on him. He's on some serious probation restrictions now and has relapsed over and over again. His older brother has a drinking problem and was caught up in some very bad company a few months ago. For him physical removal was the best option and I helped get him out of the country and over to England where he tried to start afresh. Angela tells me he's not doing so well, but he's twenty-three and Daniel's her number one concern right now. I spend hours with Daniel, talking, talking, talking. I do this on Saturdays and once or twice on Sundays too. I give Angela a copy of my video. I hand out my unlisted phone number. I don't say anything but I can see where the drinking gene comes from and for someone so concerned with healthy eating, the medication she's on for keeping her nerves settled is not doing her much good either. But we're concentrating on Daniel today. I spend three hours with them, drinking coffee at a hotel restaurant. She has cheesecake and Daniel has a toasted sandwich. I am exhausted when they leave and to tell the truth, not very hopeful for Daniel's future. His deep blue eyes have a dead look to them. I hope I'm wrong. When I met him my first words to him, intended to scare, are now the same words I say in my mind. You're going down, bru. You're going down.

When they've gone I go to the toilet and wash my hands. I splash water on my face and look at myself in the mirror for a long minute. Then I walk out to the carpark, slowly, bone tired, to find my car. I realise I haven't seen Claydon for two whole days.

A waiter comes running after me flapping a piece of paper.

Oh yes. The bill.

FIVE

Hey, mom! What's this stuff?

Steve – no! Don't touch! No!

But what is it? Why can't I –

It's poison. Look. Look at the picture on the box. That's a dead rat. This is Rattex. If you put any of this in your mouth, you'll be like that dead rat.

Why is that foam coming out of its mouth?

Because before the rat died it got very sick.

Why did the rat *eat* the Rattex if it was going to make it sick and die?

I don't know, Steve. Perhaps it tasted good. And rats probably aren't that clever. They can't read labels. They probably don't know it's going to kill them.

But *I* know, don't I? *I'm* clever. And *I'll* puke yellow foam too, won't I, and get sick and –

Very sick, do you hear me?

Even if I have just a tiny taste …?

Even a tiny taste. You'll *die*, Steve. Like a rat.

✳

Rattex, huh?

I wish my mother had extended the lesson just a bit, perhaps to a line of cocaine. Sniff that up, Steve, and you'll die – poisoned – just like the Rattex rat.

Drugs, rat poison – same thing, same end. The only difference is time. Fortunately for the rat, though, death is almost instant. Addicts usually take a little longer.

That conversation has stayed in my memory my whole life. It made a deep impact on me. I wouldn't have dreamt of going near rat poison after that. I always read labels – why do you think I buy the pregnant pack instead of the cancer one when I buy my cigarettes?

Would you knowingly choose death, and such an agonising one, for something that might make you feel good for just a few seconds? What can you be *thinking*?

I'll tell you what.

It won't happen to me.

What did I tell you about falling in love with your first high?

I'm not going to lie to you and anyone who tells you different is not telling the truth: make no mistake about it, in the beginning drugs are cool. Really cool. And the good feeling that some drugs will give you is a *seriously* good feeling. So good that eventually you will sell your mother, your sister, your *soul* for it, for that five second rush that is so awesome, so mind blowing that every thrill you'll have without drugs after that will pale in comparison. Bungee jumping? Forget it. That's tame. The best sex you've ever dreamed of? Sorry – not even close. That rush is like . . . it's like . . . god, I don't have the words for it. Who can describe it? Perhaps the closest I can come is to call it an orgasm in the brain, a mind-fuck so amazing that you'll want to do it again as soon as possible.

So you do, and it's amazing all over again. Five seconds of ecstasy. Worth every penny. And you're functioning, you're going to work, you've even got energy to spare. And the weekend's coming up. Recreational drugs – such a great term, isn't it? It becomes what you do, how you play. You build it into your leisure activities. And it's so manageable. What's the big deal?

And while all this rationalising is going on, you've set a behaviour pattern with movable parameters that's going to be difficult to break. It could be that there's a bit of a conflict flickering around inside you at this point. In your heart you'll know that you should be paying attention to the road sign that is flashing just out of your line of vision, advising you to Turn Back Now. Danger Ahead. But at the same time your head is telling you that you're a competent enough driver and can negotiate any sharp bends or rocks that might have tumbled into the road. You know what you're doing.

Maybe you'll even draw up a sort of management plan. Mentally you give it a label – Harmless Fun – and you restrict it to Saturday nights with close friends you can trust. It becomes a weekend thing, under your control and in its compartment. Big difference between what you're doing and that horrifying photo in the weekend papers of a dead addict with a syringe still in her hand. No relation at all. Her drugs are different, just like the alcohol my dad drank was different from the alcohol that was in plentiful supply at Brian's house, remember? Brian's was the feel good kind. Your drugs are the feel good kind too. Recreational. That's the key word. And you play at weekends only.

But hang on. Friday's part of the weekend too, isn't it, and Wednesday there's a farewell party for one of your work friends who's emigrating, and shit but you've had a stressful week and deserve a little relaxation, and you know if you work through the night this week there's a good chance you'll get that contract and then there's some serious celebrating to be done –

So what happened to Saturday nights only?

Harmless Fun has slipped quietly from the wings onto centre stage.

You wake up in the morning and it's there. It's in your head all day, no matter what day of the week it is. There's a point somewhere round about now when your heart and your head are saying the same thing: You're in trouble here. You've got to stop this. You're getting wasted too often. But your mind seems to have learnt a strange little mantra and it slides smoothly over the small voice of your heart, eventually muffling it completely. This is what it says: just one more time, just one more time, I'll do it just one more time.

Your management plan might be littered with excuses by now but hey, you got the contract. No brain damage there. Quite the opposite, in fact. You've never been so creative, so inspired. Maybe if you just scaled back to Saturday nights again . . .? They're just fun drugs, after all, not real junkie drugs, and Saturday night is party night. Why can't you have the best of both worlds?

I'll tell you why.

Subtly, so subtly you won't even have noticed it, the intellectual desire to experience the rush just one more time has been replaced with a physical need so strong that it has burrowed like a leech into the very core of you and it has embedded itself there like an alien implant and now you have to feed it, and feed it, and feed it again. It's as voracious as that monster plant in that show – The Rocky Shop of Horror Stories, or whatever. Saturday nights is history, china. And the periods in between you using get shorter and shorter, and the stuff doesn't seem to be working so well for you anymore. Don't get me wrong – the rush is still intense but now so is the physical need. And the need is relentless. It's unforgiving. It will only let up when you satisfy it.

That's craving.

✳

For a very long time I had only two feelings, both of them at the extreme opposite ends of the scale: they were high or craving. Nothing in between.

What was my drug of choice? Whatever I could lay my hands on.

You don't care. You don't care a fuck what you're putting into your body, and whether it's pure or contaminated with good old rat poison, you're not going to know in advance. It's the spin of the roulette wheel, the gun to the temple. And as you're shooting up, the needle steady in your hand – *innn*, out, *innn*, out – waiting for the silent G-force roar in your head, when you're falling forward into the abyss in the seconds before you feel as if you're being flung violently backwards with that instant *whooosh!* to the brain that's as dramatic and sudden as a rocket bursting past your eardrums into the sky, you don't know whether this is going to be The One. The one that kills you.

For me that was part of the rush.

I call it the dance of death.

With drugs there are no half measures. It's either Yes or No. It really is. Which president's wife was it who had that whole campaign running against drugs in America – Nancy Reagan, Jackie O? I forget. Anyway the slogan was dead simple: Just Say No.

Hah.

Who did she think she was talking to, I wonder?

The annoying thing is, it's true. The snag is, it's not so easy. For *her* maybe. Although I'd put money on it that some of the people who are loudest in their advice on the dangers of drugs for the 'youth of today' are putting away triple gin and tonics at any given opportunity and have a comfortable relationship with their pharmacists. But let's not go there right now.

The fact is your only real weapon against addiction is your mind and it's a powerful weapon, believe me, the most powerful you'll ever have. Be careful though – it's also a double-edged sword. It's your protection, your *only* protection, against what could be a predictable downward spiral into the pain, anguish, degradation, alienation, fear, physical deterioration etc that drugs will tip you into (and that's on a *good* day) but it can also be turned and used against you in the blink of an eye. Who grabs it away from you and turns it against you?

You do, of course.

I knew, I *knew*, the very first time I smoked, that it was a bad move and I'd regret it. I knew it – right here in my heart.

My heart said No, my head said Let's go, my buddies were watching me . . .

The deeper you get into drugging the more blurred the lines of reason and self-deception become. The only advice you will ever take, in the end, is your own, and here's a tip – it's not an intellectual conversation. There *is* no debate. Keep doing drugs and you'll die. The only part of the process that could be up for debate is When and How painfully? Your mind, however, will turn it into a debate and there will be a lot of voices trying to drown each other out in your head. Which voice do you listen to – the one that says Get out while you still can, or the one that says You can handle this.

I've had that debate with myself many times.

✳

It might have been my sixth, maybe seventh time in rehab. I thought I had got as low as I could go and I was determined to stick to the straight and narrow. I was in my twenties and didn't have a thing to call my own. This time was going to be different. I totally bought into the programme. I totally believed that I'd been given my last shot at getting clean. I totally knew that this time – this time – I could do it. There was just no question in my mind. Steve and drugs were over.

I could be wrong but I think I almost made my mother proud. Maybe she was just pretending, but anyway, I thought I had her believing in me too. She told me she was behind me, that I could kick this thing, that it wasn't too late for me to become a productive, honest citizen of my country. She'd called in a few favours and somehow lined up a job for me on the Wild Coast, in a casino and hotel complex, part of which was still being built. I was on the security staff at the construction site. Security. Who said God doesn't have a sense of humour? Well, at least I could look the supervisor in the eye and tell him without lying that this was something of an area of expertise for me. Never mind the small fact that I wasn't normally the one in charge of the handcuffs.

Part of my job was to check what was being brought onto and off the site. I had a uniform and everything. The staff was housed in bungalows and in the evenings they'd usually hang out together playing pool or cards, gambling a bit. This was a high risk area for the likes of me and I knew it, but I was singleminded and focused. I was clean and planning to stay that way.

On my first evening a couple of the guys banged on the window of my bungalow where I was lying on my bed smoking and listening to the radio.

Hey, Steve. The guys are going to braai tonight. Wake up and smell the sausages, china. You coming?

I was tired. The first day on the job had taken its toll. It was going to take some adjustment, this responsible nine to five employee business. I said thanks but no – early night for me. I had to be up and at my post at five in the morning.

The second night there was a bang on my window. We're going up to play pool and have a beer. Come join us if you feel like it.

I did feel like it, but I weighed up the dangers – pub, pool, music – and came out with Dangerous Combination. I decided against it. I had another early night but this time I battled to get to sleep much before eleven. I could hear music and men's voices coming from the pub, those sudden shouts of laughter that go with mates in a pub having a good time. I closed the windows and lay sweltering in the Wild Coast heat, smoking cigarette after cigarette in the darkness.

I'm generally a friendly guy. I like company and talking to people, but at this stage of my life I had no real friends. Drug addicts don't have friends. They have *drugging* friends and that's a different dynamic altogether, based on codependence and usefulness. They drift in and out of each other's lives and eventually fade away, sometimes to die, sometimes to rehab, usually just going wherever the drugs are. I could have done with some real friends, ordinary people who did ordinary things.

I badly wanted to fit in here. Even though I'd just arrived, I could tell they were a good group of people and I could see they had formed a close little community that worked hard during the day and partied hard at night. I longed to be one of them. When I turned down their invitation the third night in a row I could tell they thought I was a bit strange, standoffish. I was torn. I didn't want to be the outsider again.

On Friday night I took a long hard look at myself. Physically and mentally I was feeling strong. I was handling the job just fine and, which came as something of a surprise to me, I was actually beginning to enjoy the responsibility and the fairly tedious routine. I was going to be OK. I thought I could allow myself a little time out.

The pub was buzzing. The air was thick with smoke and noise and I stood squinting in the doorway, shading my eyes, to see if I could spot someone I knew. In the dense smoke haze the only thing that was clear was that the barman was being worked off his feet.

Steve!

I was punched on the shoulder a few times and then dragged into a game of pool with two of the guys I knew from the site and someone called Jake who worked in surveillance whom I hadn't met before. Jake was not entirely sober but he had a big welcoming grin and a grip that nearly cracked a knuckle when he shook my hand.

What you drinking?

Just a Coke. Thanks.

He looked at me and I smiled. Coke's good.

I drank Coke all night and got to bed, happy, tired and sober, at two in the morning. I was back with my new mates on Saturday night. We had a braai and I drank Coke. Then we played a couple of games of pool and I drank Coke, and although I didn't feel even the slightest urge to move on to alcohol, the sweetness was beginning to get to me. With apologies to the manufacturers, there really is only so much Coke a man can drink – especially in a bar surrounded by people in various stages of inebriation. Nevertheless, I felt fine, and all the voices in my head were singing in perfect harmony.

I was so chuffed with myself. I was clean. I was clean. I was in control. Mentally I gave the finger to all of those people who thought I couldn't do it. I gave a double finger to my old headmaster whose words still lurked deep inside my skull. You'll never amount to anything, Hamilton. You're just a waste of space. Well, who's a waste of space now, you old *poephol?*

A day or so later I had a slight argument with my boss. Nothing major, something to do with paperwork that I hadn't realised needed to be signed a million times by everyone in the universe. Some bags of concrete mix had gone walkabout. I found them eventually, but tempers had been a little short and I'd had to trudge all over the site in the midday sun asking questions and peering into the backs of trucks with my clipboard. My buddies joked me out of my sulk later that evening in the pub.

Where've you been, boet? It's eleven o'clock!

What you need is a *real* drink, china. Clean out the old cobwebs.

Jake was on his way to the bar and he raised an eyebrow at me.

I'll have a whisky, I said without missing a beat. Thanks.

Attaboy! We were getting worried about you. Pull in, man, pull in.

The choir in my head stopped singing. The hands on the clock above the bar said 11.05.

It's just one. You can handle just one. You deserve it after the day you've had. Stupid supervisor prick.

Press the pause button for a second. I'm clean. I am off drugs. I have had it with rehabs and psychiatric clinics. I am never sticking a needle in a vein again – never!

OK. Now press play and you're looking at Steve smiling up at Jake and putting his hand out for a glass that's slopping golden-brown liquid onto the table.

They're both laughing. Now fast forward a few frames. Where's Steve gone? The chair he was sitting on just a moment ago is empty. Oh, thank goodness. He put that whisky down, didn't he, without raising it to his lips. He put his hands in his pockets and walked back to his bungalow. Phew – that was close.

No. Wrong video, I'm afraid. Put it back on the fantasy shelf, the one the guidance teachers go to.

Start again. Step outside. Pan across the bushes at the back of the pub. If you look carefully, you will see some movement. No. It can't be. Is that *Steve*? Surely not. What's he doing out here? A minute ago he was playing pool and drinking Coke. Wasn't he? What happened in there? Check your watch. It's two minutes past 12.

Go in closer. It *is* Steve. And he's with two of his new buddies and his new best friend, a Zulu cleaner who works in the hotel. The cleaner, whose name is Vusi, is busy making a mandrax pipe from a bottleneck. Steve has had three whiskies (two of them doubles) and a triple rum and he and Jake are passing a joint between them. Jake is chuckling at something. Something's amused him, but it's hard to tell what from here. As for Steve, he seems somehow apart. He's not talking to the others. He's just sitting there quietly, a half jack of Captain Morgan between his knees, staring up at a sky that is murky with stars.

INSTITUTIONS

Here I go. I'm leaving rehab. Again. But all of a sudden the place I couldn't wait to see the back of has taken on an entirely different aspect. The noises, the voices, the guy who's temping in the reception area while the usual receptionist has gone to the dentist, the smell of floor polish mixed with Wednesday boiled cabbage, and medicine – that *medicine* smell I hate so much – all of these things have become familiar to me, and safe.

Since when did an institution become my home, my sanctuary?

I hesitate on the steps outside. It's a windy day. There are papers blowing up off the pavement. I can hear people shouting to each other from the street but I can't see them.

I can't go. I'm scared. Damn it, I'm scared of this. I am what they call 'at risk' and I know it. I know what I'll do the minute I hit the streets and it isn't buy a newspaper and look at the job columns. What a waste of space I am.

I have this thing, a superstition I suppose you could call it. If I step over this imaginary line in the driveway with my right foot, I'll be OK. If I step over it with my left foot, I'm going to die. I'm hesitating, dithering, hovering about here with my denim jacket pulled tight across my chest. I can't do it. I can't leave. Where's Andrea? Wasn't Andrea leaving today too?

Suddenly Sister Rita is beside me. She looks at me curiously. I thought you left, she says. Aren't you leaving today? I nod, but I can't look at her directly. I tuck my hands beneath my armpits and hunch my shoulders against the wind. Well, she says, Goodbye, Steve, good luck, and she turns to go back inside. She's wearing a mauve cardigan over her white uniform. I can feel, though, that she hasn't gone through the door yet.

Sister Rita, I can't, I say. I'm not ready.

Go on, Steve, she says, and there's a softness in her tone that makes me feel more afraid than before. I turn around and look at her. She nods at me and makes a small encouraging gesture with her hands as you would do to a dog that's followed you home and now needs to go back to where it came from.

I can't, I say again. I'm not ready.

Oh, Steve, she says and I think I can sense kindness in her voice, even love maybe. She's going to change her mind. She's going to come over to me and put her arms around me and lead me back inside where it's warm and – Steve, she says. *Go. We need your bed.*

I pick up my bag and go back to the streets. I step carefully over my imaginary line, making sure to use my left foot.

SIX

I love dancing. I think that's one of the good things I inherited in the Hamilton genes. That and a love of music. Perhaps in another life I'll learn to play an instrument and become an entertainer like my dad could have been if only – well, if only. For now, though, my entertaining is restricted to performing on make-shift stages, in school halls and in conference rooms, and I only know how to do one show. It doesn't have a lot of music in it – none at all in fact – and I guess if it had a soundtrack it would consist more of gunshots and tears than Celine Dion.

When I was fourteen and an apprentice alcoholic I made a discovery. Two discoveries, actually, and they were linked. The first was that not all girls were like my sister and the second was that with enough alcohol inside me on a Saturday night I lost my natural born shyness. A new Steve, the life and soul of any party, had arrived.

The contrast between how I was at home and how I was when I was with my buddies was kind of chalk and cheese. Until then I'd spent most of my life at home ducking and diving, staying out of my father's way as much as I could, fending off the odd blow and putting my skinny frame between him and my mother when things threatened to get out of control.

It wasn't a fun place to be.

I started staying out later and later on Friday and Saturday nights. Often I wouldn't go home at all, preferring to crash at Brian's house. He had his own key and we let ourselves in without anyone remarking what time it was. His mother got used to seeing me scratching around in the kitchen cupboards for cornflakes on a Saturday morning. She was very easygoing, Brian's mom, and if she noticed the smell of vomit in the bathroom and the clothes on the bedroom floor that stank of smoke she never said anything.

Sometimes, though, we'd tell our parents we were kipping at James's place and instead me and Brian would roam the streets all night, drunk and wild, kicking over dustbins and setting off car alarms just for the hell of it.

I began to slip out on the odd school night too, at first to test the reaction and ready with a story if need be. But nobody really commented. To tell the truth I don't think anyone even noticed. By nine o'clock on any given evening, if he wasn't down at the hotel, my dad was passed out in the lounge with his mouth wide open and the rest of the family had retreated into their private corners.

If, on the other hand, my father was in one of his drunken rages, I suspect my mother was only too glad to have me out of the way. I had a baby sister by this time, too, who was starting to get in the way, and it took up a lot of my mother's energy just keeping her and her toys out of the path of danger. My father had been known to rip the head off an imitation Barbie and fling it through a closed window, oblivious to agonised cries of protest, golden curls and small fingers grasping at air. I thought I was doing my mother a favour by making myself scarce.

As I grew older, more street smart and, most significantly, *taller*, my line of defence on the battlefield that was home was becoming the old favourite: attack. I still dived a lot but I ducked less often where my father was concerned. I learnt to stand my ground and to advance rather than retreat. I could raise my own voice to match his. I found I could raise my fists too. Especially my fists. And especially when I had a good shot of vodka burning in the pit of my stomach.

But when I was with my buddies on a Saturday night, with a couple of beers inside me and the music playing loud and clear out into the night – hey, then you'd see a different Steve. That was where I really came into my own. I had all the moves. Michael Jackson had nothing on me. I was the centre of attention and I *loved* it.

At home being the centre of attention meant something else entirely and usually came with a backhander or two. With my friends I was the guy who could make a party happen.

Well, my buddies were one thing, but our social circle was expanding. I discovered a whole new audience I could shine for. This audience had breasts and long tanned legs, and there was one in particular who took my breath away.

Her name was Tracey and she was the captain of the netball team. She had smooth dark hair the colour of polished mahogany and she wore it long, to her waist, and it flew about as she danced. Her eyes were full of fun and wickedness and when she laughed she threw her head back as if every part of her was flung into that one moment of pure joy. She had a thin gold chain around her ankle and she would pitch up at a party, kick off her shoes and head for the centre of the room where she would dance as if she were the only person in the world and the music was playing just for her.

I would never have admitted it to Brian or James, but I think I was already in love with Tracey when I was about twelve. Needless to say, she was completely oblivious to my existence. Now, however, that I had discovered the magic potion that gave me the confidence to enter her space, things changed dramatically – and in my favour.

Sometimes the potion came in bottles from the hotel's off licence, and sometimes it came from Brian or James's family pub. Either way it became the essential ingredient for having a good time. Without it I was the old Steve, the kid with feet of clay, the no hoper whose father the pisscat had tripped over the science teacher the one and only time he came to parents' evening. With it I could be anyone I wanted to be, and right then I wanted more than anything else to be the guy Tracey couldn't resist.

And it worked. Tracey liked me. She liked the new Steve. We became a couple and all of a sudden the world was at my feet. Steve and Tracey. Tracey and Steve. *Fuck*, that was a good time. With my arm around my girlfriend and a bottle in my hand, I felt life couldn't get any better.

I found something else that the magic potion could do. While it wasn't going away, I discovered that what was happening back home could be shoved and squeezed, most of the time at least, into a corner of my brain, pickled in alcohol, and ignored. So that's where I kept it, like a jar of fermenting fruit, preserved in Red Heart rum, and I made sure I screwed the lid on tight.

It's ironic, I realise, but strangely enough it was difficult for me to lay my hands on alcohol. Call it a peculiarity of my father's or maybe it was the Scot in him but he was scrupulous about keeping his booze to himself. He could drink himself into oblivion and still know exactly how many bottles there were in the fridge, and god help anyone who so much as relocated them to another shelf to make room for butter or cheese. Another peculiarity was that my father never let me touch a drop of alcohol. Never. Where other kids my age whose parents had a glass of wine or beer in the evening or over weekends would be allowed the occasional sip or can of lager, my father wouldn't let me near the stuff. I was allowed to fetch and carry for him, that was OK, but heaven help me if the level in his glass dropped a quarter of a centimetre between the kitchen and the La-z-Boy recliner across the passage. I wonder what he could have been thinking – that by keeping the demon drink away from me he was saving me from becoming like him? That's funny, dad. I was way ahead of you.

My parents weren't great believers in the concept of pocket money so I had to rely on my buddies to bring the booze to our weekend sessions. Usually this wasn't a problem. In that unwritten code of boyhood friendship, no words needed to be said. They understood. It was simply accepted that I'd chip in if and when I could, when I could raid my mother's handbag, steal my sister's tuck money or grab a fistful of loose change from the top of my dad's dresser before he got home. I was getting my priorities right, way back then.

One Friday night we had all congregated at Arthur's house. His parents had gone overseas for a month and left things, rather precariously in my opinion, in the hands of Art's older brother who was twenty-one and at college. At least that's where they thought he was. Mostly he was at his girlfriend's place, watching videos and drinking cane and Coke, and he hadn't yet got round to mentioning that actually he'd dropped out of college and was thinking about looking for a job. Anyway, he wasn't in evidence that evening and the word spread quickly that Art's house was where everyone was going to meet up.

It was a bit of a different crowd from the usual one. I got there late and couldn't find Brian anywhere. Brian had promised to bring a few six-packs along. He had an on-off arrangement with the delivery guy from the bottlestore his parents had an account with and, with a small commission on the side for the driver who stopped by their house every week, it was a beautiful system. At least it meant that we had a fairly regular source of supply and Brian's father never seemed to check his accounts very carefully.

I couldn't see Tracey either but there were a hell of a lot of people coming and going and I knew we'd meet up sooner or later. I sat on the floor near the speakers and lit a cigarette. I stretched my legs out in front of me and closed my eyes. I could feel the music pumping through me up through the floorboards but I didn't feel much like dancing. I needed a drink first. There was a group of girls from school I'd always found intimidating hanging together in a bunch and they glanced expectantly at me from time to time. I ignored them. I kept my eyes closed, hoping that the image I thought I was creating – cool, casual, aloof – would make them keep their distance. I didn't have anything to say to them tonight. All my slick lines had deserted me. Inside my stomach was churning with nerves and sheer irritation. Every now and then I'd open my eyes and scan the room. Where were my buddies? Where the hell was Brian?

Eventually I saw him shouldering his way through from the kitchen. Thank god – frosties!

Where the fuck you been, bru?

No, I had to do some stuff for my uncle.

Have you seen Tracey anywhere?

He shook his head. I think I heard she wasn't going to make it tonight. Her folks are giving her uphill about her marks.

Shit! Well, let's grab a beer.

Sure – where are they?

Didn't you –? Ah, *fuck*, Brian! You said – ah, *fuckit* man!

I couldn't . . . I thought . . .

I don't give a *stuff* what you thought! What we going to do now?

What about James? Where is he? Isn't he bringing tonight? We got family visiting from Joburg. I couldn't –

James never turned up that night. Brian and I separated. I think he went home. I was so angry. No Brian, no Tracey, and I couldn't just go home. On a Friday night? Hell, no. I walked outside to piss in the garden and calm down. I was fucking furious. How was I supposed to – ? What was I supposed to – ? It was Friday night, for god's sake, Friday night! And nothing to drink!

As I was going back inside I almost tripped over someone who was leaning against the wall in the darkness at the side of the house, away from the noise and the music.

Hey, watch it, man.

Sorry.

There were four of them. They looked older than the rest of the crowd and seemed apart somehow. Maybe they were Art's *boet*'s friends.

A thought struck me. You okes got anything to drink?

Someone chuckled softly.

Then, We don't drink, a voice drawled lazily out of the darkness.

And I'd thought they seemed cool! Well fuck that for a laugh. I turned to go.

We don't drink, the voice repeated. We smoke.

One of the others chuckled again. I saw the glow of a cigarette being passed from one hand to another.

Oh big fucken deal, scoffed fourteen year old Steve, who was on the way single-handedly to keeping Mr Stuyvesant in business. You smoke.

Then they all laughed, not loudly, not *at* me exactly, but in a companionable, friendly sort of way, as if they shared a private joke. A very funny private joke. I could see them more clearly now that my eyes had become accustomed to the gloom, and they weren't that much older than me. In fact I thought I recognised a Grade 11 guy who used to do woodwork and then disappeared in the middle of term. I thought he'd gone to a trade school somewhere. Mark someone. He was holding something out for me to take.

Pull in, china, he said. You ever seen shooting stars?

✳

I found out a few things that night and on the many similar nights that followed.

Dagga. Weed. Spliff. Zol. Dope.

The stuff sure had a lot of names for something so harmless.

And what a fuss about nothing.

What did I discover about weed that first time, other than that it calmed me down and made me feel a bit sleepy? Quite a lot, really. Let's see. That basically it wasn't even a drug at all. It was a plant, a herb, and an ancient medicinal one too. That it had been used for centuries in all sorts of healing ways. Even specialists use it now for cancer sufferers, I learnt, and apparently it was really good for asthma. That it wasn't addictive. That it was the whole basis of the peace-loving rastas' religion and philosophy and when did you ever see those guys starting any wars? That it relaxed you, that it released creativity, that some of the world's most brilliant art and music and poetry had come out of minds that were mellow on weed.

Where was the harm? Where was the danger? I just couldn't see it. And, come to think of it, where were the bloody shooting stars?

I never did see those shooting stars, but I learnt that everyone has a different experience with weed, so it didn't worry me. Anyway I kind of liked the idea that it was a very individual thing, something that was completely owned by and unique to me. I liked that.

But there was one other thing I learnt that night, and it was probably the most important. I took it in subliminally, through my subconscious mind, not like the half-arsed facts I was busily squirrelling away in my brain to be trotted out in due course as a means of justifying what I was doing.

Subconsciously, and because nothing happened when I smoked my first joint, or nothing discernible anyhow, I lost any fear I might up until then have had of street drugs.

A simple thing, but significant.

After the first time it was easy. I couldn't wait to share it with Brian. And my new friends were so generous. It was all about sharing and caring and I found there was no shortage of supply. I was naïve. I had yet to learn the golden rule of the supply chain, the one that would soon be taught to me, and that I in turn would teach to others.

Your first time is free. Your second time is free. Your third, your fourth time is free, but one day, my friend . . . *you owe me.*

I was keen to learn, keen as hell. The very next weekend I was back at Art's place and I went looking for Mark and his buddies. I found them in exactly the same spot as they'd been the weekend before. It was as if they hadn't moved in a whole week. I hovered about at first, suddenly not altogether sure of my welcome.

That sweetish, herby smell wasn't there tonight and I frowned, feeling awkward. One of the guys was drinking Coke out of a two-litre bottle. I wondered if I'd imagined it all but I'd been looking forward to this moment all week. The prospect had sustained me through the humiliation of a maths test I'd forgotten about as well as a particularly bad fight my parents had had that made my baby sister cry for three hours until I nearly brained her. I didn't intend to turn around and go home now. Besides, I'd already promised Brian I'd have a surprise for him.

Just wait, buddy. Just wait. No, I'm not *telling* you. Then it wouldn't be a surprise, would it?

The two cane and Cokes I had under my belt gave me confidence.

Hey, Mark. How's it going?

Mark looked up at me for a long time without speaking, squinting his eyes against the smoke of the Camel plain that dangled between his fingers and pulling bits of tobacco off his bottom lip.

Cool. Pull in.

So – um – what about –?

They said nothing. One of them, Michael, was beating a rhythm against his thighs to some song in his head and hadn't even opened his eyes when I arrived. Then, like a slow motion picture, Mark took a little box of Rizlas out of his pocket and held out his hand to the guy on his right, who stared up at me expressionlessly while he dug into his pocket. He pulled out a rolled up plastic bank bag and passed it to

Mark, all without taking his eyes off me. I could feel a sweat break out on my palms and I wiped them on my pants. If I was a dog I'd have been drooling.

Mark held out both hands to me. Visitors first, he said softly.

So I learnt something else. I learnt how easy it was to roll a joint, how to get the mix of tobacco and weed just right so that it burns quickly, how to take out the dagga pips first because that's what gives you the bloodshot eyes parents and teachers are urged to look out for in moody teenagers. And, very importantly, I began to understand the rules and the rituals.

The new boy rolls the joint and the new boy smokes first. Why? I'll tell you why. They're checking your credentials. How do they know you're not drug squad or that you won't bust them the first chance you get? So – new boy goes first.

Just a precaution.

We didn't stop drinking or smoking cigarettes. We just added weed to the menu. Friday nights, Saturday nights, and before very long we became daytime practitioners too. In summer it got blisteringly hot on the south coast and by mid morning if you were sensible you kept yourself out of the sun. Our school had a surfing team and Brian and I had always planned to try out for it. We both loved the sea. Our best practice time was before school, before it got too hot, and we would hit the beach with our surfboards at six o'clock in the morning and usually, but not always, make first assembly at quarter to eight by the skin of our teeth.

Now, though, with our new skills, we'd still hit the beach before school but we wouldn't always hit the waves. Sometimes we'd surf, but more often than not we'd just sit among the rocks looking out across the water, talking about Life and passing a joint around. Before we rolled it we'd take the dagga pips out like I'd been shown but our eyes were still red and I took to carrying eyedrops around with me in my pants pocket. They helped a bit but when the effect wore off we had to be ready for any comments and questions that might be tossed at us. We weren't too inventive, but then fourteen year old boys get creative in other ways.

The surf was rough today, sir, makes the salt more potent.

Sitting too close to the TV, sir.

We stayed in the water a bit long.

Got an eye infection, sir. Pink eye. My mom says it's contagious so don't come too close, sir.

Sir? No, I'm fine, sir. Really.

A Day in the Life ...

It struck me recently, over the end of year holiday period, when I was having what people told me was a well-deserved break from the schools and the talks and the crisis calls, that I'm fortunate to have my family close by. Not just Candy and Claydon – that goes way beyond fortunate. I mean my mother, my sisters and various aunts, uncles and cousins – who are all, for better or worse, still in my life. They all do relatively normal things, like have you over on Sunday for a braai, or ask you to help them do the shopping. I still find this kind of stuff strange, startling even. That I can push a trolley round Pick 'n Pay and buy food for my dog are minor miracles in themselves. That I'm around to do these things at all is extraordinary.

Anyway. It was New Year's Eve. Family gathering – everyone was coming and my cousin had promised to make his famous potjie, a rich, succulent meat and veg stew you'd never get in any restaurant. Candy and I arrived later than we'd intended and hunger and festive cheer had got the better of the rest of the party. They'd all but cleaned out the potjie and demolished the salads, but my mother had managed to save some stew for us and had kept the pot simmering. Soon we had piled up plates and Claydon was galloping around on the lawn outside with his cousins and a Christmas cracker hat slipping down over his nose. Inside my uncle was talking gloomily about the cricket to anyone who would listen, the television was on in one part of the lounge and Candy was pulled into a game of Trivial Pursuit in the other.

I don't understand cricket. I can't sit still long enough to try by myself to figure out what the hell they're all doing anyhow. And it's too late to ask really. Too embarrassing. The depth of my ignorance about ordinary things that are general knowledge to men my age is the downside about trying to take part in normal social interaction. It only draws attention – everyone's attention, but especially mine – to my inadequacies. I hate just sitting there, nodding, as if I know what a right arm spinner is, let alone who might be the specialist in the Australian team.

In a nutshell, I'm ashamed. I'm ashamed to admit not knowing all sorts of things, the kind of day to day information that gets you by in normal life. Like the sports boycott. I didn't even know about the sports boycott. And how can I ask someone to explain it all to me, now, at my age?

What do you mean, you never heard about the sports boycott? What were you – unconscious? Well, yes, probably.

The finer points of sporting achievements or defeats, that unifying male bond that can turn any conversation into an animated argument in most of the country's living rooms, passed me by long, long ago. I can't relate. I don't fit in. It's just too difficult to go back to the beginning. He's a right arm spinner. His speciality is the effortless cover drive. Remember when Jonty

Rhodes dived at the wickets in that match against . . .?

No. I don't.

I don't remember.

I went outside for some fresh air. I smoked one cigarette, then another. Claydon was kicking wildly at a plastic soccer ball. Watch me, Dadda, watch me. Yes, Claydon, I'm watching. That's good. Very good. My mother put her head round the back door. You OK, Steve? You want some pudding? I shook my head and tapped another cigarette out of the packet. The sun was hurting my eyes and I wandered round to the garage and sat down in a plastic garden chair. I could hear bursts of laughter coming from the house and the sound of the fridge door slamming shut, followed by the distinctive crack of a beercan opening.

I felt tired and old and suddenly overwhelmingly depressed. The laughter from the house grated on my ears. What was so funny back in there anyway? How long had we been here? Wasn't it time to go home yet? I clasped my upper arms tightly and started rocking, just to calm myself down a bit. It didn't help. So I got up instead and walked around the garage a bit, and then back out onto the lawn. All my muscles were aching, as if I'd been running. Dadda! Yeah, Claydie, I see you. But watch me, Dadda, you're not watching me. Was it just me or was my child developing a whine in his voice that would irritate Mother Teresa herself? Dadda's got a headache, Claydon. I'll watch you just now. Back in the garage I realised I really did have the beginnings of a headache, down at the base of my skull, and I was feeling slightly dizzy and nauseous. I sat down and rocked some more, trying to take my mind off the vicious feeling of self-pity I could sense welling up inside me.

Hey, bru, there's coffee and Christmas cake. What you doing out here? You all right?

And Candy. It's a bit rude to sit out here by yourself, hey. We're playing board games and actually it's fun. Come back inside and join in. Your mother's asking if you're OK. Are you OK? Can I bring you another Coke?

Board games. Yeah, right. Bored games. What can someone like me do with games?

My mother again, with a cigarette in her hand and that anxious look. Steve. You haven't been dabbling, have you? Are you sure?

I'm sure. I'm sure. I'm sure. I'm just not feeling very well, is that such a big deal? And no, I don't want another Coke. Thank you. Or leftover Christmas cake. And if anyone offers me a mince pie I'll throw up. I just want a bit of peace, is that too much to ask . . .

Back on my chair in the garage after another walk round the garden and two more cigarettes, it wasn't difficult to picture the group inside – the quick glances, the lowered tone – Steve's really OK, is he? He hasn't, you know –? And my wife shaking her head. Just leave him, he's fine.

I knew I was probably embarrassing Candy. It was my family after all, not hers, and it wasn't fair of me to distance myself like that.

Eventually, we got away. Claydon fell asleep in the car and Candy looked out the window at the sea while I apologised. I told her I wasn't feeling too good. I was nauseous and sweaty. Maybe there were carrots in the potjie. I'm allergic to carrots. Maybe that's what was making me so sick. Candy was relieved to be able to focus on the possibility of carrots. It gave us something safe and neutral to talk about for the rest of the drive home.

The next day I phoned my cousin. Carrots? No, Steve. I don't put carrots in that particular dish. Just a splash or two of beer to give it flavour . . .

Perhaps I need to tell my family – again: if you want to include me in your lunch party, there's only one very simple fact you need to remember.

There's no cure for addiction. It's a sentence for life.

So forget the name of the right arm spinner. Forget the capital of Mogadishu.

But most of all – forget the beer in the potjie.

That's the bottom line, I'm afraid, bru. Either that, or don't invite me. Your choice. I already made my choice way back when I was young and in control, and I live with the consequences every day.

Every. Single. Day.

SEVEN

Escape.

Nearly all of my daytime fantasies and most of my dreams at night involved some form or other of escape. Whether I was watching the swallows gathering in the sky, getting ready to fly north when autumn began to close in on us, or fixing the broken wing of a gull with a homemade splint, it was always there in my subconscious.

Prepare to fly. Fly away. Take your marks, get set, and get the hell out.

When I was younger I fantasised about my parents not actually being my *real* parents and running away from home to find the perfect nuclear family to which I truly belonged. I kept my bicycle oiled and had a small, completely inappropriate stockpile of food in an old school rucksack I kept hidden in the garage for the moment when I would take off. Chips, biscuits, chewing gum. Staple stuff.

I never did it, of course, although my instinct then, and now, when confronted by trouble was to pick up my heels and run for the hills. Unless I was high, when an aggressive, violent, ugly Steve emerged, ready to take out anyone and everyone, and able to do it too.

But that desire to escape, to remove my soul to a place of safety, is so basic to me that to this day I recognise it instantly in others. One time, a very bad time, when I was deep into drugging and pimping in Point Road, the very sleaziest part of Durban's dock-lands, a young runaway from Pretoria hooked up with us. I don't think I ever knew her name, or not her real one anyway. There were so many of them, those kids who came and went at that time, that you never struck up any proper kind of relationship with any one of them. This one couldn't have been more than about thirteen but she already had the flat, blank eyes of someone who's cut herself loose from hope. She'd put space, physical miles, between whatever it was that had caused her to run in the first place but it obviously wasn't far enough. She needed a deeper hiding place and the drugs she'd been using for that up until she found herself in Durban weren't doing it for her any longer. She'd come down to the coast with one thing in mind: she wanted to spike and she wanted to shoot up Wellconal. Pinks. She needed to get really wasted.

I'd like to believe that I still retained some tattered shreds of conscience somewhere because every time this kid pestered me or pleaded with me to help her shoot up, I told her to get lost. Probably she just irritated me though. I'd chase her away and she'd move around and eventually come full circle and back to me. It was enough to wear a person down so eventually we agreed to give her what she wanted. And besides, she was a favourite with the businessmen from uptown who cruised the streets late at night looking for the young anonymous runaways with a short life expectancy. No one could say she wasn't paying her way.

I chose the vein in her groin. My buddy Phil held her face. You don't want to watch, your first time, and he needed to see her eyes. I mixed up the shot – I don't think it was more than half a tab, but I can't really remember – and eased the needle smoothly into her vein. She didn't flinch but she was tense and scared and trying not to show it. The skin around the entry point I'd chosen was soft and white and unmarked, the skin of a child, like my little sister's skin. *Innn*, out, *innn*, out. A couple of seconds and I saw the rush hit. I felt her body relax and she fell backwards onto the couch we were sitting on. Phil let go of her face and moved out of the way before her bowels loosened.

That's the immediate result of shooting up pinks, by the way. Everything relaxes and I mean *everything*. It gives the term 'letting go' a whole new meaning.

Foul-smelling watery shit and piss spurted out of her with soft farting sounds and ran down her legs and onto the filthy rug and the racing section of somebody's three week old *Natal Mercury*. She lay there, half slipping down the couch with her legs splayed out and her skirt rucked up to her waist. Her head had flopped back on her neck and she wasn't moving at all. She looked like she wasn't breathing.

Wait, I called to Phil who was already halfway out the door. Wait! I think the fucking chick's OD'd on us.

Ah, shit. He came back and stood looking down at her, taking quick nervous swigs from the bottle of beer in his hand. He was quite drunk.

Let's get the hell out of here, I said.

No, she's OK. She's OK.

She's not moving, Phil. Look at her eyes.

Someone else had come into the room, a woman we knew only as Blommetjie, although any resemblance to a little flower had long since been erased.

Give her a *klap*, she suggested. Now.

We smacked her and Phil gave her a whack in the chest for good measure, in the general vicinity of her heart, but she just lay there.

I was sweating. Sometimes even half a tab can cause an overdose, you just never know, but Phil still didn't seem bothered. Easy for him. He wasn't the one who'd stuck the needle in. I felt responsible and angry at the same time. Bloody idiot child. What was she doing here anyway? Where were her damn parents? Phil left the room again and I heard him turning taps on in the bathroom next door, while Blommetjie slapped the girl's cheeks a few more times and tried to pull her upright. She was as floppy as a ragdoll. Then

Phil came back and jerked his thumb towards the door.

Cold bath, he said. That's all she needs. She'll be fine. Stupid little cow.

We all helped carry her into the bathroom where we dumped her unceremoniously in her clothes into the couple of inches of cold water that was pooling slowly in the bottom of the rusted, grimy tub. Blommetjie turned the taps on full and we watched in silence as the water crept up her thighs and onto her stomach. Stringy bits of shit floated to the surface. Then we turned the taps off and left.

And if she slips down and drowns, I said.

Phil took no notice of me. Instead he pushed me ahead of him, quite roughly, and out of the front door. We squinted in the harsh glare of sunlight. Another hot Durban morning.

Maak a skyf, bru? I nodded. Sure.

We walked on down to the beachfront where we met up with a few people we spent the rest of the day with. I don't think I ever gave the kid another thought and hardly registered when she turned up again, back on the block and seemingly no worse for wear, a few days later.

What happened to her in the end? Your guess is as good as mine and to be honest I couldn't have cared less. She was just one more customer out on the streets chasing after that place to escape to, just for a while, just till she'd got her life back together. And just like the hundreds of other nameless young girls who passed through my hands, one thing I do know for sure is this:

if she's still alive, which I doubt, she's not thinking back on me with affection. And what she might have believed was an escape route turned out to be a cul de sac. At both ends of the road.

※

Actually, I did leave home a few times while I was still at school, but never seriously and never for any longer than a couple of days. Mostly I was kipping at a mate's house, so that didn't count, but I do remember one time when I camped in the dunes for a weekend and got bitten to pieces by insects, and that other time when – well, more of that later.

I suppose, deep down, the practical side of me didn't actually see any place to go, while the responsibility of looking out for my sisters and my mother, and for keeping an eye on my father so that he wouldn't cause too much damage played its part in making me stick around. It was a responsibility that I took seriously and the weight of it was sometimes so real, so physically heavy, that I would get a stiff neck from it and blinding headaches where even the softest sunlight would hit me like a hammer blow between the eyes. My sister would slip me the odd Grandpa headache powder sometimes and that helped a bit.

Responsibility versus escape. Those two opposites have been trying to split me in half for as long as I can remember, and the thing that really gets to me is that whatever I do or have done in my life, because drugs was my escape hatch of choice I have been branded forever as someone of weak character who cannot face up to responsibility by the very people who never faced up to theirs. Perhaps some of them might read these words some day and I'd ask them to pause and think for a minute. Take one small image, that of a small boy driving his drunk father home in time for supper when his legs weren't long enough to reach the pedals, and then give me a lecture on responsibility.

✳

For a little while after my father died, just before I went into the army, my mother's father moved in with us. It was terrible. As it was, we were all struggling to come to terms with the emotional gap that had opened up in our lives. On top of that our house had very little extra space and my mother had to give up her bedroom. I was drugging heavily then and was unpleasant to have around at the best of times. I came and went at all hours. If I was at home I slept till lunchtime. If I went out nobody dared ask me if I'd be back for supper. If I lost my house keys I thought nothing of breaking a window to get in at four in the morning. When my mother tried to suggest that I do anything around the house I'd swear at her and tell her to ask my sisters. I stole money shamelessly from my grandfather's wallet and silently cursed him for not having anything of real value, like war medals, I could steal and pawn.

My behaviour drove him crazy and when he

could see my mother wasn't going to do anything about it, he wasn't afraid to speak up. My mother did try to defend me. She never wanted to believe the worst in me. He's just growing up, she'd tell him. Leave him. Let him go. He's taking his father's death hard. He's just finding his way.

Actually, I was doing exactly the opposite. I was so busy losing my way and knocking down all the signposts in the process, I was caught up in a dizzying downward spiral of self-destruction.

My grandfather wouldn't stop hounding me. He followed me around the house, talking to my back.

It's high time you grew up, son, he'd say. Time to start taking a bit of responsibility round here, help your mother shoulder the load. She hasn't got it easy, you know, bringing up three children without a husband, a breadwinner. You've got to act the man around here now. Look to the future.

I ignored him, but he'd hit the wrong nerve. His words scraped away at me like a blade whittling down a piece of wood until the white pith at its core was raw and exposed like a wound. Luckily I knew all about how to deal with wounds. Treat them with alcohol and drugs until a good scab forms. Never, ever pick the scab. I had so many scabs I was a walking example of living scar tissue.

One night my mother sat beside me on my bed, a bundle of dirty clothes on her lap she'd been busy scooping up off my floor for the wash.

You should listen to your grandfather, Steve, she

said. He's only trying to help you.

Despite myself, I could feel tears burning at the back of my eyes. It's not fair, I blurted out, aware of how much like a petulant child I probably sounded. It's not *fair*. What does he know about responsibility? What does he know about me, about us? It's all just bullshit. He doesn't know anything. *I'm* not your husband. I'm *not* the man of the house. I'm so *tired* of being the responsible one. I've been the responsible one in this family since I was ten years old for fucksake. If he can't see that, don't tell me *you* can't? I'm not your husband and it's not my job to play that role. I'm a drug addict, mom, a drug addict.

I went away to the army soon after that and my grandfather stayed on for a while longer. When I came home on a weekend pass I found that he had sold my father's car. My father had loved that car. It was supposed to be mine after he died. It was the only thing of his I had. My mother had said I could keep it in the garage until I was home long enough to give the engine an overhaul and make sure it was roadworthy.

I guess my grandfather thought it was a waste of space.

✳

Meanwhile in class at school I spent hours looking out of the window and daydreaming about being some-where else, somewhere exotic. At home I couldn't concentrate on homework when my parents were yelling at each other, which was most of the time, so I didn't do much of that. As a result I struggled academically and my father, when he wasn't crapping on me at top drunken volume for poor results and less than complimentary report cards, concluded that I was probably more suited to the factory workbench than the ivory tower.

When I was younger I'd made my dad a woodcut, a perfect replica of the dog that was the symbol of the company he worked for. It took me days of precise and careful drawing, shaping, carving and scraping. As a finishing touch I took a match and gave it a burnt-edged effect all around the outside. I gave it to him, hesitating, but he seemed to like it, and I saw that he put it in his briefcase before he went to work that morning.

Very occasionally, he would take me with him to his office and these, I remember, were special occasions for me, probably because they were so rare. Anyway, they stand out in my memory as little islands of promise, of hope, perhaps, that there could be a father and son bond between us and I concentrated hard on not doing anything that might annoy him. One time he took me in with him I saw my woodcut on his desk. I think I nearly burst with pride. If I close my eyes today I can feel that moment of secret pleasure all over again. My work of art, right there on display, for all his buddies to admire.

I liked to draw. I still do. Just like I write poems and songs in my head, all the time.

After the heady success of the dog woodcut, I got

busy again. This time I really outdid myself. I drew a bird of paradise, resplendent in every colour in my pencil case, each feather extravagantly bright and outlined in bold, contrasting shades. I gave that to my dad too, holding my breath, knowing that I was probably chancing my luck and that it would more than likely get thrown out with the Sunday newspapers. Still I looked for it next time I was allowed to go with him to his office and it was there! Something about it was different, though, and when I took a closer look I saw that my dad had added his own personal touch.

He'd drawn a cage around the bird.

Anyway, my father had made up his mind. He believed that his son belonged in the ranks of the blue collar workers. Steve is practical, good with his hands, was what he told his friends down at the hotel. He's technical.

He wasn't altogether wrong, although he'd never actually discussed this with me personally, nor did I ever share with him (or anyone else for that matter) my dream of one day becoming a pilot and flying round the world without stopping. But my marks at school were dreadful and he drew his own conclusion from that. As far as my father was concerned, average grades meant an average brain. End of story. In his mind there was no question of anything else being behind my spectacular record of non-achievement. The fact that me and my sisters lived our lives in a state of wound up tension and sometimes abject fear seven days a week and that this might have had something to do with it would never have occurred to him.

Whether in fact I was 'technical' and good with my hands or not, the academic or arty side of life was not going to be for me. And because I wanted to please my father, despite everything, and was pathetically grateful that he seemed to be taking an interest in me, even if I only heard about it second hand, I went along with it.

I was a 'fixer' by nature. Give me something broken and I would want to make it whole again. Don't get me wrong. I did enjoy the mechanical side of this natural inclination to mend and rebuild things. I enjoyed taking things apart and putting them together again, and I knew I was good at it. By the time I was fifteen I would be able to strip and clean an engine, repair a toaster or get a broken lawnmower to cut the toughest grass. I could also roll a joint faster than anyone I knew and remove all evidence in a nanosecond at the first sniff of trouble.

One time, though, I wasn't fast enough, but that came later.

＊

My father's drinking was heavy and continuous. His job suited his lifestyle perfectly. Being an area manager meant that he was on the road a fair amount, and he didn't have to keep regular office hours. He was off calling on clients in different centres several days a week and this meant lunchtime drinks and sundowners and after work drinks, and probably morning teatime drinks too. Sometimes, if he'd finished all his calls for the day and he'd run out of drinking buddies, he'd come home and continue drinking there until he passed out or my mother came home from work. If he passed out before she got in it didn't matter if she screamed abuse at him because he'd be none the wiser. If he was just drunk and she screamed at him then he had an excuse to get back in his car and go down to the hotel just to get away from her.

It even became safe for me to smoke with my buddies in our garage at home after school. If my dad did happen to come home in the middle of the afternoon, the chances of him noticing us at all, never mind what we were up to, were remote, he was that out of it. He didn't even notice me much when he was *sober* so what the fuck did I care? I was fifteen and my buddies were all the family I needed.

The good thing about friends when you're that age and you're joined at the hip is their loyalty – up to a point, that is. I would discover soon enough just how far that unshakeable loyalty went when the chips were well and truly down.

More than once when we pulled in to the garage after school to drink and smoke, we'd see my father's car in the driveway, door wide open, keys in the ignition, and my dad lying with his face in the flowerbed. We'd just walk on by and nobody'd say a word. Such a scene would have completely humiliated me when I was younger but I'd found the cure for humiliation now, *and* the cure for pain, hurt and despair, and every other sad emotion I seemed to be especially prone to.

I turned to that cure more and more frequently.

Like a painkiller that relieves the shooting *zing!* of an abscess beneath a tooth, being stoned brought blessed relief to the constant ache in my chest. But everybody knows the effect of a painkiller wears off and unless the abscess is excised the tooth will start to throb again. But perhaps you can't get to a dentist so, just in the meantime, you'll carry on with the painkiller, treating the symptom. Sooner or later, though, you'll find that the pills are not having the same effect anymore. This is because your body is getting used to their chemicals and the abscess is winning. So you try some other painkiller, a stronger one, and that works just fine for a while. But you still haven't got to the dentist, and anyway you hate the dentist and you're sure the abscess will die down by itself. And then you won't need the painkillers anymore.

I've laboured the metaphor, I know, but I get like that sometimes so live with it. I'm not wrong, though. Everybody knows that the only real solution is to ditch the painkillers and get rid of the abscess, but what if you can't? What if you're a fifteen year old schoolboy and the abscess is your *life*? What then? You go looking for an even stronger painkiller, of course, or you double your dosage at the very least.

My father was a pugnacious Scot with a violent temper, and to be fair, it wasn't always directed at his family. Sometimes he needed his family at his side.

Steve, I'd hear his voice, low and urgent, on the phone from the hotel's callbox. Steve. Come quickly. We got shit.

That would be the signal for me and my mates to race down to the pub and pile into whatever brawl my old man and his cronies had started. There'd be a general free for all, a few smashed bottles, some over-turned chairs and tables and at least one red-veined face flat out on the barroom floor. When it was all over and my dad had sworn me not to breathe a word about it to my mother, he might even give me a hug. This was our quality time. Then he'd treat my buddies to a round in the pub. Me he'd send outside to sit on the pavement and blow on my bruised knuckles until it was time to drive him home.

You're under age, mate, he'd apologise. I'll send you out a Coke with Shadrack.

Sometimes our brawls would be one on one and take place inside our house. One weekend when I was out in the back garden, stoned and trying unsuccess-fully to put a new chain on my bicycle, I heard my mother screaming, *screaming* at the top of her voice.

Steve! Steve! For the love of god – Steeeeve! Where are you? Heeelp!

All the small hairs on the back of my neck stood up. I flung my bike down and ran for the back door. It was like a scene from a kitchen sink melodrama. My mother was cowering against the wall with her hands shielding her face and my father was roaring wild and charging down the stairs straight at her in his vest and socks with his fists raised. His bloodshot eyes were wide open and terrifying and he looked like a murderer. I could hear my little sister crying hysterically somewhere offstage.

I intercepted him at the bottom of the stairs and there we were, Steve and his dad, in a frenzied thrashing of fists, tearing flesh and the sickening crunch of bone on bone. In seconds I had him face down on the floor by his hair and I started pounding his forehead into the parquet tiles, over and over again like a man possessed. Then I let him go and started kicking him but he grabbed my ankles and I went over and we rolled all over the living room and I heard things breaking and crashing and above it all my mother and sister crying and shouting and trying to pull us apart. I was like a man three times my size with a lifetime of rage pouring out of me in one molten rush.

My father managed to stagger to his feet and he took off, out of the front door and out into the road. By this time, though, I was completely out of control and I hardly noticed that my adversary was gone. In fact now I could feel someone else attacking me, kicking me black and blue and raining blows down on my head until I was demented with pain and fury. I hit out wildly, grabbing and biting, and I started smashing everything that I could lay my hands on in that house, shouting I hate you! I hate you! I hate you! while my mother fell onto her knees on the carpet and sobbed into her hands.

Suddenly my little sister darted over to me with something in her hand. She clutched me round the top of my thighs and pushed her nose into my leg and held on for dear life. She thrust her hand up at me until I was forced to stand still and look at what she was holding up to me.

Take it, she said. Take it!

It was an old army bible. I'd never clapped eyes on it before that moment or since, and don't know who it belonged to or where she found it. Or for that matter why she felt she had to give it to me. She was about five years old. I asked her about it many years later, and she could remember neither the incident nor the bible. I suspect she thought I was making the whole thing up, that it was just one of those hallucinations or bad trips that are so jumbled up in my damaged brain. Perhaps she's right. Perhaps there never was a fight. Looking back even now, though, and remembering, it still seems pretty real to me.

I stopped shouting and kicking and throwing myself about, and I looked at the small black book in my hand. It meant nothing to me but something had brought me back to myself. I picked up one of the coffee tables that had been knocked over and was now minus a leg and I laid the bible down on it. Then I knelt down in front of my sister and put my arms round her for a minute. She held herself stiffly and stared at me with big round eyes. She was so small and so scared. Perhaps she was bracing herself for a blow.

Then I walked out of the front door and down

the road. My father was nowhere in sight, not that I was looking for him. I was just walking. I think I walked for a long time that night but I can't really remember it too well anymore, or where I went for the next couple of days. I know I didn't go home and I can't remember whether the incident was ever spoken about again within the family.

While I walked I spent a while thinking about violence and in particular the extreme violence I'd discovered myself capable of. In later years I would come to associate it with mandrax – I'd call it a mandrax fit – and I would experience it again, many times. Sometimes it would get me out of trouble, but mostly it would result in a prolonged period of involuntary incarceration in one kind of prison or another, a psychiatric institution or a gaol. Either way, they all had bars on the windows.

I felt bruised all over, especially in the region of my kidneys, as if I'd been kicked there, really hard, with hobnailed boots. My father's blows had all been to the front of my body, though, and he'd been wearing only his socks anyway. It was as if I'd received a much harder beating after he'd gone, when it was just me going wild in my own living room. I didn't dwell too long on it, but I gave the experience a name in my mind: God's hiding. I think God beat me up that day, as a warning or something.

Needless to say, I paid no attention.

※

One afternoon I came home from school, threw my bag down in the hallway and headed for my room. I was surprised to see my mother there. She wasn't due home from work for another hour or so. I stopped short in the doorway. My mother was sitting on the edge of my bed with a whisky bottle in her hands. She had a defeated look about her. Her shoulders were slumped and she was staring down at the floor. She didn't straighten up when she heard me. She just turned her head sideways and looked at me. I could see she'd been crying. Her face was puffy and her nose was red.

I can't take your father's drinking anymore, she said. I'm leaving.

Mom, no. You can't –

I'm leaving.

She moved out the very next week, taking my little sister with her. She gave my other sister and me a choice but we had to decide quickly.

You can come with me, if you like, she said. It's not you I'm leaving. I hope you both understand that?

We didn't but we nodded our heads anyway. We thought that if we agreed with everything she said she'd change her mind and stay. My sister had just started high school and had made some good friends. She was reluctant to pack up again and head off north to a city she didn't know and cousins on my mother's side of the family she didn't really know either.

I spoke for both of us. We'll stay here with dad, I told my mother.

I think she was surprised, and perhaps even a

little hurt, when we turned down the escape route she was offering us. Although god knows she had borne the brunt of it, she knew only too well the ripple effect of harbouring an alcoholic in the home and now she was all out of energy. She must have recognised at last that nothing was ever going to change. Her choices were tough ones. She could stay and watch what little fabric of our family that was left disintegrate completely, or she could take us away and try to start over somewhere else. She'd thought it was a done deal, that my sister and I would choose to leave with her. After all, she knew we were damaged kids. She had stood by helplessly and watched my sister grow more and more introspective, see how she would flinch and tense up whenever my father entered the house, drunk and belligerent. She had seen bruises on my face bloom and change colour when I'd got in the path of an argument once too often. Why, she must have wondered, why on earth would we choose to stay?

The answer was simple. I knew if we stayed my father would have a reason to come home at night. No matter how late, no matter how drunk, I knew as long as we were there he would still come home.

INSTITUTIONS

I can't move my arms. There is something in this bed that is wet and slimy. It's vomit. Jesus, it's vomit. God! Is it mine or someone else's? It stinks. Fuck – that smell! I hate that smell. It's on my face, my hands. I can feel it between my fingers. Soft, slippery lumps between my fingers. Get this stuff off me. GET THIS STUFF OFF ME. Where is everybody? Where am I? If I turn my face . . . oh Christ it's all over the pillow. The pillow is wet too. Jesus. Fuck! Where am I? Where am I this time?

I can't move my arms. I'm strapped down for fucksake. They strapped madmen down in One Flew Over the Cuckoo's Nest. I'm not mad, I'm a drug addict, and I'm coming down, man, I'm coming DOOOOOWN. And I need . . . thank God – my mother's here. Mom. Mom, tell them. Who's that? This doesn't feel – No. This is not good. This is not good. I'm an addict for fucksake. My veins are full of . . . *Nobody's asked me what I'm on. I'm on – I'm on* . . . No! Don't you know you never mix . . . DON'T YOU KNOW –

My mother knows. Tell them, Mom. Mom? *Tell* them. No, no, it's *not* all right. They *don't* know what they're doing. That's where you're wrong. They don't know what they're doing. Don't shake your head. Don't turn away. They're drugging me, Mom. They're *drugging* me. Shit! Don't let that fucker – Shit! Let me . . . If I could just get up. *I* know what I need. I need to get *out* of here, that's what I need. They don't know what they're doing. They're experimenting on me, can't you see that? Am I the only one who – No – don't look at me like that – Mom. Mom – no, stay! Please stay. Tell them. Tell them, for pity's sake.

They're going to kill me. *Again.*

EIGHT

Those were dark days, after my mother left home.

Before, bad as it was, there had been a certain pattern and order to our lives. All that had gone now. We found that a lot of the things we'd taken for granted just didn't get done. Laundry, for example. How often did the sheets get changed? What got ironed and what didn't? Who paid the maid and how much? Where was the form for my sister's school hockey tour and was it OK if I signed it because dad was semi-conscious and it had to be in tomorrow? Should I leave food out for the dog or only feed him in the evenings? If I forgot to put the garbage out in the road on Friday morning, would it have to stay where it was for another week or would they come back for it if you called someone?

So much to think about.

I was on the phone to my mother a lot.

Food was another thing. Meals became infrequent and haphazard and my sister and I lived alternately on her speciality, burnt scrambled eggs, and mine, dodgy pies from the café (until Brian told me that he had it on good authority that they contained pigs' eyelids). After that it was cereal, bowls and bowls of it. I began to look like the Coco Pops monkey. We also began to do a kind of circuit thing among our friends' families, and in the end we got fed well enough, I suppose. It was a smallish neighbourhood and it was no secret that my mother had hit the road. I guess they felt sorry for us, but it wasn't a subject that anyone brought up. Often my sister would spend a whole week at a time with her friend Lisa down the road and that was something of a relief to me. At least it gave me a bit of a breather and left me and my father to our own, separate devices. Lisa's mother Anne, a nurse, and our mother had been good friends and I think my mom might have had a word with her before she left.

At home my father was changing right before my eyes. Without my mother you'd have thought there was no need for pretence anymore, no need to get defensive about the difference between the number of beers in the fridge yesterday and the number in there today, but his behaviour had changed. He became furtive and hunted looking, skulking around the house in his vest and socks like a guest who knows he's outstayed his welcome. He was drunk almost all the time, even early in the morning. Either he was still pissed from the night before or already on the way there from the cheap whisky he probably rinsed out his toothpaste with. It was hard to tell. He mumbled to himself, he swore at me and he tripped and stumbled wherever he went. One night I found him crumpled up at the bottom of the stairs and I didn't know whether he'd fallen on his way up or crashed down to the bottom. No use asking him, of course. He wouldn't have known.

Although I never knew him to miss a single day's work, all the same I was anxious. I began to fear that he might lose his job because he was leaving for the office later and later each morning, sometimes still pissed from the night before. He grew flabby and haggard and his eyes were permanently bloodshot. He would even wear the same safari suit, badly pressed, for three days in a row.

There was hardly any need to hide them, but he started stashing bottles all over the show. I'd come across them, full, half-full and empty, in the unlikeliest places: the linen cupboard, behind the charcoal bag out by the braai, wrapped in his pyjamas under his pillow, in the washing machine, and tucked down between the cushions on the sofa. If they were full I emptied them down the sink, but I don't know why I bothered. It was a futile gesture and it just pissed him off.

I grew more and more depressed and scared.

I phoned my mother.

Mom, please come home. We need you here.

Is your father still drinking?

A bit, but he'll stop if you come home. He's promised to try.

No, son. I can't come home. I'm sorry.

At first I sought consolation in my own brands of alcohol and my special cigarettes, the hand-rolled kind, but it would be naïve and inaccurate to say that consolation was all I was looking for. Remember what I told you about falling in love with your first high? It's not the *drug* itself you fall in love with, remember, it's the *feeling*, and by then I was seriously head over heels in love. But that high, that level you want – no, *need* – to get to, is fucking elusive and you can't just go the same route that you went before to reach it because it doesn't work like that. So you start to experiment, mixing and matching, and trying different combinations of drugs, anything to find that perfect place – *yesss* . . . – and stay there, just for a few minutes.

By now for me and my buddies dagga and alcohol were child's play and they weren't doing enough for us anymore. We were trying anything and everything, in different combinations and quantities. We smoked tea leaves, papaw leaves, whatever vegetation looked promising, crushed up and mixed in with weed, and soon we added thins – diet tablets – that gave you an amazing buzz not unlike E. Couple of those, a couple more, and a joint or two, and that's one hell of a buzz. Thins also give you a kind of clenched jaw as well as the chats. You just want to talk and talk, you have all this energy and you can't sit still, you can't sleep, you can drink as much as you like and you won't get drunk. It's amazing. At least that's what you think at the time. Quite soon you'll find, though, that it's not amazing enough and the two tabs you were taking turn to three and then four at a time, just to have the same effect.

You've got to remember that addicts are incredibly inventive. We'll try anything. That's one area where all of the rehab clinics kind of miss the point. They're not getting us *off* drugs. They're keeping us *on* them, just expanding our options. They mean well but they're playing right into our hands. They're just giving us different drugs and different combinations, only these ones are all above board and legitimate because we have permission for them and we get them from the pharmacy.

When you leave rehab after completing your 28-day programme or whatever, with a packet of prescription drugs in your pocket and careful instructions to have three pills a day and only after meals . . . Come *on*. Whose hands are these pills *in*, for heaven's sake? Think about it.

The very last clinic I left, my pockets weighed down with good intentions and lots of little packets of medicines designed to keep me sane and stable and – hah! – drug free, what do you think I did on the bus on the way down to Durban?

Let's just say that by the time I'd reached my destination a few hours later, my pockets were a lot lighter, so was my mood, and the good intentions were simmering somewhere out of sight on a back burner.

And I'd done really well on the programme and put my life of drugging behind me once and for all. Honest.

※

Still, consolation was a substantial reason for my drugging during this rough period when me and my sister were alone with my dad. The strain of trying to keep it all together, making sure my sister got to school on time and had everything she needed, from sanitary pads to nail polish, was getting to me. Drinking relaxed me. Coupled with a decent joint in the company of my friends, or even on my own, I found that being stoned was the only thing that could take the edge off my anxiety and, not to beat about the bush, my deep-seated, near all-consuming fear. It was the only thing that could take it away, that feeling of tightness in my chest, when my heart hammered like crazy, and I felt lightheaded with terror for no reason at all.

I was afraid all the time. Afraid that my father would not wake up from one of his binges. Afraid that he would get fired for drinking on the job. Afraid that he would plough into oncoming traffic on the highway. Afraid that my mother would forget all about us and never come home again.

Me and my buddies roamed the streets at night, usually drunk and high and looking for trouble. It was a small town and the cops got to know us well. They were forever pulling us in, especially me, checking for drugs and generally giving us a hard time. They knew what we were up to, they knew we were drugging, but we were clever and cool and they couldn't pin anything on us, no matter how hard they tried. We laughed at them. We were invincible.

One night James scaled the keys to his dad's car when his parents were away for the weekend. We thought we'd go into Durban and score but we needed petrol and didn't want to waste what little money we'd pooled for drugs on filling up at the local garage.

There was an old age home in our town, quite close to where I lived. Logic told us that given the age and, hopefully, deafness of the inhabitants, we could help ourselves to some petrol from one of the residents' cars in the parking lot without too much risk. Light-fingered Steve was given the job. My buddies kept watch while I trawled the parking lot. I selected an old Peugeot, the kind that has the petrol tank at the back, sort of behind the number plate. When the coast was clear I got down on my haunches and set to work. I'd hardly got the cap off when all hell broke loose. I nearly shat myself. Out of the darkness came what I can only describe as the walking stick brigade, a long unsteady row of pensioners, wild-eyed with triumph and blood-lust, and brandishing sticks, crutches and god knows what other scary weapons, probably *bedpans*, as they advanced upon me from their hiding place in the shrubbery. Christ, it was like something out of a horror movie, the Night of the Living Dead or something.

Adrenalin pumping, I took off like a shot, my buddies nowhere in sight, of course, and headed deep into the suburbs, hoping against hope that James's granny hadn't been among the ambushers. Just to be on the safe side, I stayed out all night.

In the morning, tired and hung over from the remains of the halfjack of Mellowwood brandy I'd discovered in the side pocket of my pants, I stumbled home. If I saw the white car parked in the street opposite our driveway, it didn't register. It hardly registered either when I found myself grabbed unceremoniously by the arm and bundled into its back seat.

Busy night, the cop said without looking at me. And it's not over yet. Let's go, shall we?

Where to?

Oh, just a little drive. We'll chat on the way. I thought stolen goods as a topic might interest you.

I don't know what you're talking about. I haven't –

Oh ja? Tell that to the uncle whose car radio just got ripped off. He's very upset, you know.

What car radio? I don't know what you're talking about. You've got the wrong guy. I'm telling you.

I was quite cocky, feeling secure for once at least that he really *had* got the wrong guy. But I still wasn't off the hook. I learnt that it wasn't the first time that the old age home had had nocturnal visitors and in fact the very Peugeot I'd had the bad luck to pick out had had its radio and speakers stolen the night before. Talk about being in the wrong place at the wrong time. It didn't look good for me from anyone's perspective and I soon realised that my innocent protesting was falling on deaf ears.

So who were you with last night?

No one.

OK. No one and who else?

We played this game for a while until we both got bored with it. I didn't know it at the time but they'd already picked up the others. He was just messing with me. All I could see was that this unmarked Datsun Laurel had a full tank of petrol and we looked set to be cruising the streets all day. I still felt relatively safe until it dawned on me: I was the last link in the chain, not the first. My buddies had shopped *me*.

But we didn't steal any radio, I told the cop.

Pull the other one, he said. I'm taking you in.

I'm *telling* you, I insisted. I promise. Search my house. Search my *buddies'* houses. You won't find any radio or any other of your so-called stolen goods.

He was getting pissed off with me now.

You think I'm stupid? You were *recognised*, sunshine, at the scene of the *crime*. Plain as day.

I weighed up a couple of possible responses to this one but in the end I kept quiet. *Damn* James's granny. And I thought she was the one with the cataracts in her eyes. I decided to change tack.

You know what, hey, I told the cop. I was there, OK? I was there. But all I was trying to do was borrow a litre of petrol and that's the truth. You check for fingerprints, you won't find mine anywhere on that car but on the petrol cap.

He looked at me for a long minute before he spoke. We're checking, he said. Oh, we're checking. And you just better not be lying. You kids are running out of chances very quickly. You especially.

He did a u-turn and, miraculously, we headed

back towards my house, the opposite direction from the cop station. I looked at my watch. It was past lunchtime, but the cop seemed in no hurry to get back to his Sunday braai. He seemed intent on taking the scenic route and did a few twists and turns around the suburban streets.

You smoke dagga, he said to the road in front of us.

No, I –

Don't fuck with me, kid. You smoke dagga, I know you do, so don't try and bullshit me. Take this as a friendly warning. You continue on the path you've chosen and you'll be sorry one day. Is this your house?

It was and I realised, with a sinking feeling, as he pulled into the driveway and turned off the engine, that he was planning to escort me inside. He opened his door.

Let's go, he said.

My father was in the lounge, half passed out on the couch, well on the way to oblivion. I could see he got a bit of a fright when he saw the friend I'd brought home with me this time and he struggled to a half sitting position and wiped a hand across his eyes.

There was no preliminary chit-chat, no pleasantries. The cop stood silently for a minute, his eyes moving over the room. I was conscious of the bottles, the glasses, the overflowing ashtrays, but he didn't comment.

Instead, Where's your son been this weekend, he asked my father in a flat tone.

What? Right here. In his room.

No, he hasn't. He was arrested this morning. On suspicion of theft. You didn't know that, did you, sir?

My father turned a furious face to me and tried to get up but on his second attempt the cop pushed him back down onto the couch with the tips of his fingers.

I'm not finished, he said.

My father subsided, knocking an empty glass off the coffee table in front of him. He looked down at the carpet, his arms resting on his knees, hands dangling between his legs. I felt depressed and very tired.

Your son didn't come home last night, the cop told him, and you don't have any idea where he was or what he was doing. I'm willing to bet that I know more about this kid right now than you do. He's going to get himself into some serious trouble one of these days and if he does – *if he does* – and if anything else happens to him –

He paused.

Anything at all. I'm coming looking for *you*, china, do you understand me? *For you.*

A Day in the Life …

Just one. It'll be OK.

No, it won't. You know it won't. There's no such thing as just one and you of all people know that.

Yeah, but –

There is no but. End of story.

I know that. Of course I know that, but you don't know what it's like. I've got a lot on my mind.

So deal with it. You know what will happen if you go back there.

Yes, I know. You're right, but –

So?

You don't understand. You don't know what it's like.

What do you mean I don't know what it's like? Who do you think you're talking to? One is too many. A thousand is never enough. Remember? Remember?

It's all I think about, for chrissake. Do you know how boring that is? How tedious, day after day to – I just need a bit of a break, you know? I've been working my guts out for ten days without stopping. I'm not sleeping well. My teeth are giving me problems. In fact, you know what? My life sucks.

No, it doesn't. Look at what you do have. You have Candy. You have Claydon. Aren't they enough for you?

Yes. You're right. They are. More than enough.

Good. See? That's better.

Or are they? Are they enough for me?

Don't think like that. You can't afford to think like that. You know exactly what will happen if you let your guard down. You can't afford to get complacent.

Oh, please. Complacent? Me? It's not that complicated. If I could just relax for half an hour, to get my mind straight. One joint is not going to kill me.

Yes, it is.

Listen. I know what my system can take. I know what my limit is after all this time. It's not like I'd be mainlining, you know. Fuck! Do you know how self-righteous you sound? And paranoid. People already think you're paranoid – did you know that?

Don't do it. Walk away. Have a cup of coffee.

I don't want a cup of coffee. Do you know how many cups –

Yes, I do know.

Just one. I can handle just one. I haven't had a fucken joint in I don't know how long. No one even has to know.

Yes, but you'll know.

That's irrelevant.

No, it's not.

Come on – how bad can it be?

You know how bad. Don't go there.

Just one . . .

Steve, in conversation with Steve. Yesterday.

NINE

Sometimes I get things muddled. It's that old mental filing system problem I have. Time sequences, especially, are hard for me. I backtrack and go off at tangents all the time, trying to remember, struggling to get things into chronological order as I piece together the story of my life so far.

I know now that trauma does peculiar things to your head, especially when you put drugs into the mix, and in retrospect now, as an adult, that time when I was fifteen or sixteen and my mother had left us was obviously a very traumatic period for me and is responsible for a lot of the *kak* that still churns around in my mind. Like the endless debris that you read about that floats around in space, cluttering up the universe? That's what my head feels like sometimes.

I could have talked to someone, I suppose, but in

those days kids weren't much encouraged to spill their guts about emotional stuff. For one thing, we didn't know how. We didn't know those emotions were acceptable. Kids were expected to sharpen up and deal. Depression. Anxiety. Panic attacks. Those were adult things. Weak things. And even if there *had* been an option of asking for help and guidance, I was too proud and too stubborn to have gone that route. My dealer was my therapist.

One particular weekend, though, stands out in very sharp focus in my mind and I have no problem with the time sequence. It started on a Friday.

Brian and I had been smoking down at the beach before school and we'd stayed longer than we should have done. I'd missed my ride and if I was late for assembly again I knew I'd be in deep shit. I'd had several warnings already that week and I wasn't anxious to be called up and crapped on in front of the whole school. I looked at my watch – seven o'clock – and decided that if I jogged home it was still early enough for me to catch my dad before he left for work and get a ride with him.

His car was still in the driveway, wedged rather tightly against the gatepost, I noticed, but still movable.

Dad?

No answer.

Then I heard loud retching noises coming from upstairs. I was used to the ghastly sounds my father made sometimes but this was worse than usual. I felt a small flutter of alarm. I took the stairs two at a time. The bathroom door was half open and as I was going past it, I caught a movement from inside. I stopped. My father was leaning against the basin retching, his whole body rigid in spasm. He didn't see me. Then he threw his head back, stumbled towards the toilet and puked up a stream of thick red blood. It splattered into the bowl and he retched some more and puked up more blood. I stood watching. Then he raised to his lips the bottle I hadn't noticed in his hand and he did something I'd never seen him do before. He didn't take a sip or even a swig. He just opened his mouth wide and poured the brown liquid down his throat. It splashed all over the floor.

I was conscious of a sentence that was playing itself over and over in my head like a continuous, monotonous tape recording.

I will never be like this man I will never be like this man I will never be like this man.

My father pushed the bathroom door open and went right past me without seeing me. He went into my parents' bedroom and out of my line of vision. I heard him puking again. Then I heard him trip on the edge of the rug on the floor and watched as he flopped face down onto the double bed like a fallen tree.

I waited a minute, watching him.

Then I went to the kitchen and got a bucket of water and a rag and I cleaned up the puke on the bedroom floor. I went into the bathroom and flushed the toilet several times. The water in the bowl was pink. I wiped the rim clean with the puke rag and then threw it in the bin.

I splashed water on my face without looking at my reflection in the mirror above the basin. Then I put on my blazer and I walked to school.

✳

When I got home in the afternoon I fully expected to find my father's car still in the driveway. I couldn't imagine that he had actually made it to work, not in the state he'd been in when I left him. But the car was gone. The woman who worked for us and cleaned up our shit a couple of days a week was in the kitchen.

Where is he, I asked her.

Gone to his meeting, she said.

His meeting?

She looked at me, no expression on her face, and nodded. Gone to his meeting, she repeated.

We both knew where his meeting was. I got on my bike and pedalled slowly down to the hotel. It was Friday afternoon. Weekend ahead. Pocket money. Two rand could buy you a lot of dagga in those days and I wasn't intending to deprive myself.

My father was there at the bar, at his usual place at the counter with his buddies, looking a little pasty faced but otherwise none the worse for wear. We didn't speak but he couldn't meet my eyes. He dug in his pocket and gave me some money. I didn't ask him how his day had been, but then he didn't ask me about my day at school either. Hadn't done for about a year anyway, so why start now?

I hooked up with James and Brian and that night we got trashed. The next day, Saturday, I didn't get out of bed until noon and by then my father was already very drunk. We ignored each other and I stayed out of his way. He drank steadily all afternoon in front of the television but that night, unusually, he didn't go down to the hotel. When I went out myself, I left him in the lounge, exactly where he'd been all day, sprawled on the couch with a glass in his hand.

On Sunday morning, as I was struggling to the surface through my own bad hangover, with my bedroom curtains drawn and the pillow over my head to keep out the sharp, bright sunlight, I heard my sister screaming. Fuck! I shot upright, my heart thudding, trying to work out where the sound was coming from. It was closer than I thought. I ran, slipping and stumbling, into my parents' bedroom across the landing. My sister screamed again and I lunged at her and grabbed her by the arm, gripping her so tightly I knew I must have been hurting her. She seemed rooted to the spot and I pulled her, *dragged* her, towards the door, away from our father, with his whisky breath and bloodshot eyes. She started sobbing then, those big heaving sobs of someone who's just about to lose it. I could feel her shaking.

I stopped in the doorway and looked back at the man on the bed.

Why, I said, and I could feel a horrible thickness

in my throat as if I had something big and ugly stuck in it. *Why, dad? Why are you abusing us?*

I didn't wait for an answer. I knew he wouldn't have one. I wondered if he even knew who we were right then. Instead I took my sister along to her bedroom, helped her shove enough clothes for a few days into a small bag and then sent her down to Lisa's house.

I thought of phoning Lisa's mother, Auntie Anne. I thought of phoning my mother. In the end I did neither. I just went back to bed.

✳

I think in those days pubs were closed on Sundays so my father belonged to something called the Scotsman's Social Club which amounted to the same thing as a pub anyway. He and his buddies would get together on a Sunday and drink and play darts and stuff.

This Sunday, though, my dad didn't go out and I stayed in my room most of the day, just lying on my bed and listening to the radio, trying not to think. About anything.

Later that evening I heard him calling me.

Steve. Jesus . . . Steve!

What? I put my head round the corner of his room. He was doubled over, gasping, and clutching his chest. What, I repeated, not moving.

Call Auntie Anne. Please. I think I'm having a –

So I did. Automatic pilot. I got on the phone and I called Lisa's mother and told her that I thought my father might be having a heart attack and asked if she would come and look at him. By the time she arrived, my father had stopped gasping and groaning, but he seemed to be struggling for breath and his skin was clammy. He was very pale. I began to feel panicky and I hovered about uselessly in the passage, getting in the way and feeling sweat break out in my armpits. Auntie Anne put her head round the doorway.

Phone the doctor, Steve.

I did, and luckily he was at home. He said he would come right away. While Anne stayed with my father I ran down the road to wait on the corner, to kind of speed things up, I guess, or just to feel that I was doing something. The doctor was everybody in the neighbourhood's family GP but it was late and dark and I thought if he saw me waving at him he wouldn't have to drive slowly and peer at house numbers on the way down our road.

I was standing there, smoking a cigarette, and pacing up and down when a cop van turned the corner and pulled up beside me.

No way – I protested, but before I could say anything else there were two of them leaping out of the van on either side of me and I found myself pinned up against the vehicle with my hands on the roof. I tried to turn around but I got a swipe against the back of my head for my trouble. They knew me, these guys. They picked me up frequently.

Listen, I said. My father's having a heart attack. I'm waiting here for the doctor. I'm telling you.

Praat kak, said one cop. Don't talk rubbish to me. We're taking you in.

Ja, ja, said the other as he finished frisking me. We know you and your bloody nonsense.

He started shoving me ahead of him, small painful pushes with his hand on my back. The first cop unhooked the catch on the back doors of the van. I struggled and shouted, panicking now. I couldn't see past their ugly big bodies to the end of the road where I knew the doctor's Jag should be appearing any minute and I was freaking out.

I'm serious, I shouted desperately. My father just had a heart attack. I need to – the doctor –

It was absolutely no good. I got another smack on the side of the head and was pitched forward into the back of the van. As the driver's door slammed I saw headlights and a car cruise slowly into our street. I banged on the window.

There, you cunts! I shouted. There's the doctor's car!

They looked at each other, then turned and looked at my frantic face up against the window. The passenger cop got out again as if it was a great big effort and he still knew that somehow I was conning them, but he let me out and I panted up the road, following the doctor's tail lights while the cops revved their engine, did a wheelie and ducked.

It was a heart attack, but a mild one. At least I'm pretty sure that was what it was, even if the doctor told me it was heartburn. I saw the look he and Auntie

Anne exchanged when they came to talk to me in the lounge. I don't know how much or what she told the doctor before I got home, breathing heavily and with a cut on my knee from the metal edge of one of the police van's back doors, but I'm sure I looked wrecked. Perhaps they thought I'd been running away and changed my mind and came back.

Shouldn't I take him to the hospital, I heard Auntie Anne say.

The doctor shook his head. Not this time, he said.

He was looking at me.

＊

Steve – how's your mother doing?

No, fine, sir. She's doing great. We talk on the phone every day, and she writes –

And the little one – settling down?

Oh, yeah. She's doing well. She misses the dog though.

I'm a bit concerned about your other sister. I haven't seen her in class since Monday. Is everything all right at home?

Oh, yes, sir. I forgot to bring a note, sir. She's just got a bit of the flu. She'll be back at school in a couple of days.

So everything's all right at home? Your dad –?

He's fine. We're all fine. Thanks for asking, sir.

It was unthinkable to tell anyone about the events of the previous weekend. It was unthinkable even to talk about it, with anyone, not least my sister herself. Even though I was only fifteen, I knew instinctively that I had to keep up appearances or everything would fall apart. My mother had left me in charge and I wasn't about to let her down. I couldn't allow anyone to know what was really going on or to see things as they really were. The shame would kill me and I knew if my mother found out how badly I was handling things, she'd *never* come home. I couldn't risk anyone snooping round our property, a teacher or – heaven forbid – a social worker or the pathetic guidance woman from school nobody would dream of confiding in. Besides Auntie Anne, and even her only on a strictly once-off, emergency basis, no one, but *no one*, was going to be permitted access to the Hamilton home to survey the wreckage. Apart from the humiliation of seeing my father on one of his truly awful days, the mess in the kitchen was enough to get the health department out, not to mention the takeout boxes lying all over the lounge, unmade beds and a general stench in the air that I came to recognise as despair. So I pulled on one of my many masks, the good student and responsible older brother one, and we got on with things.

We just got on with things.

My sister came home from Lisa's and the incident was never mentioned and when my mother phoned to see how we were doing we said we were OK but we all missed her and wished she'd come home.

Is your father –?

Yes, but he's trying –

I'm sorry, Steve. I can't.

We did go and visit her once and my father made a big effort. He had a haircut and bought a new shirt that was a size too large for him and the colour made his face look tired. Although his hands shook and we all noticed it, no one said anything. He was really trying and if he drank on that holiday, it was top-up stuff. He didn't pass out once and I became breathless with hope. I even saw traces of clearly deep affection between my parents. Surely, surely . . .

The one subject that was on all of our minds was the one that was never brought up. It was as if it would jinx the whole thing if we brought it out into the open. It's like talking about my clean time – I hate to do it and I always do it with my fingers mentally crossed. It's tempting fate, I think. Just saying the words out loud is asking for trouble.

Anyway, the possibility of my mother having a change of heart and coming home with us was something I clung to the whole of the week or so we were there. I willed it to happen. I knew it would. It had to.

But it didn't. I don't know why it didn't or what was said between my parents in the privacy of their own room, but all of the pieces that were beginning to slot into place for me simply burst apart again, like atoms or something bouncing off each other and spinning away in their own stupid orbits.

I have a photograph from that holiday. It was taken by my mother from the balcony of her apartment, after she'd said goodbye to us. It's a picture of me and my dad standing together, looking up at her, the sun in our eyes.

Both of us are smiling.

I love you, dad . . .

INSTITUTIONS

The blue of the sky and the blue of the sea are practically the same colour. The only way you can tell where one ends and the other begins is the tanker on the horizon. And the seagull. Against the sun one minute it's dark as it wheels away, the next pure white when the sun catches its breast. I watch it swoop and glide, this way and that. It's not going anywhere. It's just chilling, out there over the Indian Ocean, minding its own business and accountable to nobody. So easy. So FREE. It's not even moving its wings. It holds them out, stiff and straight, like a kid on a beach playing at being an aeroplane, as it soars upwards on an invisible cushion of air. I think I can hear its cry, loud and harsh, but that's my imagination at work. I can't hear anything in here except the blood rushing in my brain and unintelligible voices somewhere far away, nothing to do with me.

This is Addington. Psych ward. I'm twenty-seven years old and I'm trying to die.

I'm aware of someone behind me. I take my eyes off the bird for a second and turn my head. A woman, at a guess in her early fifties, is standing there, with her arms at her sides. She's looking out the window, frowning, trying to see what it is I've been gazing at so intently. She smiles at me.

What are you looking at?

I indicate the gull with my chin and turn back to the window. I don't want company. Definitely not from a twin-set and pearls auntie from the suburbs who's suffering from stress because her maid quit. The gull is flying higher and higher. I thought only swallows could get up so high. I have to squint to keep my eyes trained on it. I want to be that bird. I wish I could just lift my wings and fly, up, up and away. Like the song. Away from everything.

It's beautiful, isn't it?

God, she's still here.

I ignore her. I don't want her to see how the stupid bird has affected me, how its pure simplicity has brought home to me the basics of freedom and has me questioning why it's me locked up in here, trapped and broken, while it's out there, flying its stupid heart out, just because it can.

Isn't it, she repeats. Beautiful.

I shrug indifferently. I suppose so, I say.

You looked so far away, she says, coming closer. What are you thinking about?

I don't know why I say it but I do. What am I thinking about? That that bird out there got high and guess what, it never took drugs.

Is that why you're here?

Grudgingly, I am drawn into conversation with

this woman. At least it passes the time. I tell her I'm a drug addict and I'm waiting to be moved to a rehab clinic called Lulama. I don't tell her that I'm just going through the motions because I have no choice, that it's not going to work this time and that I've had enough of it all.

You're so young, she says. You don't look well. I'm sorry.

For the first time I look at her properly. She is thin and very pale, with greying hair and fine lines around her mouth and at the corners of her eyes. She might have been pretty once. She looks as if she hasn't slept for a while. I can relate to that. Sleep has not been a refuge for me much lately either. I ask her what she's in for.

Nervous breakdown, she says. Not the first one.

Before the words are properly out of her mouth I've already lost interest. More lies. I am so SICK of the lies. Suddenly it makes me angry.

Crap, I tell her. You're a drug addict like me. No different. I can tell it a mile off.

Anger has made my tone scornful. I don't mean it to be quite so rough, though, and the way she flinches makes me swear at her under my breath and turn back to the window again.

But she's not going away.

You're wrong, she says quietly, but firmly. I'm not a drug addict. I'm on medication, yes, but the doctors –

Oh, medi-*cation*, right, I drawl sarcastically. Of course you are.

155

I need the pills, she explains, enunciating care-fully for the lowlife junkie who doesn't understand that not everyone's like him. I can't cope without them. The doctors say if I stopped –

She's really pissing me off now. So what's your drug of choice, I interrupt her, and this time my voice is just as harsh as I intend it. Ativan? Valium? Etomine? I reel off a whole bunch of drugs, all tranquillisers, or antidepressants, or anti-anxiety pills the shrinks dish out to keep us calm and manageable. I can see I've hit home and I relent, but only slightly. She needs to know what she's up against and if it's a losing battle for me, perhaps it needn't be for her. That stuff's going to kill you, I tell her. Believe me. I know what I'm talking about. You think you've seen doctors? Well, now you're talking to a specialist. Drugs. That's my area of exper-tise. And if there's one thing I can tell you, it's that you're in the wrong place. You don't need to be in a psych ward. They're not going to help you here. They'll just adjust your 'medication'.

She's staring at me strangely and for a second I catch a glimpse of myself as she must see me. I weigh 45 kilos, my clothes are filthy, I probably don't smell great and there's a tremor in my hands that I can't con-trol. I realise in my desire to convince her that I've been shouting too. Some specialist. It's almost funny.

She changes course. What's your name, she asks me. Steve, I tell her. No last names. I'm Steve. She's June. June with the nineteenth nervous breakdown.

I should go, she says. It's getting late. She's

pushed back her sleeve and I mentally calculate the value of the gold watch on her wrist and convert it into mandrax tablets. Old habit. My husband – she adds. She's looking anxious now.

Sure. I shrug. Whatever.

She smiles at me again and gives a silly little wave as if she doesn't know what else to do. She walks slowly to the door.

Come with me, I say suddenly.

What? She turns back to me and suddenly it's terribly important to me that June should understand who she really is.

Come with me. To Lulama. They can help you fight your addiction there. I've got contacts, I can arrange a bed, I'll help you. Let me help you . . .

I told you, she says coldly. I've had a nervous break-down. I don't belong in a rehab clinic. The doctors –

The doctors don't know what they're doing, I tell her stubbornly. Haven't you heard anything I've said? They're lying to you, June.

Perhaps she's humouring me, at least at first, but when I shift over an inch she comes back and sits down and before I know it I realise we're exchanging life stories. I realise something else too. I like June. She has a quiet sadness around her that makes me alternately want to hit her or hug her. She talks fast, quickly and urgently, as if she has to get it all out before someone stops her. And her story is so unoriginal and mundane. The cliché of the straying husband, the under-mining of her self-esteem, the verbal abuse. Blah blah

blah. It's the basic plotline of a million marriages, my own parents' marriage included – with variations, of course. And where do the stressed out, anxious, depressed wives seek the solution nine times out of ten? In a tidy little blister pack handed over by the family GP who's running late and has double booked all of his patients and still has to make time for the pharmaceutical rep before five. That's where June's addiction started. No possession rap in school for her. Hers was all above board and perfectly respectable. Even socially acceptable, after a fashion.

Until now, where I can see the spectre of withdrawal like a shadow behind her eyes. It takes one to know one. But I *know* I can help June and I want to help her. More than anything.

I've got to go, Steve, she says. My husband is coming to visit me.

She's gone all formal on me again. Maybe it was the thought of her husband coming. Maybe we've come too close to intimacy and it's too raw for her. June is a woman no longer comfortable with intimacy. She's edgy and agitated, both of which states I recognise all too well.

Tomorrow, I call after her. Lulama.

But I'm not holding my breath.

✳

I'm waiting for David to pick me up and take me through to the clinic. I have all my worldly goods in a togbag between my feet: a T-shirt and a pair of takkies. Not much to show for twenty-seven years. I think of Ronan in his black Porsche and his seven fucking companies.

Hey, drug addict.

It's June, with what she probably thinks is a brave smile. Actually she looks dreadful. Her face is very white and there are big dark bags beneath her eyes. I'm coming with you, Steve, she says. If that's OK?

I smile back. Pull in, June, I say.

It's an addict moment. You had to be there.

In Lulama this time I know I'm going to die. I forget about June completely as the terrifying phantoms of my own withdrawal move in to claim my soul. I've been through this before, many times, but this is the worst, the worst it can ever be. I want to die but I can't. I beg, I cry, I pray for death. The tears that come are blood, not water. I can feel them scorching, skidding in burning furrows down my cheeks. I curse everyone who comes near me, my mother, my father, God, the sisters who watch indifferently as my vomit hits the wall over and over again and my bowels loosen and the stench of death mixes with shit and piss and fear and makes me crawl to the corner of the room and whimper for my mother.

When the shaking starts and the sweat pours off my chest and I'm freezing and the crawling things come, in my crotch up my arms my legs my ears, I scream for help. I scream and scream and tear at my skin, raking with bitten nails at my arms and legs and no one hears, no one comes.

Then my brain is on fire – no, not my brain, it goes much, much deeper than that. I don't have a name for it, this place that is being *consumed* from the inside out. My soul, perhaps, or whatever is the very essence of me, the core of me, the private, hidden place. Pain is not a word that can describe this. It's every kind of physical and mental anguish that can possibly be experienced and it's all concentrated on me. On Steve. Every excruciating blowtorch breath I pray is the last. But I am beyond prayer, beyond help. I am Steve. Beyond beyond. I can not come back from this.

I can't breathe. I am suffocating. My body is going to explode, and then it does and I'm covered in foul smelling shit, thin brown watery shit and it stinks and my stomach goes into spasm and the cold sweat breaks out again and a jet of vomit jerks me upright like a puppet and then drops me face down in it where I lie, burning and shaking and knowing nothing except that I'm not dying and I'm all alone and no one gives a damn.

For two days I don't know who or where I am. On the third day I'm feeling better but I'm still disorientated. I'm weak and when I stand up too quickly I black out. My hands shake violently, spasmodically. I have to be helped to the toilet. One of the volunteer sisters tells me to take it easy. I have a vitamin deficiency and am suffering from malnutrition. I need building up, she tells me solemnly.

I find that I am also practically a cripple. Standing is painful, so is walking. I do the addict's shuffle, bent over like an old man, holding onto the walls and fighting down waves of nausea. The pain and the stiffness, I understand, are from excessive shooting up behind my knees and in my groin. I have sores there still, black and crusting over. They smell too – a mixture of disinfectant and old blood.

It's Saturday and I'm managing better. I get as far as the TV lounge and June is sitting there. I've forgotten about June and it takes me a few minutes to rewind the tape and to react when she says Hullo, Steve. She's the only other person in the room but she's not watching TV. The sound is off anyway and the picture is snowy.

I can see that June is dying. Her face is the colour of day old ash and her eyes are huge and full of fear. She looks straight into mine and says, I can't do this, Steve. I'm too old.

Crap, I tell her. June, that's crap. You can beat this, you can, I *know* you can. Didn't I promise I would help you? Well, I'm here now. You don't have to do this on your own. Let me help you.

I'm frightened, Steve, she says.

I offer her a cigarette and she shakes her head. I have a quick one-sided conversation with God as I struggle with a match. I tell him I think he's been getting his wires crossed lately. June doesn't deserve this, I explain urgently. Please. I'm asking you. I'm asking you for this *one thing*. Take me instead. I *mean* it – I'm finished anyway. But not June. *Please*, God. Not this woman.

The next day, it's Sunday, I go looking for June in

the TV lounge. She's not there, and she's not in the residents' lounge either, or the dining room. One of the sisters comes to find me. June's not well today. She's asking for you.

June isn't really there. Just this thin, kind-faced woman on a white pillow, too weak to sit up.

Hey, drug addict, I say. Or try to say. No words come out at first because I'm trying to suppress a hot flush of anger that seems to start at my toes and race through to my chest in one swift movement, where it lodges like a splinter. *This is not right.* Before I can speak June lifts an arm and calls me over. I stand beside her bed.

Steve, she says. I'm dying. Pray for me.

I lose it then. Three people have to pin my arms to my sides and drag me out of there before I can smash every last item in that small, cold room.

✳

They give me permission to go to the funeral. The therapists escort me. I understand that I am crazy. I am violent. I am unpredictable. God knows what I would do if they let me loose.

God knows.

A Day in the Life ...

Hey, Steve. Long time no see. How are you?

   Fine.

   $\boxed{F}$ *ucked up.*

   $\boxed{I}$ *rrational.*

   $\boxed{N}$ *eurotic.*

   $\boxed{E}$ *motional.*

   I'm fine. Just fine.

TEN

Addicts are relationship time bombs. I found that out over and over again, and I'm still discovering it today.

Remember that whenever you do drugs, whether it's regular, 'harmless' weed smoking, or shrooms, or something more hectic, like acid or crack cocaine, you undergo a personality change. Might not be radical, perhaps not even noticeable to most people at first, probably not to you. I believed, for instance, when I was smoking and drinking at fifteen that the Steve who emerged then was the real Steve. It was the Steve someone as special as Tracey could be drawn to, after all, the Steve she was crazy about, who could make her laugh and was so affectionate and caring. Who wouldn't want to be that person? But think about it – right from the beginning my relationship with Tracey was based on a lie. It may have been great but it wasn't real. Reality lurked in another place that wasn't cool to be in.

Round about that time I also discovered something else that would become central to my lifestyle and behaviour from then onwards. I discovered the lure of power and *shit*, it was seductive. I was completely sucked in by the heady *feeling* that comes with knowing that you have something that someone else wants and that you have the ability and the means to satisfy their desire or to deny it. That's a potent mix. It's dynamite in anyone's hands and I would come to use it, ruthlessly, shamelessly, knowing the consequences and not giving a damn about them. I must have ruined hundreds of young lives, not only the kids I got onto drugs, with cold deliberation, but the lives of their families and friends too, and I did it all with my eyes wide open and without a qualm of conscience.

Looking back, it's all such basic psychology really. Remember what I told you – high or craving? Nothing in between? I was talking about drugs, of course, but I think I can apply these two extremes to my childhood too and to my own stunted emotional growth. What was it that I craved so badly? I didn't know it then but I do now, and there's lots of words for it. The two that are most arm's length and palatable, perhaps, that won't make you run a mile and think oh god he's gone all touchy feely, are approval and affection. Kinda basic really, when you think about it.

Approval and affection.

I craved those two things. I think we all do. I looked for them from my father, even in the worst times, and I'm still looking for them from him today, even though he's been dead so many years. The craving starts early, right back in the cradle. Think about the reaction of a parent the first time he sees his baby smile. Approval and affection all round. The baby does it again and it has the same magical effect. I think we spend the rest of our lives doing whatever it takes to have that reaction repeated.

I'm going to go out on a limb here, at the risk of alienating you. There's only one word for it, actually, and that word is love. It's love we're all looking for, that's all, in one form or another. We're high on love or we're craving it. Nothing in between. That's my theory anyway, and I've got brain damage, remember. I just know that when I had it, I was as high on it as anyone could be, and because it was so rare a commodity in my family, I looked for it – or a substitute for it when I thought it wasn't there – any place I could. If I had to buy it, manufacture it, cheat and steal to get it, change my personality to fool someone into giving it to me, barter drugs for it, hell, I'd do it.

I thought I could find my way to it through drugs.

It's important to understand this fundamental thing about doing drugs: it's not the drug itself that you want. It's the *feeling* you're after. The good feeling. Perhaps it's your substitute for love. The tragedy, of course, though, is that by the time you realise that it's only a substitute, and a poor one at that, it's too late to turn around and say Oh, well, let me go looking for the real thing then. By then it's got you. It's got you good.

And walking away is an impossible option.

It's pathetic in its simplicity when you think about it. Just like the song says: all you need is love.

At fifteen, though, I didn't know that was what it was. In the beginning it was more of a game than anything more sinister. It was a mixture of fun and bravado and a hefty leg-up for my non-existent self-esteem. In my home life I was a pawn in a struggle that was much bigger than me, and I was hopelessly out of my depth. I was disempowered, if you like. Outside of that environment I was someone else entirely. I was a person people wanted to be around. The sad thing, I suppose, in retrospect was that perhaps even *then* I was deluding myself. Perhaps it wasn't really me they wanted at all. I knew I was the route and the means to the good feeling and that everyone wanted a piece of that, but was that all that I represented to my friends? I'll never know now. Way too much water's gone under that particular bridge and most of those friends are dead.

That's the trouble with drugs. None of it's real in the end. The whole thing is one big lie. I wish every day that I could start over, turn back that damn clock and see what the real Steve was like and what he could have accomplished without his dangerous toys and dubious playmates. That's another reason why I want my life back.

✳

Tracey nagged at me. She knew what I was doing and she wanted to try it too. Back then my instincts were still reasonably sound and I hadn't yet tossed my conscience onto the garbage heap. I was protective of Tracey. I didn't want to get her involved in what was a risky business altogether. She was in line for prefect, even head girl.

No, man, Trace. You're captain of the netball team. You don't want to go messing with that stuff.

You do it.

Yes, but only now and then. It's no big deal. It doesn't even affect me.

Well, if it's no big deal, let me try it. It probably won't affect me either. Just once. I just want to see what it's like. Please? Just for the experience.

I don't know . . .

What's the worst that can happen?

Well, OK. Just once though.

Cross my heart, Steve.

Needless to say it's never just once. You'll know that by now. If you don't, you haven't been paying attention.

We started rolling joints for our girlfriends, me, Brian and James, small, one-bladed Rizlas, and they started smoking with us down on the beach to start with and later anywhere else that was relatively private. Our garage at home became a favourite drugging place. Drugs became what we did, how we socialised. We didn't know it then but we couldn't really function or relate to one another properly without them.

That's what I mean about relationship time bombs. When your emotions and moods are dictated by drugs, that's a slippery set of rocks to use as a foundation for a relationship. You're different on drugs. You behave one way when you're doing drugs and another when you're not. The highs are very high, the lows are ghastly, and the in between times are spent calculating and scheming how to get back to the highs. It's an interesting cycle and it doesn't really matter what drugs or combination of drugs you use. They all follow a similar pattern. What's different is the intensity, the time it takes to get there, the effect on your energy and your mood, and the gamble on a good or bad trip if you're on something like acid. The intention is always the same, to reach that plateau of euphoria and stay there as long as possible. Trust me, it *is* euphoria and don't let anyone tell you different. And when you do reach it, it's truly amazing. When you're high everything seems possible. The solutions to all your problems are so obvious, in fact to all the *world's* problems too. Everything is gentle and peaceful.

Then you start to come down from the beautiful plateau and now the only thing that's amazing is how drab, dull and ordinary everything is. And it's all a lot more drab, dull and ordinary than you remembered it. Simple problems are magnified. People you usually like to be with, you don't want to hang around with anymore. You become antisocial at best and unpleasant and obnoxious at worst. You get no pleasure out of anything and the business of living becomes a chore with very little going for it.

If you have a girlfriend, whether she is using too or not, she's your passenger on this switchback road. When you're down she's down there with you. When you're high and tripping on the good feeling again everything between you is fine. In fact it's better than fine. Making love when you're stoned – better yet, when you're *both* stoned – can be the most erotic and intense lovemaking you will ever experience because when you're high everything, every *sense* is exaggerated ten-fold, your emotions especially, but sexually too.

But what happens when you're not stoned? I'll tell you what happens. It's a let down and guess what – very possibly a let down in the literal sense as well. Bet they don't tell you that part in the drug talks, do they? If you can get it together, lovemaking is not as good as it was before, even disappointing, mechanical. There's a vital element missing.

And all of those other elements that are part of any relationship are affected too. Your moods veer first one way and then another. You get angry, depressed, anxious, paranoid, restless, you name it. Is your girl-friend really being faithful to you? Why is she tapping her fingers on the table and looking bored? You have an argument over something trivial and all of a sudden it's a BIG argument. You have a misunderstanding and before you know it it's grown out of all proportion until you're not talking to each other and there's a hairline fracture in the precious trust you thought you shared. So what do you do? What do you do to get your relationship back to where it was before? Ah, yes. *That's* what you do. Of course.

Then there's another thing, and it relates to that little mantra every dealer knows off by heart. Your first time is free, your second time is free, your third, your fourth time is free and then one day . . . *you owe me*. Remember it? A dealer's generosity has a limit and business is business.

Drugs cost money. What if you haven't got enough? Well, there's a few options open to you, but the most important thing to remember is that you're going to pay. You are going to pay. You can borrow. You can have an extended loan. You can pawn something. You can steal something of value and hand it over. Or you can get a commission deal going, if you like. Just pass some weed around among your friends, bring in the cash for that and the commission you earn will pay for the drugs you bought two weeks ago. Well, almost. There's a bit still outstanding, but that's cool. You can bring that tomorrow. The day after? No, *tomorrow*. But what if – ? We know where you live. We know who your friends are. We know –

OK, OK! Tomorrow.

After I came out of the army, when I discovered that I couldn't get a job because I was a drug addict, had a criminal record, no matric and no other qualifications to speak of, someone suggested I go see Mikey.

Mikey?

You know Mikey . . . with the black BM?

Oh sure, Mikey.

I went to see him. I explained how I was battling a bit, not able to find work, how I'd just got out the army, been on the border, how I had no money. He listened to my hard luck story with a stony expression.

So how can I help you, bru?

Well, I – I thought – I need something, Mikey.

So what you got?

Well . . . if you could . . . I just need . . . Fuck, I *need* something, Mikey. Whatever you got. Just one pill. Just one. I'll pay you. I promise.

With what?

I'll give you my denim jacket, bru. It's new. It's almost new.

Mikey laughed but there was no humour in the sound. I got ten denim jackets, he told me.

Just give me a couple of days. I'll get the money.

Round about then I was easily working through a thousand bucks worth of drugs in a week and I knew I was heading for some serious withdrawal. I felt nauseous, my head ached, I had a million worries jostling each other for space in my head. I was close to panicking even before I got to Mikey's place. I knew I had to make a plan and soon.

Mikey jerked his head towards the face-brick walls of the high school down the road. You know that place, he asked me.

I nodded. I was sweating. I didn't have time for small talk.

That place is paying for my house, bru.

I was a bit slow on the uptake and I looked at

him blankly. Then he waggled a fat hand beneath my nose. He had a gold band on every pudgy finger.

What you telling me, Mikey? You been married five times?

He shot me a look, smiled and looked away again. He had a gold front tooth. I'm not married, he said, gazing over my shoulder, but I have a fondness for glitter.

I dug deep into my pocket for the one thing I'd kept for a severe emergency. The way I was feeling, I reckoned, was pretty damn severe.

This do, Mikey?

He took my mother's wedding ring and turned it around in the sunlight. He didn't look all that impressed, but he slipped it into his pocket all the same. Tell you what, he said. I give you press outs, R8 a tab, and you sell them at the school over there, R15 a tab. You take the difference – you can do the maths, bru? – and we're in business.

Mandrax had only just hit Durban. Up till then it had largely been a Cape drug, originally used as a prescription painkiller but soon the main ingredient for a white pipe. Mandrax crushed and mixed with dagga and smoked through a bottleneck gave you a rush unlike any other. I knew I'd have customers moving through the fancy wrought iron school gates in droves. They'd be queuing up, day and night.

And when my mother shed bitter tears over her lost wedding ring, I blamed the maid next door, who came to visit our maid sometimes.

Never did trust that woman, I told her.

INSTITUTIONS

Andrea arrives in rehab at the same time as me. We are in admissions together. I can't remember how many times she's tried to get clean, but this is my eleventh institution and when they bring me in I'm in pretty bad shape. Apparently my heart keeps stopping. This will happen three or four times over the next couple of days. There is panic every time I arrest – the first time is right there in the reception area where my head hits the floor as I'm taking a pen from the sister on duty to sign in. My mentor, a guy who's in Phase four of the three-month programme, someone they assign to you when you arrive, raises the alarm. He realises quickly that I haven't just passed out, but that I'm actually about to die on him. This won't look too good on his CV when he gets to the job interview phase of his recovery.

Doctors and nurses come running. They jab a needle into me and start to work on me right there on the floor until they get my heart going again. I'm vaguely aware of all this activity and I wish they wouldn't bother, but no one's listening to me as usual. I don't actually know where I am although I think it might be Phoenix. All I have in my head right now is a dim memory of tripping on the bus on the way here. LSD. I'm not on this planet anymore, that's for sure.

And I've had enough. I've had enough of it all. None of this is new for me. None of it works anymore. This is the end, and thank God for that.

For two days I listen to Andrea's withdrawal in a room just down the passage from mine. The screaming, the swearing, the crying – and the hideous, desperate *ka-klung!* of the bars on the side of the bed as she wrestles with the restraints that keep her tied to it. I don't know what damage they think she can do really. Andrea has had all the tips of her fingers amputated. She got gangrene from shooting up under her nails too many times. That's what you do when you've got no veins left to speak of.

I have an open, suppurating sore in my groin the size of a fifty cent coin. It's a crusty black hole and it won't close anymore. Lately I've had to dig hard to find an entry point for a needle, there's so much dried blood to scrape away. It's only the sticky ooze of greenish-black pus that guides me to the spot where I can gouge the wound open properly. It smells bad though. I'm rotting. My body is in a state of decay. My mind too.

When I'm stable they pump me full of psychiatric drugs and give me plastic cups of pills to swallow and they gradually begin to integrate me into a group. Phase one. Steve is back in Phase one and nobody's saying Welcome home. How many times can a person slide down the big monster snake on the snakes and ladders board and start over right at the bottom in the Phase one block? I'm sick of it. Sick and weary. I can't keep up this pretence anymore. It doesn't work. *Why* doesn't it work? I don't know. I just know it doesn't. I suppose they've got to do *something*, and maybe for one or two people it's not all a waste of time. Perhaps, though, they're giving hope where there isn't any? Maybe that's their first mistake. They've given me hope enough times, told me I can live a drug-free life. I know now they were lying. That's how I feel about it anyway. And they're lying still. I feel like getting up and shouting at the bland-faced group of 'problem children' sitting around me: YOU'RE ALL GOING TO RELAPSE THE MINUTE YOU WALK OUT OF THAT DOOR WHEN YOU'VE COMPLETED THE PROGRAMME AND DON'T LET THEM TELL YOU OTHERWISE. But we don't talk about relapse in Phase one. I know that much. Maybe *that's* their first mistake. The possibility of relapsing is way higher than the possibility of not. Why not put it out on the table and deal with it?

I'm not responding in this group. Fuck, I'm still coming *down*, for chrissake. What's the big hurry – a shortage of beds again? Anyway, I'm not interested in participating this time, playing the new boy, waiting politely to be introduced, listening to instructions about my chores. I've done this so many times I can't go on anymore. I sit on the fringe of the group and stare out of the window. You know what? I realise suddenly – I'm done here.

And I make a conscious decision. Even though I am drugged to the eyeballs and so depressed even the smallest effort like lighting a cigarette is too much for me, I am able to make this one completely lucid decision.

I decide to die. Not to kill myself. *To die.*

I close my eyes and begin. It's easier than I think. Slowly, slowly, slo-o-owly my system starts to shut down. My breathing slows, my heartbeat grows fainter – softly, gently, it's fading away. I am letting go. This is not suicide. I am simply letting go of life. I am surprised at how easy it is.

I am aware of voices but they are far away, some-where off in the distance. I can hear my name. I have a sensation of being carried, clumsy hands underneath me, and a soft blur of faces. The voices are getting further and further away. And then. Nothing.

A strange kind of hush comes over the place while I lie in my bed with my organs shutting down and, I learn later, much later, that the members of my group come in and out of my room every day. They bring cards and other small offerings and put them where they hope I will see them when I wake up. If I wake up. It seems that I have the doctors puzzled. Someone, perhaps it is Andrea, sits beside me for a long time each day holding my hand. Pete, who is a GP addicted to peth-idine, sits in a chair next to my head and sings to me in Afrikaans, strange old lullabies he must have dredged up from god knows where.

And Miriam, beautiful Miriam the beauty queen from Israel, brings me a picture she's drawn for me. She sticks it with Prestik on the side of my locker so that if I were to turn my head I would see it. To Steve, it says. Love Miriam. She's used a piece of thick cream coloured paper, cardboard almost, about the size of a postcard, and on it she's drawn a heart. It is outlined in thick black koki and filled in with deep blood red ink. The heart doesn't close off neatly to a point at the bottom like the hearts you see on Valentine cards. This one is damaged. The red blood flows right out of the bottom where it begins to pool and congeal. The drawing isn't finished. The red koki sort of trickles away – perhaps it just ran out or maybe she didn't know how to finish it – before the bottom bit is completely filled in. Down the centre of the heart she has drawn a jagged line, carved deep with the black pen. This sad, bleeding heart is cracked right through from top to bottom. Whose heart is it? Hers? Mine? All of ours?

To Steve. Love Miriam.

ELEVEN

My mother had a lot to cope with. If I had my life back the way I dream of having it and lived ten lifetimes one after the other, I could never make it up to her. I can see how the damage and pain I caused her for so many years have taken their toll and I cannot find it in my heart to lay any of the blame for the paths I chose at her feet. I will carry guilt for my mother's tears with me forever. It's the albatross around my neck, a sorry pendant if ever there was one, and its rotten carcass is my constant reminder of the depths I sank to and to which I beckoned my mother to follow me. And she did. No matter what trouble I was in she followed me, plodding stoically after her wild and wayward son and hauling him back to his feet time and time again.

She was there on the hard wooden benches in court when I was sentenced to prison.

She was there at the graveside beside me to witness yet another of my friends being lowered into the ground.

She was there to wipe the vomit from my mouth during my withdrawals in one rehab after another.

When I had nowhere to go she took me in, without question, without accusation.

And through it all I cursed her.

I abused her home and I abused her love. I stole from her. I lied to her. I told her how much I hated her and took pleasure in the way her eyes would fill with tears when I said it.

Did you hear me, mom? I hate you! I hate you! I hate you . . .

You're like a Christmas tree, Steve, she told me once. You know how it is on Christmas morning, the pine needles fresh and green, the decorations sparkling new. And the lights! That moment when you switch on the lights and the whole tree comes alive? Isn't that the best thing? And the presents laid out beneath the tree on the floor, wrapped in colour and ribbons and mystery. That was you – once. So full of sparkle and promise. I watched you and I was proud. So proud. And then I watched the lights on that Christmas tree go out, one by one, and I saw how the branches began to droop and turn brown and the pine needles fell onto the floor. And finally, when I picked up the presents, they were all empty and hollow. That's how I see you, Steve. Just like that Christmas tree.

✳

Whether we'd ever have another family Christmas together I didn't know, but in the meantime my father was going through periods where he seemed to have eased up a bit on his drinking. I think the black weekend, his heart attack scare and the visit to my mother all contributed in their own way to a genuine intention to cut back and get his life back on track somehow. It wasn't enough to scare him off the booze altogether, that would have been optimistic, but I thought I could detect a small change. It was probably just wishful thinking, but there were times when he could hold a conversation and other times when he sat and paged through the newspaper he always brought home in the evening and there weren't as many empties in the garbage as before. Gradually, though, his intake increased again and before long he was spending more time down at the hotel than he was at home.

I took to the streets with my buddies. We were drugging every day. If you lived close to the school, as I did, you could get what they called a lunch exit. This meant that you could go home at break time and have lunch. We used our lunch exits to go home and drug and quite often I didn't make it back to school in the afternoon.

I don't have a good recall of that time but it was bad. We were smoking pipes all day and drinking up a storm at weekends. Quite how we didn't get kicked out of school I don't know. I guess there was never any real hard evidence, only suspicions, truancy and a complete lack of academic interest. I suppose we turned up in class just often enough to keep one step ahead of trouble.

One time I got picked up in the street by the cops where I was fighting drunk, tripping, and 'causing a public disturbance' and I spent a night in the cells. It was a Saturday night and an especially busy one for them. I was chucked into a holding cell with all the other drunks and rowdies. It was crowded and filthy, with the splatter of someone's puke on the concrete floor, a bucket to pee in and a fluorescent strip in the corridor outside that they kept on night and day. It made my eyeballs ache.

I recognised a guy I knew across the way from me, where he stood propped against the wall, swaying a bit and mumbling to himself.

It was my father, pissed as an owl.

He didn't see me. By the state of him, I reckoned he wouldn't have been able to focus further than a foot in front of his nose anyway. I wondered where his car was, whether he'd driven it into a tree or had been pulled off the road by the cops. Maybe the same cops who'd given me a lift to this popular downtown stop-over. I started to laugh. It was so fucking funny, I laughed and laughed until the guy next to me tried to stub his cigarette out on my hand and that shut me up quite smartly.

The routine is that they let the drunks out first in the morning, when they've sobered up, before they release the other offenders, so by the time they shoved me out into the bright morning light, the sun was riding high in the sky and my father had gone. He was sitting at the kitchen table with a beer and the Sunday papers when I walked through the door. I could smell Old Spice. Soap on a Rope. My sister's present to him on his birthdays.

He looked me up and down.

And where the hell have *you* been, he greeted me. He was in a foul mood.

I paused in the doorway and took in the crushed beer cans on the floor, aimed roughly in the direction of the trash can, and the dog's food bowl, crusted over and crawling with flies.

I stared my father down.

Then I shook my head, slowly, and gave a small laugh.

I could ask you the same question, I said, and I turned and went up to my room.

※

Before the end of the last term at school, with the summer holidays stretching in front of us, I came home one afternoon and saw that my father had got home before me. Our driveway was on a slope and I saw his car parked there with the bonnet open. I got a strange feeling in my chest, a sort of bad, ominous feeling unlike anything else I'd ever experienced. Something wasn't right but I couldn't identify it. Instinctively I quickened my pace and was almost jogging and out of breath by the time I reached the gate and the driveway.

I stopped, with my hand on the gatepost, and let my backpack drop onto the ground. I glanced at the front door. It was open. I could hear the dog whining from the back garden where she was locked up. She wasn't usually locked up when my father was home. She was flopping around his feet if he was passed out drunk or chewing on her basket in the kitchen out of harm's way if he was foul temper drunk.

With the bonnet up and the engine idling, perhaps there was something wrong with the car but my father didn't seem to be around. Then I saw that he was sitting in the car. I could see the top of his head sticking out above the backrest of the driver's seat and as I got closer it looked like he was asleep. His head kept nodding forward onto his chest, and even when I tapped on the window right next to him he didn't look up.

I don't know why it took me so long to work it out really. It was pretty obvious what was going on. Maybe I just didn't want to see it at first, but there was the hosepipe plain as day. I saw how it had been cut and stretched over the exhaust pipe and secured with an old rag and some string. I could see it all clearly, logically. I followed it with my eyes, the way the hose was looped around the back wheel, then up the back passenger door and squashed into the top of the window like a green grooved snake, and I just stood staring at it like some dumbass fool, not even asking myself what was wrong with the picture. In retrospect it was probably only a matter of seconds before the implication hit me and my limbs started to move of their own accord, but somehow it felt like I was rooted to the spot for a long time, just a disinterested onlooker, watching my dad kill himself in the most clichéd of ways.

Then I was moving, taking in at a glance that the car doors were all locked, that the radio in the dashboard was still on and that my father's breath had made a small foggy circle on the window. I banged hard on the pane with the flat of my hand until my palm stung but my father took no notice of me.

Suddenly I was six years old again, frantic with panic at what my mother would say when she found out that I'd let him get into trouble again. Not *again*, Steve. She was going to *kill* me this time, for sure. I banged and banged and pulled stupidly on the door handle at the same time, but still my father took no notice. His hands were resting neatly on his knees.

I looked around. There was nobody anywhere, not even a curious neighbour or a gardener. I saw a big chunk of stone on the ground by my feet where it must have come loose from the border of the flowerbed and I picked it up and in one movement smashed the back passenger window. Bits of glass flew everywhere and my father's head fell forward onto his chest. I reached past him and got the door open and dragged him out by the armpits as if he was one of my little sister's dolls. His eyes flew open then but they were unfocused and although he looked at me I'm not sure whether he knew who I was at first. I could feel his muscles stiffen and resist and so I punched him and punched him again, and then we were rolling together on the lawn in a tight, desperate ball, clinging to each other for balance and aiming wild blows all over the place.

In this weird silent jumble of thrashing arms and legs I remember only a feeling of such helpless and debilitating anger that no sounds or words would ever have been able to express it. As we broke apart, gasping, wheezing, coughing and sobbing for breath, I struggled to get a steady picture in my mind of what had just happened there. It was like a scene in one of those low-budget movies where they use only hand-held cameras and everything bobs about and zooms in and out of focus and cuts to seemingly irrelevant pieces of the landscape. I was the shaky lens trying to get a fix on which part of the jigsaw I was clinging to and how I fitted into my own life, let alone the life of the man in the vest sitting crying on the lawn with his head between his knees.

He looked at me and there were tears running down his face. Help me, Steve, he said. I can't stop drinking. Can you help me?

I felt so useless, such a failure. I can't, dad, I said. I've tried. I can't.

It was as if every emotion inside me was melting and just draining away. I didn't know whether I'd even spoken the words out loud because he just turned his desperate face to me and kept begging.

Help me, Steve. *Help me*. I can't stop *drinking* . . .

That night I phoned my mother.

You have to come home, I told her. You have to. We need you here.

I put my sister on the phone too. Please, she said. Please, mom. Please come home.

Dad's going into a clinic, I told her. He's promised. And this time he's serious. He's going to stop drinking. You said if he stopped drinking you'd come home.

So she did. My mother came home. My father checked himself into a clinic and began the process of drying out.

He never drank again.

*

Down on the beach one morning before school, James, Brian and I made a quick *skyf*.

Take the pips out, James, like I showed you, man. That's what turns your bloody eyes red.

We're gonna be late. We haven't got time –

Drug squad! Don't move!

Fuck.

Talk about caught red handed. And in our school uniforms too. Before any one of us could drop the evidence and scuff it into the sand while at the same time opening our mouths to protest complete innocence and indignation, we found ourselves slapped with unexpected fashion accessories in addition to the surfing charms and bracelets we already wore on our wrists: handcuffs!

At first we were all three stunned into dumb silence. Then Brian and James were both talking at once and pointing at me.

It wasn't me, it was him!

Steve bought the weed. It's him! The dagga's Steve's.

And my good buddies looked from one cop to the other with unblinking eyes and pale, innocent faces while I stood by helplessly and listened to them.

We'd have been naïve never to have anticipated that we'd get caught one day. We all knew the risks. Whether it was a stupid law or not – and everyone knew it was a stupid law and it was only a matter of time before smoking dope was legalised anyway – possession of dagga was against the law and we were well and truly busted. We'd discussed many times what we'd do if we ever were caught, *rehearsed* it even. I was completely astonished to discover that apparently Brian and James had entirely forgotten the script. We'd all agreed. We would never rat on one another. Not in a million years. You'd just never do that. What had happened to the code – the code of honour, loyalty and undivided friendship? Out the window, clearly.

It wasn't me, it was him.

We were split up and questioned separately. Brian told them everything. He just couldn't volunteer enough information. He made it very plain, though, that none of it was his doing. It was all Steve. Steve was the one who smoked dagga. Steve was the one who bought it. Brian had never touched – actually never even *seen* – the stuff till that very morning. Yes – that very morning. He wasn't even planning to smoke. He had no idea Steve had anything with him. You could have knocked him over with a –

James wasn't much better. I could tell because neither he nor Brian would meet my eyes when they bundled us into the unmarked police car, still hand-cuffed, and chucked our school backpacks any old how into the boot. I wanted to *klap* them both. I knew exactly what had gone down.

What I couldn't know was what would happen next. Would they drop us off at the top of the road to school and let us off with a warning? Surely that's what they'd do. We were just kids, for chrissake, experimen-ting for the first and only time with weed (I knew our separate stories would have agreed *that* much at least) and we'd definitely never do it again. They'd drop us off. It would all blow over. No one would even have to know about this. And I was through with dagga anyway. I really was. I'd already decided. I was going to stop just as soon as –

See that house over there, one of the cops turned and said. He was looking at me, squashed into the middle of the back seat between the two silent traitors.

What?

That house there. With the green door.

What about it?

We'd pulled over to the side of the road near some old boarded up takeout stores. The house he was indicating looked just as run down and neglected. Paint was peeling off the green door and all the windows were shut. There was litter in the front garden and half a car on bricks in the driveway.

You take this R10 note and go knock on the door. Tell them you want to buy dagga.

What? No way.

I didn't understand what was going on, but I understood enough from the morning's events so far to know by now that I was in deep shit. My little fantasy of being let off with a Don't do it again, son, was fading fast. Already we'd taken a different road to the one that led to our school and we were in unfamiliar territory.

You don't get a choice, sunshine. Take the money. Knock on the door.

No. You can't make me do that.

I looked at James – he'd know if I had a democratic right or something – but he was staring out of the window as if he hadn't heard a word of this bizarre exchange. Brian was biting the corners of his nails.

The cop took an ugly looking gun from the holster at his hip and I felt my heart begin to thud somewhere up near my throat.

You'll do what I say, he said quietly, or you'll run from my gun.

✳

Down at the station we had to do something called a *tong tippie toets* – the tongue tip test. Nothing as sophisticated as a urine or blood sample for us and it wasn't

190

necessary anyway. They already had the plastic bankie with the weed in it. Now the brown stains on my fingers completed the formal part of the investigation.

You got one phonecall, the cop behind the charge office desk said. Who you gonna call – Ghostbusters? And he sniggered a bit as if he thought I might like to join in.

One phonecall. Two choices. Mom or dad? If I call mom she's going to really freak out. If I call dad he's going to kill me. Mom – freak out. Dad – kill me.

I'm calling mom.

Steve? What's the matter? Why aren't you at school?

Mom – I'm at the police station.

Oh no. Did you get your bike stolen again? Steve, I warned you –

No, it's not my bike, mom. It's me.

You? I don't understand. What are you talking about?

I was down on the beach and . . . I . . . We . . .

Steve? You've been in an accident?

They found me with dagga, mom. Drugs. They caught me with drugs.

Weed. Dagga. Grass. Ganja. Grows in the ground. It's a herb, man. God made it.

That was my litany.

Now, for the first time, I had called dagga drugs.

I was driven home in a squad car. The cop who drove me was a different guy from the one who'd wanted to make my feet dance to the tune of his bullets.

He told me, staring straight ahead as he drove the couple of kilometres to my home, that there was no point in telling him or anyone else that I'd learnt my lesson, that I had only smoked a joint as an experiment, that I wouldn't do it again.

Because you will, he said. And not only dagga. If you haven't done so already, you will experiment with other drugs, harder drugs one day. You will. I'm telling you the truth. So just don't fool yourself, OK? And don't think you can fool anyone else either.

✳

Accused number one – how do you plead?

Guilty, your honour.

There's a first time for everything, I believe, and this was another first for me, pleading guilty to a drug-related charge before a magistrate. I was supremely conscious of my mother's red-rimmed eyes on my back. She'd had to take a day off work to be here. God knows what she'd told her new boss. She hadn't even told my aunt yet and she was usually on the phone to her instantly when I'd done something dreadful. My father didn't put in an appearance in court. I had a heavy feeling that he might be down at the hotel drowning the sorrows of having a disgraced son. He was not wearing his new sobriety mantle lightly and I knew in my heart of hearts that he was walking a very shaky tightrope. It wouldn't take much to make him lose his balance.

Call it beginner's bad luck but nothing was going

my way. The magistrate was not at all sympathetic to the scrubbed young faces in front of him. He wasn't swayed for a minute by our clean, neat clothes, brushed hair and earnestly contrite expressions.

Never, your honour. Never again will I touch drugs, sir. I've learnt my lesson. It was just that one time and that's it.

Actually, I believed myself too. I wasn't just saying it. Cooling my heels in the cells at the back of the cop shop, I'd made a decision. My father could quit drinking, and I could quit smoking weed. I was sick of it anyway. It was expensive and getting boring. I'd rolled my last joint that weekday morning on the beach.

The magistrate was determined to make an example out of us. What we were doing was dangerous and illegal and the court was taking it seriously. He wanted there to be no doubt in our minds about that. Because of our youth and because we were first offenders and he was taking that into account, we would not be doing time in prison or reform school. But we would carry around with us a four year suspended sentence.

Let me make it clear to you, he said, what a suspended sentence means. Suspended. That's something that can fall on you at any moment, and you need to know that for the next four years it's hanging by a thread right above your heads. If you are caught again – for *anything* – you will pick up this drug charge and serve these four years in prison, plus any other sentence that is handed down to you. Do you understand?

We did. *I* certainly did anyway. Just let me outta there and I would stop. I wasn't sure that Brian, James and I would have much to say to each other after this either.

And just in case we didn't feel disgraced enough, our headmaster felt it would be a useful lesson for everyone if we were paraded at assembly like the criminals we were in front of the whole school in our new silver bracelets. A word to the friendly neighbourhood police officers and we were led, handcuffed, up to the stage in the school hall where we were made to stand for half an hour while another drug squad cop gave a lecture about the dangers of drug abuse and the headmaster's eyes raked the rows of pupils in front of him for signs of nervous twitching.

As far as my parents were concerned, our headmaster was the neighbourhood saint because instead of expelling me, he gave me a second chance. He made it very clear, though, that there would be no third chance and I had to shape up, pull myself together and put my head down, all at the same time. Anyone would think I was made of plasticine. I agreed to everything. I promised my mother I would never, ever touch the dreaded weed again.

This was my mother's blind spot. In the beginning she never did believe that I was actively, willingly using drugs. All she had to do was look in my eyes and she'd have known, but she never did. Perhaps she didn't want to see.

He's just growing up, I heard her telling my aunt

194

in a low voice on the telephone. Experimenting, you know. All kids do it. They need a bit of space to bump their heads. Steve's fine really. He got a big fright, I think. He's learnt his lesson.

In parading us in front of the school I suppose the headmaster was doing what he thought was sensible – the hot hand on the stove routine again. And I suppose there might have been kids in our school who got enough of a scare to keep them away from drugs, but they were probably kids who wouldn't have gone in that direction anyway, when you think about it. But sometimes that sort of display can backfire badly and the kids who might have been wavering on the weed smoking issue, those who were slightly tempted or intrigued – what effect did our fashion show have on those borderline ones?

I have a few little mantras, you must have noticed by now, little rhythmic phrases that I repeat to myself and to others as reminders of who we are and what we do.

One of them is One wrong word can kill a kid.

After that assembly I'm afraid to say that far from being shunned and outlawed by our peers, our status at school shot up dramatically. Everybody loves a rebel, especially one who's outwitted the law, flouted authority (with an apologetic smirk and a clink of handcuffs) and mingles among the common folk just like one of them.

By the time the school bell rang at the end of that day, I could have filled an order book, and Brian, James and I had made peace and bonded all over again. Where there had been fear, now there was bravado. Before long we were outdoing one another with our wit and piss-taking re-enactment of the bust. I could do a great imitation of the magistrate's heavily accented English. James called me Your honour until I threatened to break his nose for him.

We stopped at the bottlestore on the way home.

A Day in the Life ...

This is how a normal day goes for me now, as my 40th birthday approaches.

If there's work, I'll be on the road with Joe, my stage manager, staying in Protea hotels wherever we are in the country, courtesy of the amazing Arthur Gillis, my mentor and sometime guardian angel.

Usually, whether I'm on the road or at home, the first thing I do when I open my eyes in the morning – actually, even before I open my eyes – is feel around on the bedside table for my packet of cigarettes and my lighter. I light my first cigarette of the day while I'm still lying on my back with my head on the pillow.

Nowadays, though, as I'm getting older and my health is not great, I first do my exercises. These consist of a gentle walk round my room to get the old heart going, make sure it's still beating.

Then I light up my first cigarette of the day. While I'm getting dressed I'll probably smoke a couple more.

Then I'll have my vitamins. This involves a whole battery of pills to boost my ailing immune system which, as I get older, doesn't kick in too good anymore when there are flu bugs circulating. (Addiction is a progressive disease, remember.) After that it's a quick cup of strong coffee – maybe two – and then I'm off to meet up with Joe.

On our way to the gig we'll stop off at a garage and pick up a couple of energy drinks and make sure we've got enough smokes to get Steve through his day. If it's cold we might grab a polystyrene mug of instant coffee with lots of sugar and drink it leaning against the car with the smoke from our breath curling up against the sky. Finally, I'll pop a couple of headache powders and swallow them down with the dregs of the energy drink.

I don't have a headache.

Back at the wheel, cigarette in hand, I'm ready for the day. Off to our first school and our first show to educate young people about the dangers of dependence.

This is my clean time.

TWELVE

A history of drug addiction – even a very *short* history – creates all sorts of trust issues that will shadow you for most of your life.

When you're drugging you will betray the trust of just about everybody you know, not to mention yourself. You'll begin with your family and move on to your friends until there are no relationships that remain unaffected.

When you stop drugging and you want things to return to the way they were before – tough shit. They won't. Not easily and not in the trust department anyway. Regaining people's trust is a much longer road than losing it and it's a damn steep climb into the bargain.

I was once, a couple of years ago, on a sort of Lions road show circuit, doing my show for schools as a guest of the Lions. They arranged my transport and set up a great schedule for me. While I was travelling they put me up in members' homes.

My stage manager at the time, Ollie, and I stayed over a weekend with Mr and Mrs F. They were gracious hosts and made us feel very welcome, almost part of the family. We slept in their guest bedroom and they cooked us wonderful meals.

But they didn't trust us.

We were drug free. We were sober. We washed our hands before dinner. But they didn't trust us.

We're just popping out to the shops, they told us on Saturday morning. Can we drop you chaps off anywhere?

Oh, no, thank you. We're cool.

You sure you don't need anything?

Not a thing, I told them. We'll be fine. Don't worry about us.

We'll only be half an hour. Less, probably.

Enjoy yourselves. We'll be fine.

Ten minutes, even. Be back before you know it.

We knew what was going on. They didn't want to leave us alone in their house, in case – what? In case we made a quick pipe in the bathroom? In case we used Mrs F's silk stockings to tie round our upper arms while we spiked? In case we cleaned the place out and ducked without leaving a note?

We were 'reformed' drug addicts performing at schools, urging the youth of today not to do drugs. We were the *good* guys now. We were on the same side, weren't we?

But still . . . You just never know, do you?

Five minutes after they'd gone Mrs F came back inside for her cellphone and seemed a little embarrassed to find Ollie pouring me a cup of tea while I watched TV.

I was embarrassed too. I had my shoes on the coffee table.

I've been doing my show for a dozen years or more and I'm sponsored by some high profile companies whose continuing generosity enables me to stay on the road and do the work that I do. Right up to now I think some of them still have moments of doubt. Call me paranoid but I have a feeling no one's ever entirely sure about me. Not *entirely*. There's always a niggle somewhere at the back of someone's mind. A rumour starts, there are a few meetings, an apologetic suggestion that the rumour can easily be squashed if I underwent a simple urine test. I have to understand that their name cannot be associated . . . *They* know I'm really clean, but just for the doubters . . .

So I take it upon myself to have regular urine and blood tests, to save them the embarrassment of having to keep asking or to have to insist on putting a clause in a contract. Actually, I'd put it in for them, gladly. That clause is there for me too.

They're right not to trust me. I don't blame them actually. Although I might be clean, that's just for today.

I can't guarantee tomorrow.

There's something else too. You'd be amazed at

how deeply the superiority complex is entrenched in the subconscious of people – and how close to the surface it actually is – who don't do drugs or never have had anything to do with *addiction* of any sort, or so they believe anyway. They think they're better than us. They really do. If you accused them of this they would be astounded and you'd watch them falling over themselves to set you right. They'd simply hate to be accused of discrimination of any kind. They'll overcompensate by being extra attentive, extra understanding, just to prove their shallow humanity.

Alcoholics get off more lightly. By comparison, they're respectable. Alcoholism is accepted as an illness and people who suffer from it should be cared about and understood rather than censured. Drugging causes a different reaction. A hollow-eyed twenty-five year old who sits on a bathroom floor and eases a needle into a vein is not the same as a twenty-five year old who passes out in front of the television with his mouth open after a bottle of the famous grouse.

Why? Why should they be viewed differently?

It's *addiction* that's the illness, not the substance they're introducing into their bloodstreams. So why do we make allowances for one and not the other? Why is one just a social misfit and the other a social outcast?

As an addict in the public eye and one who sits sipping tea with guidance counsellors in the country's school staffrooms, I am hyper-aware of the difference between Them and Us. Don't get me wrong – they're by no means all like this, and most of the schools I get invited to over and over again are genuinely appreciative and supportive, and they applaud what I try to do. It's certain individuals on their staffs whose jaws must simply ache from having to smile with clenched teeth as they entertain me before and after my show. Sometimes they don't even bother to hide their disdain. It's all in the body language, which tells a different story from the We're so grateful you could make the time platitudes that slip out of their mouths. It's as if what I have is catching. They might say they want me in their schools, and congratulate me on the work I'm doing, but they're not always anxious to have me hanging around too long. Perhaps it's that trust thing again. Is it because they don't altogether trust that I'm not infiltrating the ranks and actually doing the opposite of what I say I'm doing? I could be recruiting, couldn't I? Once a druggie always a druggie. Or is it because I'm tainted somehow and they don't want any of what I've done to rub off on their nice clean clothes?

Whatever it is, I know I'm a lesser being in their eyes and they're doing me something of a favour by letting me into their schools. There are subtle ways of letting me know how they feel. Some schools will haggle over the fee I charge for my show (never more than the cost of a packet of cigarettes per child), even though it falls right off the bottom of the scale when compared to the fees some motivational speakers charge when they tell you how they got their lives back. Some schools will position members of staff at strategic points in the halls to keep an eye on what I do and say.

I can see them signalling to each other with their eyes. Some schools will press an envelope into my hand at the end of the show and when I look inside it later on I find they've underpaid me.

It's as if I don't really matter, as if there doesn't have to be a professional transaction between us because I'm only a junkie who should be grateful for anything I can get. I sometimes get the impression they think I should be paying *them* to allow me to enter their hallowed grounds. Ironically, these are often the schools with the worst drug problems and it's going on right there under their noses. I once watched a drug deal go down in the middle rows of a high school I was performing at while the headmistress and local police forum guests chatted amiably to one side of the stage, blissfully oblivious.

Do I deserve better treatment than this?

Maybe. Maybe not.

Hey – check back on my cover shot. Would *you* trust this guy in your school?

Addicts become masters in two areas of expertise: manipulation and denial. There is no one more convincing than a neatly dressed alcoholic who looks you in the eye and tells you she hasn't touched anything but orange juice in three months and just needs a bit of help in the finance department to get her business going. Or the sixteen year old former maths boff whose baby blue eyes brim with real tears at the merest suggestion that her worrying mood swings are something more sinister than the stress of too much homework. Or the crushed, hurt look of the colleague just out of rehab at your raised eyebrow over a glass of wine ordered at lunchtime – It's just a glass of *wine*. I can handle a glass of *wine*, thank you very much.

✳

After we got busted at school our habits changed. All of the promises and sincere protestations of regret for our foolish, *stupid* actions – what were we *thinking*? – and the shame we'd brought to our families fell by the wayside almost immediately.

Right after the bottlestore me, James and Brian rolled a joint, popped a handful of pills and were high as kites before suppertime. Perhaps it was meant as a single defiant act – just once more! – just to show ourselves that we were cool. We hadn't been that freaked by the whole thing, and anyway it had been blown out of all proportion. Anyone would think we were criminals the shabby way we'd been treated. We were self-righteous, indignant and untouchable.

Privately, I *was* actually planning to quit and I'd set myself a target date: the end of the year. I could have stopped right away but . . . what the hell, just one more.

There never is just one more, of course, but you know that by now, right?

So we began undercover drugging. This meant exit Steve the showman and enter Steve the secret agent. From now on we were very, very careful. I for one definitely didn't plan to get caught again and the four year suspended sentence was a strong deterrent. Not from *using* drugs, you understand, *that* we could stop anytime we wanted to – but a deterrent from getting caught.

We used the usual tactics: eyedrops for the bloodshot eyes, breath mints, deodorant sprayed around bathrooms, joss sticks burning in our bedrooms while we pretended we'd taken up meditation (James's bright idea) – anything to disguise what we were really doing. And, drawing easily on my early training, I began in earnest to lie until it came to me so naturally that I even had myself believing the crap that came out of my mouth on a daily basis. I lied about where I was going, who I was with, what was going on or not going on at school, about the money that disappeared from wallets and desk drawers, about the holiday job I didn't have that kept me out till the early hours of the morning. My mother gave me money for textbooks I didn't need, for a holiday soccer clinic that was pure fabrication, for taking my steady girlfriend out to dinner for our six month anniversary. She was pleased with my interest in extramural activities, but sad that I was never at home.

I avoided my father.

I hardly ever saw my sisters anymore.

❋

A few other things happened round about then, but I

might have them in the wrong order. It's that crazy filing system problem in my brain again. I think I have a drug in that particular cabinet for every letter of the alphabet, starting with A for acid and ending with Z for Zyprexa . . .

Although my mother never once found my drugs, and I'm sure she went looking for them, I could tell she was worried about me. One day she came right out and said it. Well, almost said it.

I'm not accusing you of anything, Steve, she said, but if you're using drugs, or even if you think you might be tempted to experiment again, you must tell me if you need help.

Mom –

I'm just saying. There *is* help out there. I worry about you, that's all. So does your father.

Mom, I wish you wouldn't always jump to –

I'm not, Steve. I'm not jumping to anything. I'm just saying.

She let it go for a while and I stocked up on incense and eyedrops and thought I had her under control. Still she pestered me.

Are you all right?

I'm fine, mom. Things are just a bit hectic at school. You know?

Well, you don't seem fine to me. Are you sure you're not –?

I tried to throw her off the scent by pleading slight depression. I told her me and Tracey were going through a bit of a dodgy spell and I wasn't feeling too good about it, that was all.

I know someone who can help you with that, she offered helpfully. She's good. She's really nice. I think you should talk to someone.

Mom –

What have you got to lose? Just give it a try. You don't have to –

All right. Jesus!

My mother was big on support networks. She'd been going to Al Anon meetings because of my father's drinking for as long as I could remember. I think that was why she put up with him for as long as she did, until she couldn't take it anymore. Without their help and support she'd never have got through the week. Perhaps they were even responsible for her packing up and getting the hell out in the end, I dunno. She never said.

I went with her to an AA meeting once, I think it might have been when I was in the army. I don't know why I went, just to get her off my back, I suppose. She can *really* nag, my mother. I mean, really nag. Anyway, whenever it was it was at a very low point in my life after I'd been busted yet again and had told my parole officer that I was going to kill myself. Oh, OK, he'd said, but do you think you could wait till after the weekend? I've got a heavy workload on my desk and the state psychiatrist needs to assess you first. Just to complete the paperwork, you understand.

I was very weak, having just come out of another 'observation' spell in a psychiatric hospital, courtesy of the same parole officer. I was so out of it that I couldn't walk. My buddies had half carried, half dragged me to the train that would take me to the hospital. On the platform as we made our way down to where the third class carriages were, the ones reserved for poor people and those whose skin was darker than mine, all these Zulu mamas came over to me. They formed a circle and walked around me in total silence, each one of them reaching out in turn and touching me gently on the head.

I think they were praying for me. I was too. I was praying to die.

Anyway, over the weekend before I killed myself, I went to this AA meeting with my mother. There was an oldish guy there called Joe, who knew my mother, probably from the million meetings she'd attended over the years. When he stood up to say his spiel – you know, the little ritual speech – I pulled my cap down over my eyes and slid as low as I could go in my chair. My mother jabbed me in the ribs but I ignored her.

My name is Joe, I heard him say. And I am a recovering alcoholic and drug addict.

That got me sitting straight up in my chair. I looked at him immediately with deep suspicion but caught no exchange of glances between him and my mother. I was convinced she'd set me up, but she, too, was staring innocently ahead of her as if she was unaware of the significance of the words he'd just said – specifically for my benefit, or so I believed: a recovering alcoholic *and drug addict*. That was me.

His admission shook me. It was the first time I'd made the connection or heard anyone else make it. Drugs or alcohol. Same difference. Addiction is the disease. Afterwards I spoke to Joe.

You're a junkie, man, I said. Not just a *juice* junkie.

Yes, sir, he said, and smiled. Guilty as charged.

We started talking and discovered we had a lot in common. Joe was into God though. Let me tell you a story, he said, and I caught myself in time before he saw me rolling my eyes, but I listened all the same. I kind of liked him.

There was this valley, he said, and it was coming down in flood, so the people living down there all started piling into boats and getting out as soon as the water started to rise. This one guy, though, he just stood there, waving the boats on. People kept urging him to get in and save himself, but he just shook his head. Tomorrow, he told them. Tomorrow. Don't worry, God will save me. The water rose steadily higher and still the boats kept coming, but there were fewer of them now. Still people reached out their hands to help him in. No, thanks, he said. It's OK. You go ahead. God will save me. I'll wait. Finally the last boat came by. Get in, they urged him. This is the very last boat. But even then he shook his head. Don't worry about me, he said. God's on top of it. He'll save me.

Joe paused and took a long drag on his cigarette. Then he drowned, he said.

That's it? That's the end of the story? I was interested in spite of myself.

Oh, no, said Joe. He got up to the pearly gates and God came out. The man was indignant. You let me drown! he said. How could you let me drown? God just gave him a look. How many boats must I send you, he asked.

✳

My parole officer sent me off to the state psychiatrist for another assessment and I played along. I could see the man didn't intend to waste much time on me. Maybe he had a shitload of work on his desk too, more deserving of his attention than a suicide-shamming junkie. I could be doing him an injustice but before I'd even sat down his fingers were reaching for his prescription pad.

I've started going to AA, I said.

AA? He narrowed his eyes at me.

I nodded. He pushed the pad away and steepled his fingers beneath his chin. I think he'd seen too many movies. He even had the white coat. Well, then, he said, standing up. That's good. That's very good. In that case, you don't need me.

At the risk of stating the obvious, I didn't go to another AA meeting. I was busy building an ark of my own with more than two of everything.

I did start going to therapy, though. I had to do something to get my mother off my case. I could tell she was disappointed that I didn't go with her again to an AA meeting so she was thrilled when I said she could go ahead and set up an appointment with a psychologist for me. She didn't make a big deal about it. She just set it up and left me to it, reluctant, I guess, to interfere or ask too many questions in case it had the wrong effect. We'd hit on something that worked for both of us. She thought I was getting the support I needed to stay away from the edge of the cliff; I got into my own little weekly therapy routine. I'd smoke a joint before my session, *gooi* eyedrops in my eyes and then go in and pour my heart out for an hour to this sweet woman who made notes and nodded sympathetically and told me how well I was doing.

You've been drug free for how long now, Steve?

I'd do a quick mental calculation. I'd been seeing her for, um, six weeks, I reckoned.

Five weeks and three days, I'd tell her, nodding proudly, and she'd write it down.

That's great. That's really great. One day at a time, right?

I'd give her a beautiful smile and a thumbs up. One day at a time.

I discovered I had a brilliant gift for bullshit. Some of my problems got a bit elaborate and then I had to check myself and pull back and focus on the more mundane aspects of my troubled life, like how badly my father's drinking had damaged our family. She liked that avenue. Her fingers positively flew along her notepad.

I got bored with it in the end and stopped going and my mother's disappointment was palpable. By then

I think she had very few illusions left about what I was doing. She and my father were called in by the headmaster of my school and that interview probably shattered the last of them. He told them that I was conspicuous only by my absence from nearly all of my classes and if I didn't pull up my socks very swiftly I would have to repeat a year, and preferably at another school.

Then James died.

His mother suffered from anxiety attacks and insomnia and one night before a party a kilometre or so down the beach he raided the medicine cabinet and took a handful of her prescription drugs before he arrived. Our mixing and matching was mostly alcohol, weed and thins and we didn't know what James had done. After we'd shared a bottle of vodka James didn't look too good. When he started puking we didn't think too much of it – we thought he'd had more to drink than the rest of us – and when he passed out, we just carried on with the party. It wasn't that late and we were sure he'd be OK by the time we were ready to go home.

He wasn't though. He wasn't OK at all. James drowned at the beach that summer. Drowned in his own vomit.

His tearful mother told our tearful mothers what the doctors said they found in his bloodstream and I can tell you it was not a pretty sight.

Neither Brian nor I were impressed with James. We talked about it after the funeral.

He was fucking stupid.

What the hell was he doing messing with that kind of medicine? That's *medicine*, for heaven's sake. You have to have a *prescription* for that stuff.

I know. You can't just *take* it. Not with booze anyway. Any asshole knows that.

He only has himself to blame.

Cunt.

Idiot.

Dickhead.

INSTITUTIONS

Apparently it's Christmas. The big news is that we're going on an outing, but nobody knows where yet. At least there's a certain amount of anticipation in the air, which gives us something to talk about and goes some way to livening up our generally lethargic days.

There's a lot of speculation.

Church, probably, someone offers gloomily. And hold the communion wine.

I'm Jewish, says Nathan. No, thanks.

Movies, someone else says, with popcorn if we're good.

What's popcorn got in it? Anything interesting?

Popcorn's mealies, you cunt. Don't you know anything? And movies aren't open on Christmas Day. Asshole.

Then it's the zoo, someone else says. We were taken to the zoo once but that was another clinic and it was closer. We walked there.

Animals looking at animals. That figures.

That's Nathan again. He hates being here but his family says this time it's not negotiable and he's got to complete the programme or he loses his job in his father's factory. He's been labelled uncooperative from day one.

It isn't the zoo or church or movies, we soon learn. It's the old age home in a nextdoor suburb. It will be an uplifting experience, we're told sternly, a chance for us to bring some cheer into lonely old people's lives. We should be grateful for this opportunity, to put something back. Some of these pensioners don't have anyone in the world to care about them anymore. Some never get a single visitor from one year to the next. Others don't even know when they've had visitors or who their visitors are. They forget as soon as they're left alone again. Whole families forget, they move away, they're only too relieved to leave the responsibility to someone else.

So it's come to this, has it? The junkies and the wrinklies at a Christmas party. Whoo-hoo. The more I think about it, though, the more I see the similarities. Senile old *toppies* dribbling their apple juice onto their jerseys, clinking glasses with a whole bunch of brain damaged Steves.

We should have a lot to talk about.

Only difference is they're probably all in their eighties and deaf as posts, while the oldest among our group is twenty-three and there's nothing wrong with our hearing. In fact I'm *still* hearing Nathan's howling screams the night he was brought in. And there's another sound that haunts me constantly – it's the rumble of the trolleys in the middle of the night when they wheel out the dead addicts. They always do it at night so as not to upset us and they think we don't know. As if a stripped mattress and freshly mopped lino in the morning isn't evidence enough. Oh, and the fact that the girl you saw projectile vomiting in admissions hasn't turned up for her therapy session. Never will.

At least I know when I've had visitors, although there aren't very many beside my mother. My sister came to see me once, not here though, another rehab, I think it was Addington Psych ward. It was the only time she ever came to see me in rehab, and you could hardly call it a visit. She never even sat down. The whole time she stood in the corridor outside my room, shifting from one foot to the other, as if she might catch something terminal if she came any closer. With her arms folded and her handbag looped over one shoulder, she just stood there staring at me with an expression on her face that I can only describe as pure and un-disguised disgust.

No compassion there, not even pity, not that I deserved either, I suppose.

I remember I was too weak to get up and too high on psychiatric drugs to so much as hold a conversation about the weather. I was having a problem keeping my mouth closed properly too. It kept flopping open like I didn't have any muscles in my jaw. Fish-mouth. My tongue tasted of metal and I couldn't control the saliva that dribbled constantly out of the corners of my mouth. Perhaps I reminded her of our father, drunk and para-lytic on a Saturday night, reeking of sweat and booze. Anyway. She just stood there. She didn't have to speak.

The eyes said everything she wanted to say. If she'd stepped forward and spat in my face that would probably have been the most eloquent statement of all.

This Christmas, though, I know not to expect anyone. My mother is on holiday in Mombasa with my aunt. I heard my sister was going to join them. They booked their tickets the day after I was brought in here, dying in my own puke, without sticking around to see if I was going to make it. Part of me hopes they'll get fatally stung by killer jellyfish but that's only on a bad day. I don't really blame my mother. She's seen me in this situation so many times I suppose the novelty has worn off for her. Best she hardens her heart, I guess, and takes a break up there under the palm trees, a thousand miles away from the delinquent, suicidal son and heir. Pina colada and giant prawns fresh from the warm ocean. Perhaps they'll send me a postcard. Dear Steve. Having a wonderful time. So glad you're not here.

So it's the junkies and the oldies who'll be pulling crackers and wearing funny hats and tucking into the turkey this year. I can visualise it already – the bang of a cracker causing at least one fatal heart attack, a wishbone stuck in the throat of a ninety year old and none of us having more than a passing acquaintance with the Heimlich manoeuvre. I suppose there could be worse ways to go. Personally I could name half a dozen. But I should swallow my cynicism. It might even be OK.

In fact it turns out better than OK. They're really quite nice and not nearly as loopy as I imagined. They're thrilled to have us join them, which makes me wonder for a minute whether they have actually been told where we're from. Perhaps they think we're a church youth group or something.

We're put at long trestle tables with white table-cloths, and only a couple of them have bibs. There are crackers all right, but they've removed the bang things inside so no chance of an entertaining coronary, and the paper hats are those same hats that have been inside cracker boxes since Jesus was a boy. Yellow on one side, green on the other, and flimsy and ready to tear at the smallest mishandling. I remember them well, from Christmas at Brian's house one time, I think.

There's turkey but it's already sliced. No sharp bones for this lot, them or us. That would be way too risky. I heard a rumour that another time with another group from the clinic a couple of years before, a crack addict had slit her wrists in the toilet with that thin, very sharp piece of bone you get in a drumstick, so maybe that's why too. You can't be too careful.

There's a piano in the dining room and a fairly ugly nurse with thick ankles plonks away on the keys, bashing out carols while we're waiting for some un-identifiable boiled veg to be dished onto our plates. They've split us up and slotted the rehab people in between the pensioners. On my left I have a white haired lady who tells me in the first five minutes that her husband passed away on Christmas Day the year before and that her daughter in Perth is coming to see her any minute with their five grandchildren. She's made an effort with the lipstick but you can see that the tremor in her hands makes this tricky for her. Letterbox red and bleeding into the deep lines of her upper lip. Where the sun pours through the high windows behind us it makes her hair look like candyfloss. It's so fine and thin I can see her scalp and it causes a sort of ache in my chest as if I've just seen something I shouldn't. Or perhaps it's indigestion. I seem to have found an appetite somewhere and have eaten three rolls one after the other that weren't quite defrosted yet. My companion hasn't eaten much at all. She tells me she suffers from crushing migraines, always has, and the medication she's on makes her nauseous but the nurses don't listen to her when she tells them this.

Medication, I ask, leaning in closer. Is that so? What are you taking?

I wouldn't swear to it but I think Nathan's having a similar conversation with his lunch buddy across the way from us. He's adopted a concerned expression that is immediately suspicious in itself. Everyone knows that Nathan's only and overriding concern is how and when he can next score so it's not like him at all to give a stuff about anyone else. Anyway, he's deep in conversation with one of the bib wearers, an eighty year old with outsized ears and one of those sad, bulbous noses that old men sometimes get. I pick up the words 'heart condition' and as I watch them I see the old man reach into first one shirt pocket then another, and then his trouser pocket and finally draw out a plastic bottle of pink pills which he shows to the kind young man beside him. Nathan is frowning with interest and reading the label intently. They're both nodding hard, as if they've found a hobby they have in common. Well, I guess they have.

Brenda is a rehab veteran like me and a survivor of two suicide attempts and three overdoses. She's moving her food around on her plate with a fork and talking to the man on her left while she's busy with her free hand feeling about carefully in the handbag of the woman on her other side who seems to have fallen asleep. I feel like applauding. That's multi-tasking all right. Go, Brenda.

I scan the room and begin to marvel at the extraordinary show and tell session that's going down right under the noses of the nurses and the people serving the food. Actually it's more like show and tell and hand over the drugs, gramps. And it's working.

It's true what they told us at the clinic. These old people are starved of companionship. They have no one to talk to, no one who will take the time to listen to the details of their ailments and their treatments. Well, they've found a willing and attentive audience today, that's for sure. It's mutual too. We've really cheered each other up.

In the combi on the way home we compare notes and loot. Painkillers and tranquillisers form the bulk of our haul. Nathan's already not with us. He's smiling gently, his head bumping against the windowpane and his eyes blissfully closed. Brenda's brought the small plastic whistle she got in her cracker and she toots it in my ear with annoying repetitiveness. I'm trying to read the joke I got in mine – Confucius he say . . . – but I'm holding it upside down and I can't say Confucius and anyway no one's listening.

Back at the clinic there's a great deal of head shaking and tight-lipped staff. In a couple of days there will be a halfhearted disciplinary inquiry that'll lead precisely nowhere. They can't for the life of them work it out.

We don't care and we're not telling.

After lights out I lie on my hard narrow mattress and I'm tripping, high as a kite on Valium and a handful of yellow and green painkillers I've never seen before that I swopped with Brenda for some Aropax. I'm looking for the Star of Bethlehem outside my window in the night sky and I think I've almost located it when I hear Nathan's strong baritone voice start up two doors away from me. We WISH you a Merry Christmas, We WISH you a Merry Christmas, We WISH you a Merry – and then there's an irritable shout and a bang and he stops abruptly and someone starts to giggle. As he starts up again I hear Franco, the only Catholic among us who'd insisted on being allowed to go to Mass this morning, shout in no uncertain terms: Will Mary's boy child please SHUT THE FUCK UP!

And if the trolleys move along the corridor in the night I don't hear them. We are all present and correct the next morning. Well, present anyway. Definitely not correct.

THIRTEEN

Jail time. Been there. Done that. Got the tattoos. And what nugget of wisdom did I take away with me when I stepped out from behind the bars? A prisoner gets a key. An addict gets a life sentence.

It seems like such a stretch of the imagination to make the connection between a skinny-legged kid from the south coast getting busted on a beach for smoking weed to a desperate man defending himself with a broom handle against 'the General' in Zonderwater lockup.

It happened though, believe it, and it's not such a stretch either.

I've thought long and hard about how much, if any, I want to reflect in this book on the time I served in prison for drug-related crimes, and because it's my story and for once in my life I'm the one in charge here,

I've decided that it's a part of my life I will not shy away from but will not dwell on either. I will acknowledge the time I served, of course I will – that's the risk you take when you use or deal drugs, make no mistake about it, and I got caught, sentenced and locked away for it more than once – but I still have nightmares when I think of those black periods. And if I spend too much time with them in my head, the emotions and the memories that are stirred up are almost more than I can bear.

The things that happened to me in prison, the appalling violence and cruelty I witnessed and the things I in my turn inflicted on others, I've decided, are best left alone now, so forgive me if I play censor in my own life story. If you're wanting graphic detail, go to a video store and take out all of the worst tough prison movies you can find. Add them all together and multiply the violence and the fear by a hundred and you'll have come a little closer to what prison is really like.

The point I need to make here, for my own sake and for anyone doing drugs or thinking of doing drugs who might be reading this, is this: *prison is hell*. It's an awfully long way from the good feeling you're trying to reach through drugging, trust me. The old cliché of Don't do the crime if you can't do the time doesn't even begin to come close to what 'the time' actually entails.

Prison will damage you – that's a given. You will not come out the same person you went in. You do not want to go there. But every day you're walking around with a bankie of weed in your pocket or travelling in a car as the passenger of someone who has a gram of cocaine in his cubbyhole, prison is what you're risking.

But I didn't know –

I was only –

I've never done this before and –

That doesn't belong to me. I swear –

It wasn't me, it was him.

Make a choice, but make an informed one because in prison you will have no choices at all. Once you are inside the rules all get rewritten but there's no actual rulebook you can consult to see how the game is played, and none of the writers of these rules is employed by the government either. Gangs run the prisons, that's the bottom line, and no matter who you are, what colour you are, what your background is or how rich your parents may be, when you are stripped of your outside identity and ushered into your cell, be under no illusions whatsoever.

You are *nobody.*

If you are physically attacked or feel threatened or victimised, you may of course appeal to the authorities for help or protection, but you're taking a big risk doing that. Not only are you running the risk of retaliation or reprisals from the jail buddies you're about to tell tales on, but you may find that you just hit a blank wall anyway – and where does *that* get you? You can rattle the bars all you like, but you're still on the inside, bru, and everyone's watching you.

And if you imagine that you will just sit it out

and be back on the street eventually after two months, six months, four years, whatever – think again, china. That's not how it works either.

For one thing, if you buck the system (the inmates' system, that is, and the only one that counts), you will pay. Horribly. You may even pay with your life in the end, and no one will tell, no one will help you, no one will give a damn.

If you are male, the chances of you being raped are pretty damn high. That's not a myth. It's the truth. And when you do come out, dressed in your street clothes again, having paid your debt to society and ready to face the world, you are changed, changed forever.

Zonderwater. Kroonstad. Westville.

I don't associate these names with places of scenic interest. I associate them with dark, desolate periods in my life.

I associate them with drugs. So should you.

※

One thing, at least, about prison is that it does come with a key eventually, unless you're a serial killer or something when they throw the key into the ocean. Drugs, on the other hand, are a prison of the mind. Getting out of that prison is a real challenge and it's a challenge I failed over and over again. But knowing what I know now, about prison and about drugs, if you gave me a choice – ten years in jail or an addiction to drugs – even now, after everything I've been through in my life, I would take the ten years in jail every time. In a heartbeat.

At sixteen jail was where I was heading. School was giving up on me and I was definitely giving up on school. My time and my chances were rapidly running out. My parents could do nothing with me. Every curfew, every rule they tried to impose on me I broke or I ignored. I spoke to no one but my friends and Tracey. The days of the little joints I rolled for my girlfriend by the rocks on the beach were long gone. Tracey was as caught in the drug web as I was. We spent all of our time together, experimenting with whatever we could lay our hands on, thins mostly, and weed and alcohol. We used different combinations, different brands, mixing and matching like there was no tomorrow. Anything to get to that feeling, that level where you felt like *Yeah, this is it. This is the place I was trying to find.*

How to get money to pay for our drugs consumed every waking hour. When it came to stealing, we weren't fussy about keeping it in the family. We moved onto the street. We stole, we cheated, we lied through our teeth. We sold or pawned anything and everything we could and we didn't care who we hurt in the process. We justified it all to ourselves and to each other, but the truth is we lived on lies.

I knew in my heart that I was in trouble, though, and so I planned to get clean. I thought I could. I really did. I even set myself deadlines.

I'll start by cutting back, just a joint or so at the weekend. Gradually ease up and then stop completely by the end of the month . . . well, maybe next month. Or hey, when I turn seventeen, that's it. I'm out. I'm done. I'm done with this stuff. I'll begin in the summer holidays, concentrate on my surfing, keeping my place in the team. I'll surf every day. And school, if they chuck me out, so what? Who needs school anyway? I'll surf for my nation. I'll – But in the meantime, just until I get my head around some of my shit, just one more . . .

At the end of that school year the headmaster suggested, rather forcefully, to my parents that I shouldn't come back after the holidays. It was not only my lack of effort and poor results. By now I was notorious. I was all of the clichés: a disaster waiting to happen, a kid already halfway down the slippery slope, a troublemaker, a con artist and a thief. The cops knew me. Everyone knew me. There was no argument, no discussion. The headmaster was not to be swayed.

And so I learnt that I was to be sent to the army where I would be taught a skill that was not currently on offer at schools.

I would be taught how to kill people.

I was sixteen years old.

Actually, when you think about it, killing people was a skill I was already acquiring on the street, although I didn't know it then, and my weapon of choice was mind altering chemicals.

In the army I would learn how to use a gun and

would be told that it was legitimate to turn it on an enemy yet to be identified. That would entail mind altering of a different kind.

For a time before I went off to do my two year basic training, I got quite famous in our town and a Natal newspaper even sent a journalist to interview me. The article that was published was all about me – the teenage drug addict who claimed to be smoking up to thirty pipes a day, nothing to it. As depressing as it is to think about it now, at the time I was quite chuffed to be such a celebrity. To protect the family name, however, I used a pseudonym and the picture they printed of me in the middle of the article was one of those darkened, half-profile to the camera shots. When my dad came home from work with the evening newspaper under his arm I was waiting. He slapped it down on the kitchen table and his only comment, when he jabbed at the article with his finger, was What the fuck is this? At first I didn't know what he meant and it took a while for me to work it out. It was all to do with the single line his finger was busy stabbing at. What upset him more than the fact that his son was a drug addict was the fact that I was ashamed of the Hamilton name and had used a made up one . . .

But that was OK. I was giving up on my dad too. I acquired a surrogate, a man who became both friend and brother to me for a long time. I grew to love him like a father and I trusted him with my life.

His name was John and he was my dealer.

John was our maid's boyfriend and he lived with

her in the servants' quarters at the back of our property. Our relationship was not only emotionally satisfying for both of us, but also mutually beneficial. He introduced me to other dealers in the townships – places completely out of bounds for a white South African boy in the seventies – and I learnt to find my way around them, the back streets, the quick way out and the signs and signals that were the common language that transcended all barriers of colour and vernacular. I have a naturally good ear for accents and languages and my street Zulu, mixed with the Afrikaans and English jumble of underworld slang, gave me credibility and easy entry into circles I would otherwise never even have known about.

I owe John bigtime and I'll never forget what he did for me. Our back premises were raided one night by cops looking for drugs. They'd certainly come to the right place and they weren't disappointed. I can't remember what it was they found, mandrax, I guess, but the thing is, they weren't John's drugs. They were mine. He knew that. I knew that. Maybe even the cops knew it too but they had nothing on me and a bust is a bust. They weren't too fussy about accuracy when it came to midnight arrests and for them it was probably a reasonable evening's work.

Through all of it, the guns, the shouting, the turning over of cheap furniture in a room no bigger than a small kitchen that contained all of John's and his girlfriend's worldly possessions, John never said a word. He was arrested, cuffed and pushed roughly out to the cop van while I stood by and waited, holding my breath, for the words I expected would come any minute: *It wasn't me it was him*. The cops probably wouldn't have believed him if he'd said them – a black man's word against a white boy's? Get real – but the point is, he didn't.

My friend gave nothing away. He didn't even glance in my direction.

John was charged and convicted for possession and he went to prison and served the time that should have been mine. Six months in the hellhole of an apartheid jail. Even a lowlife drug addict doesn't forget something like that.

Ours was a sort of apartheid friendship, if you like. It was weird how we managed to bypass some of the laws and barriers that usually prevented two people of different colours hanging out together, and how we just shrugged some of them off and accepted others without thinking about them. We used to pull in to a joint called the Showboat, down in Durban. It was whites only, of course, but we weren't politically sussed or even interested really. It's not like I would have boycotted the place out of principle, and anyway I didn't have too many principles back then. I'd go inside and buy the drinks – two Black Labels for John and two whiskies for Steve – and take John's out to him in the parking lot. Sometimes I stayed inside and drank at the bar, sometimes I took my drink out and sat on the sidewalk with him, but neither of us analysed anything over much. That was just the way it was and we worked our way around it.

As I grew older, before, during and after my not very successful career in the military, John and I became partners of a sort. We would drive all over the place together, in and out of the townships, transporting drugs to and from the Transkei across the 'border' of that so-called independent country at the time. We had some pretty close calls, I can tell you, including being shot at by drug squad police and rival dealers on more than one occasion. Like any war, in the end drugs are all about territory.

One time we were coming back into Natal from the Transkei with a shitload of dagga hidden in mealie bags. There'd been a lot of rain and the roads were slippery and dangerous. There was also a particular bridge that we discovered was underwater after the river came down in flood and it was our only route back. I knew this time God wasn't getting ready to send the fleet out, that was for sure. We learnt that the cops were out in force, though, slowing people down, getting them across the bridge and generally poking their noses into anything vaguely suspicious. They were always on the lookout for small-time traffickers like us and the route in and out was no secret.

I was very nervous about chancing it but John had a contact with a bright idea. He knew of a sangoma near Lusikisiki who could mix us some powerful muti and make us invisible. We'd cross that bridge without even being seen.

I looked at John. Oh, give me a break, I said.

Invisible?

John shook his head, chuckled and shrugged.

It's powerful muti . . . He left the sentence unfinished and sat quietly beside me in the cab, smiling to himself as if he knew something I didn't know. John was a man of few words at the best of times.

What the hell. I'll try anything once, you know me.

John chuckled, his shoulders jiggling a little, and I turned the bakkie around and we headed up into the hills on a pitch dark rainy night on a mud track so atrocious it's a wonder we didn't skid straight down into a ravine. The engine whined and strained.

I glanced across at John's barely visible profile. Are you sure about this, I asked him for probably the twentieth time, and for the twentieth time he said nothing, just gestured for me to keep driving forward into the darkness.

We were both stoned which added to the already surreal feeling of this expedition. Actually I wasn't completely convinced that John even had the faintest clue where this medicine man lived, but when I pressed him he just gave his trademark chuckle-shrug and told me that the muti was very powerful

It better be, I told him. We're going to be *very* invisible if we go crashing down this mountain.

We found our way eventually, miraculously, and arrived at a mud rondavel with a thatched roof and a sangoma who looked extremely dubious. He didn't look too excited to see us either but he and John began an elaborate conversation, part of which I managed to follow and part of which was completely lost on me. What came out at the end of it, however, was his conviction, and John's, that he could, for a fee, provide us with muti that would indeed render us invisible, just as we'd hoped – unconditional guarantee.

So I suspended my disbelief and bought into the ritual, which involved beads, a block of fat, some pubic hair and I forget what else. A couple of hours later and we were on the road again. The rain had stopped but driving was still tricky. There was also a terrible smell in the bakkie.

I looked over at John sitting beside me. I can still see you, I said.

He chuckled, his shoulders moving up and down, but said nothing.

As we neared the bottom of the potholed dirt road and drew closer to the turnoff that would take us onto the tarred road and the bridge, the rain started coming down again in silver slanting sheets that made visibility all but nil and I could feel the tension across my shoulders. I breathed through my mouth. Whatever fat we had been anointed with must have belonged to something very dead or very ill. We stank.

I could see revolving blue lights up ahead and the tail lights of cars slowing down in front of us and I imagined I could hear the mealie bags in the back shrieking Search me, Search me.

Shit, I murmured. Here we go.

My faith in the sangoma's powers, which had

never been very strong to begin with, was waning fast. Maybe we should have had a word with God about a boat instead. As we drew closer, I imagined a big arrow pointing down on our bakkie from the sky in neon lights saying DAGGA HERE.

John wasn't saying anything. If he was anxious, he was damn good at concealing it. Or maybe his faith was stronger than mine.

We're dead meat, I told him, staring fixedly straight ahead of me as I changed gear. And we *smelt* like dead meat too, but I didn't say that. I was concentrating on the cop who kept appearing and disappearing as the windscreen wipers struggled to keep up with the torrent. He had a torch and he was using it to flag down some cars and pull them over and to wave others on through. There was no doubt in my mind which signal we'd be called on to obey.

Here we go, I said again as we took the dip in second gear.

But what was this? The torch was up all right, and flagging authoritatively, but it was the vehicle *behind* us it was indicating to pull over. I'd been so sure that our number was up that I was already rehearsing in my mind a couple of bullshit scenarios, but I didn't need them. The cop didn't even glance at me. It was as if we were invisible.

We eased through, wheels slipping a bit, and began to climb the steep incline on the other side of the river.

Neither of us said anything at all on the rest of

the journey home, but every now and then I was aware of John's shoulders, jiggling, just a little.

❋

Over the years we lost touch, John and me, especially once I had to start moving around the country so much. When you're in as deep as I was, dealing and drugging, and a place gets too hot or you get too well known there, you have to move on. I was doing a Joburg, Durban, Cape Town circuit, and through all of that time I was also in and out of psychiatric institutions, being called up for army camps on the border or in the townships, and in and out of jail.

I got news of John from time to time but then the trail went cold and that was that. Last year I was doing a show in Durban when I ran into a friend of John's from the old days. I think they might even have been related. Anyway, he was a waiter at the hotel I was meeting someone at and we got to talking. He said he thought he'd heard that John was in prison, then that he had got ill and had moved back into the country, near to his birthplace. He was going into the township to score and he'd make some enquiries if I wanted him to. I did and a couple of days later he came and found me again. The news was not good, but he said he knew where John's people were and if I had transport, he'd go with me to try and find them. It seemed doubtful, though, that John himself was still alive.

I knew how the communities deep in the rolling

KwaZulu-Natal hills, the area where John's family lived, were battling with AIDS and I feared the worst. On the way there I prayed and hoped and thought about everything that John and I had been through together. I remembered that rainy night when we'd been invisible, the bust at our family home when he'd gone to prison for me, drinking together, drugging together and how he had been the most stable figure in my life for a long time.

I also remembered that it was me who got John onto mandrax.

You could say that drugging in the seventies and early eighties in South Africa was regionally divided. In the Durban area, where I spent a lot of my time, and particularly in the townships there, dagga and alcohol were the main drugs of choice and mandrax was largely unknown. It started out as a Cape drug and that's where I got to know it. Gradually, as word spread and demand grew, it moved up the coast. When it hit Durban I was in my element and there was a time when I was intimately involved in the busiest and most lucrative trade in the pills up and down the south coast resort towns. Up till then John had been a mainly dagga and alcohol man but he was soon smoking as many pipes a day as I was.

I wondered how he had died and wondered how his family would receive me.

We got close to the top of a hill where the road ran out and my companion told me to pull over and park. We got out and stretched our legs – we'd been driving for over two hours – and walked to the crest where we could look over and down into the valley at our feet. There was a cluster of dwellings that I could see down below us, and small figures, kids probably, walking around.

I knew it was a long shot, but I took a chance all the same. Gathering in a deep breath, I pursed my lips and whistled. Me and John had our own whistle, our own signal. Variations of it meant different things, from watch out, trouble coming to hey, I'm here, where are you?

I was surprised at how automatically the whistle came back to me, as if I had used it just yesterday. I waited and listened as it faded away on the air. I don't know what I'd been expecting, but I took another breath, just for old time's sake, a sort of tribute or something, and whistled again.

Let's go, I said to John's friend, and as I was turning to get back into the car, suddenly feeling depressed and old and wondering what the hell I thought I was doing there, I heard what I took at first to be an echo.

It wasn't. It was a whistle. And it was a whistle just like mine.

A Kodak moment? Hardly. But we did stagger towards each other, me stumbling over stones and bushes down the hill and John, the confusion on his face clearing as, shading his eyes, he moved slowly, like a sleepwalker, in my direction. We sat together and talked for hours. I don't think I'd ever heard John say so much in all the years I knew him. He was going grey and he had some deep lines on his face. He wanted us to smoke a pipe together. When I declined he laughed and shook his head. He laughed in disbelief, too, when I told him about my work. Well, who wouldn't, in his position? I think he'd thought I was dead too and we kept touching each other and wiping away at our eyes like girls at a high school reunion.

I told him about Candy.

And I showed him a picture of my son.

A Day in the Life ...

Steve?

    Yes, Candy?

    Don't you wish sometimes we could be like normal people and just have a glass of wine in the evening, just, like, to unwind, you know, at the end of the day?

    We can, Candy.

    But –?

    We can, Candy. But we know what will happen. We're different. There's rules for normal people, and there's rules for us.

    Oh, yes.

✳

Candy.

    What?

    I'm just looking at this statement from the bank.

    What about it?

    That call account – I thought you said it was due next week?

    It is, Steve.

    No, it's not. That's not what it says on the statement. It's only due the week after next.

    You're kidding me. Hey, look at Claydon on his skateboard –

    Candy. How many bookings do we have?

    Not a lot this week, I'm afraid. I'm still waiting

for Seaview Primary to get back to me and –

    Well, did you phone them?

    Yes, I –

    Phone them again.

    It's been a bit hectic – I'm sorry . . .

    Sorry isn't going to pay the bills.

    I know . . .

    Have you seen the cellphone account this month?

    We're in shit street again, aren't we, Steve?

    It's on our letterheads, Candy.

FOURTEEN

My mother has what she calls a 'golden moment', a sort of snapshot in her mind that she treasures, and I've come to treasure with her. It's a picture of three people walking along a beach. They're going to an AA meeting. My mother is in the middle, arm in arm with her husband on one side and her brother-in-law on the other. Everyone is stone cold sober.

Click. One for the album.

Pretty pathetic, hey, but only if you haven't been where we've been as a family.

I call it awesome myself.

Towards the end of my final year at school (before I knew it was my final year) my aunt and uncle came to visit us from Kenya. My father had stopped drinking and my mother had almost allowed herself to stop holding her breath. It was a good time for them, I think, and especially for my little sister, whose whole life up to then had been one of displacement and confusion. I wasn't around much of course. I was too busy chasing after my next high to appreciate any of the family bonding that might have been going on, or even to pass the time of day with my relations. My mother seemed happier, though, and I know she has good memories of that holiday. They did holiday things – going out to dinner, early morning strolls on the beach and endless reminiscing about Mombasa and the Norfolk Hotel and my dad getting behind a microphone and singing Moon River to my mother.

It wasn't all rosy, however. My father had lost his job by then, after a final drunk driving charge, and it nearly broke him. He was so proud of that job. But you can't be an area manager and visit your branches if you aren't to be trusted behind the wheel of a car. Until the day he got fired he never missed a day's work. To his eternal credit, bad as things were for him, between the financial blow and the blow to his fierce work ethic pride, even then he didn't relapse.

My dad was finally sober.

As far as a father and son relationship went, however, his timing sucked. While he might no longer be looking at the world through a haze of booze, now it was my turn for a distorted view of life, and I had no time for or interest in anything else. My father may, for all I knew, have wanted or even attempted to patch over the cracks, but the way I saw it, it was too late for that. Years too late.

I hated my father.

And so, despite the novelty of his sobriety, things between us were, to put it mildly, strained. Looking back, I probably still craved approval and affection from him as I always had done, but I was hell bent on sabotaging any chance of that now. Too much water had gone under the Hamilton bridge. Come to think of it, foul and murky as that water was, it should probably have been contained in a sewerage pipe with a skull and crossbones Danger sign on it. Better to let it flow out to sea underground and cross fingers that it didn't poison all the fish.

So much damage, and it still hurts like hell.

Trust works both ways and while I, no doubt, betrayed my parents' trust on a daily basis during this time, my father had destroyed my faith in him a long way back. Drunk or sober, it no longer made a difference. We never had anything resembling a conversation anymore. When he spoke to me it was to find fault, to criticise or to shame. He looked at me, his son the drop-out addict, with ill-concealed contempt.

Was he aware at all of the irony of our reversed situations? Perhaps. And perhaps that was why he came down on me so hard. I doubt it, though. I don't believe I was aware of the irony either, but I am now, and cruelly so.

I think my father saw my growing addiction as a personal slap in the face, an act of rebellion and defiance. I suppose he thought I was weak and spineless, and a drain on the family's dwindling resources.

Actually, I don't know what he thought really, but when I was wasted I could *feel* his disgust. It burned me up like a white hot flame. My reaction? To pile on the coals as often as I could.

The time came for my aunt and uncle to leave for Kenya. They had an early evening flight booked and the plan was for the whole family to go to the airport to see them off. Their visits were rare and my mother was sad and a bit tearful at having to say goodbye.

Neither my sister nor I wanted to go along and it was years and years later that she confessed to me that she and my dad had had angry words about it that afternoon. I can't remember whether she went in the end or not. Me, I was in the garage, drugging with my buddies, when the suitcases were being loaded into the car. I was out of it. I'd already told my mother earlier that I wasn't going to the airport but my father came looking for me all the same.

I remember him standing in the garage entrance, a dark silhouette against the sky, taking in the scene. He could see I wasn't in any state to go anywhere and he was furious. My father's most effective weapon had always been his tongue and when he worked himself up to full spate and let fly, drunk or sober, the fallout was dangerous. He stood there and laid into me, verbally, in an attack so vicious that I could sense even my buddies shrinking back against the walls. This time, though, I shot back at him with anger of my own, not caring what I said or who heard us. I don't know where it all came from but wherever I had stored it, my anger burst its banks that day and terrible words were said.

I know what they were, but *only* I know, and I will never share them with anyone.

They were the last words my father and I ever exchanged.

I didn't go to the airport. I stayed at home, stoned, listening to music. Later on the telephone rang. It was my aunt. Somewhere in my blurry brain I registered surprise, confusion. Shouldn't she be flying over Africa round about now?

Don't be alarmed, she told me, but your father's had a heart attack. They've taken him to the hospital.

I couldn't speak. Don't be alarmed? What was that supposed to mean? She said she would call again when she knew more but I was to stay at home near the phone.

Don't be alarmed?

A little while later the phone rang again. This time it was my uncle and I managed to find my voice.

How is he, I asked.

My uncle hesitated. Then, Not good, Steve, he said, but they're working on him. He's all right though. He's going to be all right. He's in good hands. They're doing everything they can.

I suppose a couple more hours went by but the phone stayed silent. It grew dark outside and I switched on the lights in the house and drew some curtains. I sat on the stoep, then got up and walked up to the end of our road and back again. Then I sat on the stoep some more. I fed the dog. I didn't know which hospital they'd taken my father to. I didn't know who to call. I went outside again, then back into the hallway. I picked up the telephone receiver and held it to my ear. Dialling tone.

Don't be alarmed, I repeated to myself. Don't be alarmed.

Finally, I saw headlights turn into our road and the family car bumped jerkily up the slope of our driveway and stopped just short of the garage, where I'd seen my father stop so many times, two wheels in the flowerbed.

My uncle was driving. My mother and little sister got out. They were both huddling together, crying. I stood, my arms by my sides, unable to move. My aunt followed and she stopped for a minute and looked over at me and gave a slight shake of her head. I could tell she'd been crying too. My little sister bolted past me and ran inside and my mother turned and came towards me but I stopped her with a rough, clumsy gesture and she went inside too.

Then my uncle killed the lights, turned off the engine and got out of the car. He looked weary. When he saw me standing there he raised his hand in a futile, apologetic sort of way and walked slowly over to me, mouthing words as he came. I didn't hear any of them. My eyes were drawn to what he was holding in his left hand. It was a plastic shopping bag. Pick 'n Pay. I looked down and saw my dad's shoes at the bottom of it and on top of them, neatly folded, his safari suit, socks and the clear outline of a comb that must have been slipped in by a nursing sister at the last moment.

That's when I took off.

I ran out of the gate and down the road. I ran blind for three days and to this day I don't know where I went, how far I ran or what turned me around and sent me home again. I remember nothing of it. I didn't go to the funeral. I didn't ask any questions.

I do know that that was the first time I shed tears for my father and once I started it seemed as if I would never stop. I don't know what kind of weeping that is. There's probably a psychological term for it, there always is, but all I know is that the pain of my weeping went deep, deeper than anything I have ever experienced before or since.

I call it soul pain.

INSTITUTIONS

This is no good. This is no good. I got a bad feeling about this. Get these guys away from me. Get these FUCKING guys AWAY from me. I'll take you all. I'll take every last motherfucking one of you OUT, I swear it. Don't PUSH me. Don't fucking come NEAR me! DON'T –

Jesus Christ, where am I? What *is* this place? What the –? Where are my clothes? These aren't my clothes. God, the walls are weird. They're so close. Up close and personal with a wall. That's freaky. And what's that smell? Shit. Shit – it's *shit*. Gross. God! Fuck! Where *am* I? I can't stand up. Why can't I stand up?

I'm coming down. That's what it is. I'm coming down. My god, this is a bad trip. I thought for a minute – Jesus. Thank god, thank god, it's just a bad trip. It's OK. It's OK. I'll be OK. Just breathe. Just breathe through your mouth, Steve. You'll be OK. I'll be OK.

Damn. That wasn't funny. That was so not funny –

But wait a minute. Hang on. It's not a trip. It's real. I don't believe it. I don't fucking believe it. Not again! No – not *again*. I'm in a fucking padded cell, in a fucking straitjacket. Oh sweet Jesus. How did I get here? And what am I going to do now?

The smell is not going away and now I recognise the other smells too. There's urine and sperm and – Jesus! – blood, all soaked into this colourless material I'm lying on. It's on the floor, it's on the walls, it's even on the ceiling. It feels damp and cold and slimy and the only way I know this is through my bare feet. My arms are hugging my body, tied and strapped some-where behind me like you see in the movies. I'm having a problem standing upright because I have nothing to balance myself with and my head is spinning and my mouth so dry I want to cough but I can't. My feet slip on the damp, vile smelling floor and I fall over on my side. I wriggle over to the wall and manoeuvre myself up it until I'm standing again. I'm too tall for this place and the walls and ceiling are moving closer. I'm suffo-cating. I'm going to suffocate to death and no one will come and no one even knows I'm here. If my mother knew where I was she'd come and get me out. She knows I'm not good with small spaces. She'll come. She's got to come. She always comes. I sit and wait and I count to five hundred and thirty-four and then I call out but my voice is dry and cracked and I know it's useless.

I'm in the proverbial padded cell, two metres by four, filthy and airless, and as soundproof as a dungeon in the Tower of London.

I can't. I can't do this. I'm going to go mad in here.

I rock on my haunches, back and forth, with my chin on my chest. I can feel the leather buckle at the top of this idiotic jacket cutting into the skin at the back of my neck. I know what's coming next and I know I can't live through it. I won't. Not again. Not even one more time. I cannot go through another withdrawal. I'd rather die.

I stand up, take a deep breath and make a run at the opposite wall, but my feet slip on the slimy, rubbery floor and I fall over again and roll myself into a ball. I hold my breath, trying to blow my eyeballs and hopefully my brain, but I think I black out instead. When I come round I find I'm all disorientated and now my head is throbbing unbearably. I can't focus my eyes properly so I guess it nearly worked. Perhaps I just need to hold my breath for longer. They're *not* going to win. They're *not* going to keep me in here. They can come and take my body out. I try it again, holding my breath until I'm sure the veins in my eyeballs are bursting but again I black out and wake up and this time my cheek is squashed against the wall and when I open my eyes I see there are dark brown bloodstains on it, long streaks of them, like splashes of paint.

OK, so I'll break my neck instead. I'll fucking snap it in half. I ready myself and run again at the opposite wall, head down like rugby forward. But the space is too small and I can't get enough momentum going and the wall is soft and spongy and I fall back, exhausted. My nose is running and I catch the snot in my bottom lip but it's not snot, it's blood and I sit leaning against the wall and watch it run down and drip onto the white jacket.

Why, I wonder tiredly. Why am I being punished like this? What have I done that's so bad?

FIFTEEN

In the seventies and eighties, South Africa was on full military alert for the communists who were poised to swarm over our borders and take over our homes, not to mention our hearts and minds. As a white male, once you finished school, unless there was a very good reason to do otherwise, you went into the army for two years' compulsory military service, which included several spells of border duty. After that you were required to present yourself for a number of three-month camps on and off for several years, or as long as it took to rid our country of the red peril.

In fact it turned out that the authorities had not been as alert over the years as they could have been, because apparently quite a lot of the danger seemed somehow to have perforated our defences and we were told that certain areas around the country already seethed with the enemy. This meant that there were several fronts that constituted legitimate battle-grounds, and even if some of them looked like poverty-stricken urban homes in black townships, the powers that be knew better than we did and who were we to argue? Apart from having to guard the borders of South Africa, therefore, sometimes soldiers like me were des-patched to the townships like the one John and I drank and drugged in together, to quell any potential up-risings and to root out the bad guys – who also looked a lot like John, by the way, and probably drank and drugged with me too.

It was very confusing.

I'm being flippant about it here because in retro-spect it all seems so bizarre, but the reality was far from amusing. A lot of kids got killed in the seventies and eighties fighting that strange war, buddies of mine included, and a lot of the kids who weren't killed are still battling to come to grips with what it was all for in the end.

For me, just turned seventeen, by now hopelessly dependent on drugs, it was both a nightmare and a feast. Make no mistake about it, drugs were freely avail-able in the army and I didn't waste any time making the right friends and getting a supply chain organised.

Three days into basics and I was busted for poss-ession. There was a court case which, fortunately for me as I still had that four-year suspended sentence hanging over me, I won on a technicality, and back into basics I went.

Anyone who's spent time in what amounts to a war situation will tell you of long periods of boredom and inactivity as well as shorter, more intense periods of action with real guns and real blood. To my mind, both of these scenarios lent themselves to some kind of chemical tampering, either to take the edge off the boredom or the edge off the fear. Try walking along a dusty road somewhere near Angola, bayonet at the ready, expecting either to be ambushed any minute or blown to pieces by a landmine. It's easier if you're stoned, trust me. I was scared on the border, shit scared. I think a lot of guys tried out drugs in the army for the first time. You couldn't blame them really. My situation was a little more complicated. It wasn't all in my mind, not by a long shot. My body was now so physically dependent on drugs just to function, that I was a serious risk. I should never have been in the army at all. What they had in me was a soldier on drugs who was nothing more than a zombie going through the motions or a soldier off drugs who became the proverbial loose cannon. Add a dash of paranoid schizophrenia, now fully unmasked, and put live ammunition into this soldier's hands and – you're with me, right?

I should *not* have been in the army. Nevertheless, once I was there I exploited every opportunity that came my way to keep myself from having to face my own unseen demons or the ones who were really shooting at me.

High or craving, remember? Nothing in between.

The army was a time of hectic drugging for me. I

made new contacts and I tried new drugs. I discovered the wonderful, highly addictive world of morphine when, crazed and craving, I had a medic up against a wall threatening to kill him if he didn't give me something, *anything*.

You got to make a plan for me, bru. You got to make a plan.

He looked more terrified than if he'd found himself surrounded by a wall of AK-47s, but he could see this was no time to fuck with me. I shouldn't be doing this, he kept repeating. I shouldn't be doing this. He gave me what I saw as a lifeline. Morphine. Straight into my vein. No time to fuck around.

I thanked him.

I shouldn't be doing this, he said again. Just this one time, OK?

OK, I said. Just this one time.

It should be significant, the first time you spike, and I've been asked more than once what that leap was like for me. To go from inhaling and swallowing to inserting a needle into your arm, or your groin or your neck – that must have taken some thought, even courage, if you like. You must have really had to steel yourself for that one, hey, is what they say. I mean, it's different, isn't it? It must have been a milestone, sort of the point of no return? It kind of separates out the amateurs, wouldn't you say? Alcohol, pills, weed, even a line of coke – that's not quite as dangerous, is it? But shooting up, well, that's when you know you're a *real* junkie. Right?

Wrong.

But I don't have to tell you that now, do I?

And about spiking and the big leap and milestone and shit? You know what, hey? When you're facing withdrawal and it's beginning to bite, you won't think twice about what you're about to do. Slipping that needle into your arm is just the easiest thing in the world.

*

Quite early on into my basic training the opportunity of a transfer to Durban came up. I volunteered like a shot. My reasons were simple. Durban was closest to my dealer and I didn't want to take any chances of running short or getting busted again. John was in Durban and I knew I could trust him.

Another opportunity came from an unexpected source – the army's sports programme. You had to sign up for something – rugby, soccer, whatever. Surfing wasn't an option. I chose jogging. Again the choice was a logical one. Jogging meant that I could go for long runs, outside of the perimeter of the camp, and organise my own personalised water tables. My tables didn't have energy drinks lined up on them, though, or little sponsors' sachets of vitamin-containing nutrients. The pick me ups I needed had a more immediate effect and I had a 25km excuse to go and fetch them. It was a good set-up. I could arrange a meeting place at a strategic point along my route with John or another of my regular suppliers, pick up my drugs on the trot as it were and pretend to be fit and healthy all at the same time. It was a great system and it worked like a charm.

In the meantime, however, I was getting into all sorts of other trouble.

I've always loved motorbikes and I had one of my own, tended and looked after by me with great care. I got to know some guys I was doing basics with who were involved in an army motorbike theft syndicate. I wasn't directly involved myself, but these were drugging buddies and I was always on the periphery. I knew what was going on anyway and if I could help out from time to time, I'd do it.

In fact it wasn't my first taste of stealing bikes. At school, as one of the lunch exit kids, when me and my friends went home supposedly to have the milk and cookies our mothers had lovingly prepared for us, but actually to drug at whoever's house was the safest at the time, I got to leave the grounds when other guys were at school.

One lunchtime I was hanging out with this nineteen year old brother of a friend of a friend of a buddy. His name was Nick. We used to hang out now and again and on this occasion we went to one of his friends' houses to smoke a joint. The friend's father had a really nice motorbike, the kind that started with a key, not a kick. I was impressed, hey. I stroked the chrome and checked the whole machine over. It had everything. The friend wasn't much into bikes but he let me sit on it and feel the power of the engine for a couple of minutes. I'd supplied the weed, after all. But that was as far as he would let me go even though I was desperate to take it for a spin round the block.

My old man would kill me, he said apologetically, and he took the key and put it away, beneath a loose brick under the tin roof of their garage. I might have made a small mental note.

A few nights later Nick and I were out together again and it just so happened that we found ourselves close by to the place where the guy with the motorbike lived. We looked at each other. The bike was parked in full view of the street.

Are you thinking what I'm thinking, I asked.

I don't think he was, actually, but it's amazing how persuasive my thoughts can be.

We'd just be borrowing it, I said. It's not like we're –

– *stealing* it or anything? He finished my sentence for me.

Exactly.

We didn't do anything that night, but I couldn't get the bike out of my mind and a few nights later we'd formed a plan. It was theft, plain and simple. Borrowing a bike for a joyride wasn't enough of a challenge. It was my idea to keep watch while Nick would sneak up the driveway, grab the keys, and off we'd go. That's almost how it turned out. I crouched in the shrubbery and watched Nick walk lightly up the side of the garage and feel with his fingers for the keys beneath the loose brick. Safe in my hiding place, I imagined how we were mere seconds away from zooming along the south coast road, wind pulling through our hair, screaming at full throttle into the night. I was so into the fantasy, stoned as I was, that I almost forgot I was supposed to be keeping a lookout. One thing that never occurred to me, and which was in fact the case, was that Nick might not know how to ride the bike, or even how to start it. I think he only realised this too for the first time once he had the keys in his hand. He held them up for me to see and gave me a Now what look.

Now what? I was sixteen, for heaven's sake. He was nineteen. What nineteen year old wouldn't know how to drive? What was he thinking?

So there we were, the two of us, wheeling the heavy machine backwards down the driveway, holding our breath that no one would drive by or look out of a window. At one point on the seemingly endless journey to the gate an outside light came on, momentarily blinding us and pinning us to the ground in a fluorescent spotlight. It must have been one of those movement-sensitive lights because after a minute it switched off and we carried on rolling our heavy loot towards the road and freedom.

The lure of the open road had lost its appeal by then, and we were dripping with sweat after our exertions. We decided instead to hide the bike for a few days and then do some cosmetic surgery like change the plates. I stripped it of what I thought would best disguise its identity and kept the parts behind some boxes at the back of our garage. Nick took the machine away and hid it somewhere where no one was likely to go looking.

The news of the stolen bike spread quickly in our small town. As the finger of suspicion for just about anything illegal usually pointed at me sooner or later, there was absolutely nothing we could do with the damn thing other than keep it hidden. In fact the guy whose father's bike it was had a younger brother at my school and it wasn't long before he was more or less openly accusing me and threatening to bring his brother and his brother's *breker* mates to search my property for evidence.

Talk about a cock-up. Eventually, Nick and I decided to go the disaster movie route and, petrol soaked rag and all, we pushed the stupid bike over a cliff one night. All we got out of our master plan in the end was a minor special effects display.

I still had the incriminating evidence back at home, though, and I got rid of it just in time as, true to his word, the younger brother led a heavy looking posse onto our property. They found nothing of course, but I could tell they weren't altogether convinced that their instincts hadn't been right. Weeks later, when the wreckage was eventually found, burnt out and in a million metal pieces, the kid came up to me at break one day and apologised. He hauled an unrecognisable piece of scrap metal out of his bag and showed me what he'd salvaged of his father's pride and joy after thieves had taken it up the coast and lost it on a sharp bend.

I'm sorry, hey, he said, that we . . . that I . . .

I shrugged indifferently. So you should be, I told him. Cheeky shit.

✳

The motorcycle theft ring in the army was far more sophisticated than my feeble little sortie into that particular underworld. It had been going on for a long time and I didn't really know very much about it or who all was involved. One day I saw cops arriving in our camp, not Military Police who came and went all the time. This was different and I instinctively knew that some serious shit was about to go down.

I sent the word along and there was much furtive activity at one end of the camp. A guy I knew only as Happy (who was anything but) came looking for me. He asked me if I would do him a favour. A five caps of acid favour. No problem. All I had to do was take a certain bike and hide it somewhere, just for a bit until the cops had left and the dust had settled. I didn't know Happy very well, but the acid seemed like a fair trade and I took a mate, Gavin, along with me.

It wasn't difficult. Five caps of acid between us and Gav and I were tripping. We drove the bike out of camp for about ten kilometres and hid it in a sugarcane field. By the time we got back I think I noticed that the cop cars were still there. I was so high I didn't really register and I didn't really register either when I saw Happy in animated conversation with two uniformed officers. When I worked it out they were all looking at me with great interest. Where Gavin had disappeared to, who knew?

It turned out that Happy had laid the whole

bloody thing squarely on me. I was the one who had stolen the motorbike in question. I was the one who had driven away on it. So I was the one to interrogate.

It wasn't me, it was him. When would I ever learn?

Jesus. I knew I was in for it. For one thing I was still tripping and no one could have failed to notice that. For another, while I didn't exactly deny taking the bike out of the camp, I couldn't for the life of me remember where we'd hidden it either and that story no one believed. Happy had told the cops that I was in it up to my neck. He'd always had his suspicions, he said.

I was handcuffed and led to the cop car to go and retrieve the stolen motorcycle. One of the effects of acid is that you can't control the muscles of your mouth and I couldn't stop grinning. They must have thought I was mad or insolent or both, but I couldn't help it. I sat in the back of the car, tripping and grinning away, and pointing out one possible sugarcane field after another. They were fast losing patience with me.

Eventually, I think by sheer luck, we found the bike. One of the cops decided he was going to drive it back to camp. I could have told him that was a mistake but I was trying to concentrate on getting my expression under control and to work out what story I could use to get out of a spell in DB. Anyway, the bike was a bit stuffed as it was and it was also out of oil. It wasn't fit to drive. In addition, the road alongside the canefields was full of potholes and I don't think the guy had had much experience on bikes. We drove behind him and watched him wobble and jerk and eventually pick up speed, despite the bike's odd action and the unusual noise it was making. As he put on a spurt and streaked ahead of us, we drove faster to catch up with him, until a row of very bad potholes one after the other sent cop and bike tumbling ass over tip and our car ploughing into both of them.

I don't think it was the acid – I was starting to come down by then – but I definitely couldn't control my mouth muscles after that. I *pissed* myself laughing. The cop had big grazes down his arms and his shirt was torn. The bike was even more bent and twisted out of shape than he was.

As for me, I only stopped laughing when I found myself abruptly handcuffed to the broken motorcycle, thrown into the boot of the car with it and paraded through the streets of Durban. That was definitely not so funny, and nor were the six weeks I spent in detention barracks either.

The only thing that sustained me was the thought of what I would do to Happy when I got out.

I went through some bad withdrawal in DB and I was craving and spitting mad when I came out. John was close by to help me through and when I felt better, high as a kite, I went looking for Happy. He wasn't going to be so fucking happy when I'd finished with him. I'm not so sure about the accuracy of the sequence of events or what exactly was said when I accosted him, but there was a hell of a punch up. I could have taken on the whole army and then some. I was *wired*. I would have done it too. Instead, on impulse, I stole a rifle, got on my own motorbike, gunned the engine and went AWOL.

I don't know where I was heading. I was high. I was going too fast. I don't know what I hit or who hit me (I later discovered that the accident was, miraculously, not my fault) but my bike was a write off and so, nearly, was I. The car that almost took me out apparently had to be written off too and later on my mother took legal action against the driver.

My injuries were severe. I almost lost my right hand. It had been sliced practically in half. The knuckle on my ring finger was smashed and my palm was one big gaping hole. My little finger was hanging on only by some stringy bits of tissue and it was touch and go whether they amputated or not. In the end they didn't but many months of reconstructive surgery awaited me and it was doubtful whether I'd ever regain proper use of the hand.

The physical damage was one thing and although I was in excruciating pain and kept blacking out on the way to hospital, it was nothing compared to what I was soon to be introduced to for the first time: the clashing of street drugs with medicine. They might have seen that I was high, but the doctors didn't know what I was on and nobody asked me, so they didn't know I was an addict either. From subsequent bitter experience, it wouldn't have made a difference if they had.

Anyway, I was still tripping on acid when the ambulance deposited me at the hospital and I wasn't in any state to give anybody an alphabetical list of what

I'd taken that day or the day before. If the idea is to make the patient as comfortable as possible in whatever circumstances, in my case they went about it in completely the wrong way.

On admission they immediately stuck needles into me, gave me pills to swallow and put a drip in my arm. Fuck knows what they were but for me it was bad news. I was raving, violent and in the end had to be strapped down and sedated. Nobody could understand what was going on and the more I tried to tell them, the more agitated I became, the more tranquillisers they jabbed into me.

My mother was distraught. She didn't know what was going on either. I begged her, I pleaded with her, not to let the doctors or nurses come near me, but she just wouldn't understand and it freaked me out. She bore the brunt of my desperation.

They're trying to help you, Steve, she said. The doctors know what they're doing.

They *don't* know what they're doing, I screamed at her. I'm a *drug addict*, for chrissake, and they're putting *more* drugs into me and whatever those fucking drugs are, THEY'RE NOT MIXING WELL WITH THE OTHERS.

Steve, calm down. Try to rest. You need to rest. Keep still.

The more she tried to calm and reassure me, the more desperate and violent I became. Eventually, she would stand aside, her face pitiful, and let the doctors take over. I would lie helplessly, sometimes strapped down, sometimes on a pillow slimy with my vomit, and watch as she gradually receded and disappeared from my view.

This was a pattern that was to be repeated many times and it was always a no win situation for me. I would fight everyone off like a madman, trying to keep them and their psychiatric drugs as far away from me as I could. The crazier and more violent I got, the more they pumped me full of drugs until I was quiet and compliant and preferably asleep. What they couldn't know and wouldn't believe was the terrifying war that waged inside my mind and body with each drip through a tube or unidentified pill they forced me to swallow.

My body was in self-destruct mode. It was greedy for drugs. It clutched at anything. But my mind paid a hideous price.

✳

While my hand was beginning to mend, my mother was taking legal advice and there seemed to be a strong case in our favour against the driver who'd hit me. Part of the process of putting a case together meant that I had to tell my story to a whole heap of people. It was exhausting. Everyone wanted a piece of me – the army, the police, doctors, my mother. And all I wanted was to get out of the hospital and back onto the street where I could do something about the appalling withdrawal I was starting to go through. I needed to score. I had to make a plan and soon, but they wouldn't let me go. My nerves were raw and I was in constant pain. Medicine dripped into me through tubes and I lashed out at everyone who came near me. I grew terribly depressed and began to think that suicide was an attractive way out.

One of the people who had to interview me was a psychologist and it was on his recommendation, given my mental state at the time, that I was sent to a psychiatrist for assessment.

Another bad move.

The psychiatrist prescribed a stay in an institution where I could be properly medicated. I'd just got out of hospital. I was in no hurry to go back and suffer through a repeat performance. My protests, however, fell on deaf ears and the man's bland non-comprehension of the sentence he was handing down to me infuriated me beyond anything. I grew agitated. I started pacing his office. When I tried to explain, he wouldn't listen. He wouldn't *damn well listen*. When he reached for his prescription pad, I ripped it away. I swept handfuls of papers off his desk. I was scared witless, feeling helpless and defenceless in an alien place, as if I was speaking a foreign language.

Who said that the best method of defence was attack? Well, maybe it worked for that guy but all it got me that day was a couple of humourless bouncers in white takkies dragging me down to a ward and a week of sleep therapy.

I did get out in the end, with see-through plastic

packets of pills from the dispensary and a bunch of prescriptions that would ensure all the pharmaceutical reps bonuses for Christmas.

I went back to the street, nursing more than my tender, injured hand.

As soon as I got home I gave John a whistle.

INSTITUTIONS

I know where I am this time. This time they can't fool me. I have all my wits about me, every last one of them. It's advisable when you're in the army. If you haven't it could be *your* head exploding in a fountain of brains and pink bubbling blood instead of the buddy beside you whose twitching corpse you're going to have to pull out of the road when your sharpest instinct is to run away as fast as you can. Well, *he* didn't have his wits about him, that's for sure. And now his wits are spread all over the fucking border, aren't they, poor fucking sod.

I know where I am this time. This time they can't fool me. It's One Mil Hospital. Psych ward.

And I'm not winning any prizes for best dressed soldier of the year.

This hospital is so full they sometimes have to mix the loonies in with the honourably injured when there aren't enough beds or when one ward is full and there's an ambush or something somewhere and extra space has to be found in a hurry. So they've devised an interesting dress code for the freaks. That's us, the psych ward patients, the ones with *internal* injuries.

Just so we know, we're the soldiers, they keep remind-ing us, who are wasting taxpayers' money and threat-ening to let in the red tide of communism because we're stoned all the time and so shit scared when we're not that we forget that we're supposed to follow orders. The only orders a drug addict obeys when he's craving are those barked out by Captain Withdrawal. Someone ought to point this out to them.

Anyway. This is what we have to wear: our army boots, pyjamas, a striped dressing gown, and a red helmet. All the time. This is so that we're easy to spot at any given moment and can be identified when we start to run amok or something.

Unarmed and dangerous.

The psych ward gang.

I have been told, repeatedly, that I am a danger to myself and to others, that I have wild, uncontrollable bouts of rage. My aggression is unpredictable and violent.

Nobody listens to anything I say, of course, and it pisses me off. I'm *not* violent. I'm *not* aggressive. I'm *craving*, for fucksake, and scared out of my mind. I've seen some shocking stuff out there, stuff that could challenge the worst trip on acid. I could also tell them that pumping an addict full of conflicting psychiatric drugs isn't helping and it's going nowhere to improving my bad mood.

Anyone with half an eye can see I don't belong in here. In fact there's a guy in the bed opposite me who now *has* only half an eye, and half a head too, thanks to PW Botha & Co – go ask him. There's enough insanity outside the walls of this psych ward to fill a hundred hospitals. Go check out the border, man. Go on a township patrol. This is South Africa in the eighties where violence rules.

Am I the only one here who *gets* that?

If I could just find someone who'll listen long enough for me to explain. I don't *want* to use taxpayers' money, believe me. Just let me out of here and I'll be out of your hair before you can say *swart gevaar*. I'm sure someone else could use this uniform. It's an outfit to die for, after all.

Today is a bad day. Because I'm so dangerous, they've got me handcuffed to an RP. We go everywhere together, like Siamese twins, even to the bathroom, which is really irritating. I make a point of drinking a lot of water so we have to go often. It irritates him more than it does me so that's why I do it, but the game is getting boring. The cuff is tight and it chafes my wrist. He doesn't like my cigarette smoke so I blow it in his face.

We're on our third circuit of the linoleum passageways, nodding to the other walking wounds, when a moth flies into my left ear. Christ! I can feel its panicky wriggling and flapping and it freaks me out bigtime. I have a graphic image of it, wings whirring crazily, trying frantically to escape like only a trapped thing can, and its wings make a fuzzy, muffled sound deep in my head. It tickles so badly that I want to scream. I shake my head to free it but nothing comes out.

The RP isn't having any of this weirdo behaviour. *Staan stil*, he hisses.

Wag, I say. There's something in my ear. Wait while I get it out.

He sighs but stops walking and stands beside me, rolling his eyes. I'm obviously trying out some diversionary tactic. Either that or I'm hallucinating. He knows there's nothing in my damn ear. I'm just a junkie.

It's my left wrist and his right that are handcuffed together so I have to twist to the side to pull on my earlobe with my free hand. I give it a tug and a little shake. Although all of my nerves are screaming, I don't want to rub in case I squash the stupid thing. I poke my little finger gingerly inside but I can't feel anything so I put my head on one side and jump up and down on the spot, like you do when you're a kid at a swimming pool and you've gone deaf because you've got water in your ear.

The RP makes an impatient noise and jerks on my chain. I subside like an obedient dog but people are beginning to slow down as they pass us and stare curiously, some of them smiling, some giving my reluctant companion sympathetic looks. I can't help myself. The tickle and *brrrrrrr* of desperate moth wings gets louder and more frantic and I do another little jig. It's going to *brrrrrrr* right through to my brain! I don't know which one of us is panicking more now. The thought does cross my mind that I might actually *be* hallucinating and that this is another strange side effect of god knows what drugs I swallowed down with my

Jungle oats this morning. But no. This is real and now it's really getting to me. I have visions of a huge, hairy moth body stuck fast and dying in there, its wings getting feebler and feebler and me left with permanent tinnitus like those old soldiers in World War One who had imaginary shells exploding right inside their heads long after they'd been shipped off home and the war was over. Eventually they went crazy, just from the sound.

I'm going mad, I tell my twin, lifting our arms, clinking in unison, and taking another wild swipe at my ear.

Oh really, he says, jerking our arms back down. Coulda fooled me.

I jerk our arms back up again. I need to see a doctor, I say.

You got that right, he says, not moving.

I'm serious. Take me to Casualty. I'm *serious*, man. Listen for yourself, if you want. You can hear it. *Can't* you hear it?

I lean towards him so he can get an idea of the sound system I now have growing in intensity in the inner chamber of my ear. He leans back in alarm. You better be careful, he warns me. I'm not joking.

Neither am I, I say desperately.

Now I'm hopping on one foot and my red helmet is slipping. People are openly laughing at us and I can tell it's pissing him off.

You think you funny, hey, he says. Let's go. I'm taking you back to your ward.

Can we stop by in Casualty, please? I decide to act sane and make a big effort to ignore what is now the great flapping beast that has sought asylum in my head. I suppress the vision I have of it laying eggs, rows and rows of them, that will hatch one a day for the next six months. I'll be giving it a name any minute.

He sighs again, heavily. He must hate his job. I know he hates me.

But we make a right and end up in Casualty where the doctor on duty gives me a very sceptical look and reaches automatically for his prescription pad without even stepping forward. He's recognised the uniform.

Tell him, I urge the RP, as I rub madly at my ear for the ninety-third time, beyond caring if I grind the wretched thing to a fine grey powder. Tell him I'm not making this up. There's a fucking creature in my fucking ear!

What's the problem here?

I could kiss his feet. It's Dr B. I recognise him from K G Five in Durban, and after a long minute he recognises me. He even remembers my name.

I tell him what's bothering me.

Let's take a look, he says without any hesitation.

I stand still while he peers through an instrument and makes little whistling noises with his teeth. Gone in deep, he says. If you'd just given your earlobe a little tug . . .

I narrow my eyes at him.

Right, he says.

Then he calls a nurse over and after their second

or third attempt they manage to flush a really sodden, really tiny, hardly recognisable moth out of my left ear.

I am triumphant. Dr B hands me an empty matchbox so that I can keep it, as a souvenir, or proof, whatever – take your pick. He gives my captor a cool sidelong glance but the RP's expression doesn't change one iota. He's not examining what's in that matchbox, not for anyone.

We jangle off down the passage and I force his hand up in a reverse thank you salute.

The finger is for him.

SIXTEEN

When I was declared fit again, I went back to the army and finished my basic training. My hand had healed quite well, but I would never have the strength in it that I'd had before. Back home my mother didn't know what to do with me. I was drugging to stay alive and drugging not to die. I needed money but I couldn't find a job. She got me a menial position in a factory through a friend at work, but I lasted two weeks at it before I was fired for being drunk at ten in the morning.

I got another job all by myself, this time as a quality controller for a motor assembly line. I was supplied with a hammer, a screwdriver and a cloth, and it was my job to spot check welding. *Fuck* it was boring. The guy who was doing exactly the same thing to my right thought so too. His name was Sammy and he was from Newcastle. We'd be on our feet all day, clanging away at random. God knows how many cars we might have sent out onto the road ready to come apart at the seams on account of Sammy's and my casual approach to excellence. Our conversations were generally short and to the point, punctuated by the sound of metal hitting metal.

Clang.

Sidelong glance. Got a blow, bru?

Clang.

Sidelong glance. Sure, bru.

Clang.

It was unbearably mind-numbing. I'd have usually been drugging till 4 a.m. the night before, turn up for work at seven, still stoned, pissed or both, and report for duty, swaying slightly in front of the foreman, whose sour expression meant that he was onto me from day one. Sammy wasn't in any better shape than I was and we both discovered after a couple of weeks on the job that sharing a joint on our lunch break was the only thing that got us through the afternoon session. This was apparently not acceptable behaviour to the foreman or the boss. I wasn't sorry to leave. All that clanging gave me a headache anyway.

I knocked halfheartedly on a few doors and made some vague enquiries at the garages in town that might have been looking for unreliable, unqualified mechanics who might or might not show up, but somehow nobody was very keen to employ me. I don't know what happened to Sammy. I kind of missed him, in a way.

All of the sympathy that had come my way after

my accident rapidly dried up and my sisters had taken to pretending not to know me. I don't know for whose sake it was, but after a while I kept away from my family as much as I could.

Then I hooked up with an old buddy of mine who'd just got released from prison. Someone had lent him a bakkie and after closing time one night we reversed it into the plate glass windows of the local bottle store. We stole armfuls of booze before the cops got there and found, to our disgust, when we made it to his aunt's house and out of the reach of the law, that we'd managed to help ourselves to the cheapest, vilest possible brand of brandy on the market. Remarkably drinkable all the same after a couple of bottles. Then we raided his aunt's medicine cabinet – she was a Valium junkie, the 10mg tabs, and I think we took five each – and we got completely wasted for the rest of the night and most of the following day.

I had a second hand motorbike then and I was still buzzing when I set off home. I kept falling asleep at stop streets. I finally made it to our driveway at the exact same moment that my mother was being dropped off from work by her boss. I think I parked, but I couldn't get off the bike and I couldn't sit up straight either. I had a bottle of Coke in my hand and as I struggled to get my leg over and onto the ground the Coke spilt all over the engine, hissing and splattering all over the suit pants of my red-faced mother's boss. I was too out of it to know what was going on but apparently he helped to get me up to my room. I lay on my bed and I was *flying*, hey. It was terrifying and amazing at the same time. I was flying straight up, I mean *straight* up like a rocket into the sky and then CRASHING back down again, leaving my stomach somewhere up near the stars. That's what it felt like anyway. The reality was that I was lying on my back puking my guts out and I didn't even know it. My sister heard the strange choking sounds I was making and she came into my bedroom just in time and found me drowning in my vomit, unable to turn over and hurl on the floor. She called my mother and they cleaned me up. I slept for three days. After that my sister told my mother that if I didn't leave home, permanently, she would.

Once, after I'd come out of yet another rehab clinic and was trying desperately to stay clean, I tried to make my mother understand how hard it was to be me, what it was like to be an addict. I was terribly depressed, brimming over with self-pity and wanting to end it all. I admitted to her that suicide was never far from my mind.

It's not fair, I said. You don't know what it's like.

Hold it right there, said my mother. I don't know what it's like? Let me tell you something, Steve. Through all of your drugging, when you didn't know where or who you were, when you were sick and dying and craving, when you had so many punctures in your arms and legs that your veins collapsed, when you couldn't walk or breathe on your own, when your heart stopped, when your groin went septic – She stopped, breathless, and looked hard into my eyes. Through all of that, my son, remember one thing: *I was clean.*

I tried to speak but she stopped me again.

And you know what, Steve, she said. I *prayed* for your death. Sometimes I still do.

＊

My uncle had a farm down in the Cape, just outside of the city, and my mother, at her wits' end and sensibly choosing my sister over me, sent me down to stay with him and to work on the farm. Different sea air. A change of scenery. New friends. She tried, my mother, I guess, but an addict is an addict and ultimately all that the relocation did for me was introduce me to a whole new group of people and a new drug culture. I took to it like the ducks took to the water on the farm's muddy pond.

The labour on the farm was drawn largely from the Coloured community and right from the start I felt comfortable with the guys. Maybe it was my imagination, but there was an air of alienation around them and it resonated with me. Apartheid had a different effect, I felt, on these people than on anyone else. They fell somewhere in between everything somehow, a bit like me, really. Perhaps that's why we got on so well. Or perhaps it was just my well developed pain sensors at work. Anyway, who cared? We had the same remedy for pain.

Another thing I found was how warmly they welcomed me into their homes and their lives. There were no questions. There was no moralising, no judging. This was a new experience for me and it took some getting used to, I can tell you. I wasn't getting it from my blood relatives. I felt almost able to drop my defences when I was around them.

My Coloured friends introduced me to mandrax, at that time mostly used only in the Cape as a street drug. The government banned the sale of it in '74 and it would be a while before its large-scale illegal manufacture and trade would turn into the multimillion rand industry it is today. We'd get it from the old people – it was a powerful sleeping pill – who still had access to it by prescription, and a potjie mandrax became a regular thing for me.

I'm a quick learner. In no time I became an expert at crushing the tablets, mixing the powder with the right amount of dagga and tobacco and making a bottleneck, a white pipe. This new discovery gave me a high so sweet I fell in love all over again. I began spending all of my free time in and out of homes on the Cape Flats, where the poverty and overcrowding was probably not unlike my father's background in the slums of Glasgow. Alcohol and dagga were everywhere, as were gang violence and domestic abuse. I felt familiarity slip over me like an old worn glove. I fitted right in. And why wouldn't I? I was my father's son, after all.

I was asked once whether I had forgiven my father. I thought it an odd question at the time and I must have looked surprised.

Forgiven him? I don't know – why?

Well, you should. It's because of your father that you're the highly qualified expert in your field that you are today.

That's one way of looking at it, I suppose, and the guy who asked me was right. I spend sleepless nights today wondering what I could have been or could have achieved if I had put my clever mind and dextrous hands to a more intelligent purpose than making a white pipe or offering myself as a guinea pig to test the effect of a new combination of drugs.

Because I *was* an expert, hey. I was known for it. I was the tester, the one they'd try stuff out on to see how good it was. There was an expression we used – *kap om* – which I suppose, translated, means keel over or black out, but that doesn't sound quite right. It's better in Afrikaans: *As Steve kap om is die pille OK.* In other words, you'd know it was good stuff if it could drop me like a stone.

Good though it was in Cape Town, drugging at the level I needed to keep withdrawal at bay was expensive, and working on my uncle's farm wasn't exactly bringing in the bucks. I'd also got involved in some small-time dealing up in the District Six area and was getting a reputation round the cop stations as someone to watch. After a while I realised that my uncle didn't want me anymore either. I think I exasperated him. When I was on the farm I'd spend all my time with his workers, drinking and smoking with them in their quarters till the early hours and showing up late for work the next day, lethargic and hung over. Other times I'd simply disappear, sometimes for days at a time. He complained that he never knew where I was and he'd worry and wait and worry some more and then phone my mother to see if *she'd* heard from me and then *she'd* start to worry and –

Mostly when this happened I'd be in one of the townships, drinking brandy and smoking five or six pipes a day with my friends, or else hanging round outside the banks on pension pay out day, waiting to relieve some elderly woman of her monthly grocery money.

It got too much for my uncle in the end. He couldn't take the responsibility. One day he just put me on a bus and sent me home.

I wasn't too sorry to go. I missed my buddies and I missed Tracey. While I was away I heard she dropped out of school and was doing office temp work part time. Then Brian said he'd heard that she'd got a job at a pharmacy in Ramsgate or Port Edward or somewhere, Saturday mornings, which was really good until they caught her leaving one day with half the dispensary in her backpack. She moved to Durban and was staying in a flat with a buddy of hers.

Brian hadn't finished school either. He'd left at the end of Grade 10, somehow managed to avoid the army, and went to trade school for six months. He dropped out, began again and finally walked out with a certificate that everyone was quite sure he'd stolen and not qualified for. Like me, he went through a series of jobs and got fired from every one, either for drinking on the job, arriving at work tripping on acid and occasionally forgetting for a week or two that he even had a job at all.

One night, coming home from a *jol*, riding his motorbike at a speed no one as high as he was at the time in his right *mind* would have been going, except me, perhaps, Brian hit a pedestrian, catapulted into the air and died where he landed, fifty yards away, his neck broken. When I heard the news I mourned my buddy the best way an addict knows how. I didn't light a candle, send flowers or visit his parents. I got wasted. I didn't allow myself to think back to where it all began – *We don't drink. We smoke* – and how I couldn't wait to take Brian with me into that secret, members only world I'd discovered. Those thoughts came later, much later. Like yesterday. Like right now.

Still, Brian shouldn't have been going so fast. No one in his right *mind* would have . . .

❉

I got back into doing the dagga run with John again, in and out of Transkei, but I was restless and edgy and bored. I'd brought mandrax up with me from the Cape and I showed John how to make a pipe. It wasn't long before word spread and confirmed for me what I already knew – the drug, when it hit Durban, as it inevitably would, was going to be big. There were already signs. I could almost *feel* the city bracing itself for a rollercoaster ride and I, with my Cape-based contacts, was perfectly positioned to take advantage.

I got in with a dealer called Mlungu who was also quick to see the potential and over the following six months or so we had a sophisticated network up and running and were controlling the supply of mandrax up and down the south coast as far as Toti. Mlungu was an odd mixture, a big guy, light skinned, who spoke Zulu, Xhosa, English and Afrikaans equally fluently, sometimes all of them mixed in together.

We made a lot of money and we did a lot of drugs. There was money everywhere, cash spilling out of cubbyholes in the cars we drove, cash in the filthy flat we hung out in down near the docks. I reckoned at one stage we must have been moving two to three thousand tabs of mandrax a day. Our formal education might have been sketchy, but we knew all about the law of supply and demand.

We had different grades for different customers and there was method in our madness. The best grades we'd sell first and have our customers coming back for more. Then we'd give them standard grade stuff that pulled the same addiction but not the same rush as the quality tabs. The effect, of course, was that our customers kept coming back for more, desperate to get back to that first high – the one you fall in love with, remember?

Then there were the Vaalies, visitors from up Joburg way, who came to the coast in droves in search of the legendary Durban poison and whatever else was going. They were unsuspecting victims too. We loved pulling one over them and they had money to spend which made it all the more enjoyable and lucrative. We'd charge them through the nose for one stick of standard grade dagga in a thin matchstick roll – we called them *kartjies* – and they'd go away happy. Until the next day, when they'd be back, panting for more.

It was one hell of an operation we had going but the risks we ran every day carried a very high price. Drugging and dealing and keeping a heartbeat away from getting busted took a lot of energy. Luckily, energy – the chemical kind – was in plentiful supply. I only slept when I passed out.

While I was with Mlungu I worked the block with a guy called KK for a bit. We had a loose shift arrangement, where a minimum of two guys at a time would cruise the streets on a roster basis. There were three main shifts, starting in the afternoon – two to ten, ten to six and six to two again. One night it was KK's turn to drive and mine to score. We were working the ten to six shift that time. The guy in the front passenger seat is always the one who scores because he can get in and out quick. The driver keeps watch and keeps cruising while the deal goes down. First we'd circle an area a few times to check out whether it was safe, clear of cops, rival dealers or anyone we didn't know. There would be someone on the street, hanging around on a corner or in a doorway, also keeping an eye out, and we had an effective system of hand signals and short-hand conversations so that we'd know whether the coast was clear or whether to keep on driving.

Hoe's die blok?

Blok is cool.

Sometimes it was just a murmur and a shifting of something from one hand to another to alert us – *Blok's not cool* – and we'd get out of there fast. There's always a risk though. Sometimes we weren't fast enough and sometimes our lookout system fucked up.

This night was one of those. A couple of our buddies were riding with us but I was up front. KK had the car circling, nothing seemed amiss, and we pulled an Indian guy in a red bakkie. I got out of the car but even as I did something felt not quite right to me. I had the drugs in my hand behind my back and for some reason, sharply honed instincts probably, just before I got to the bakkie, I put the packet on the ground. They can't bust you for possession if you're not technically *in* possession. As I turned to run, screaming at KK, who was doing a circuit and drawing closer to me but not yet close enough, the Indian guy was out of the bakkie like a panther and I had a gun at my head.

Pick it up, he said.

I knew these guys. So did KK, who had slowed down but was still loyally circling, sizing things up, weighing up the odds.

Pick it up. The click behind my ear was unmistakable.

KK!

Call your buddies over.

I ignored the instruction, shouting instead – *KK,*

fuck it!

Shit, Steve. I got a heavy record, hey, were the last words I heard from KK as he gunned the motor and hit the freeway, leaving me with a packet of drugs in my hand, a cop with an itchy finger and a car chase I wanted no part of. KK knew what he was doing though and in no time he lost us. Soon it was just me and my friendly plainclothes drug squad mate, grinning wolfishly at me over his shoulder. He had huge teeth beneath a thick moustache.

Hey, whitey, he told me. You going to sing like a budgie.

Where we were the police station didn't have cells for white guys like me. Separate incarceration was the name of the game in apartheid SA, so we began the long ride to Amanzimtoti, five uncomfortable hours' drive away, where they had holding cells for the white scum, as opposed to the black, Coloured or Indian scum. Five hours in the back of a van that smelt like rotten fish, in the humidity of the south coast in the middle of the hottest summer in several years, and I was finished. I was coming down from whatever it was I'd been on, I forget, and by the time we pulled into the police station's parking area I was so dehydrated I thought I was dying. Hell, I *wished* I was dying. A couple of cops came out to look at me, but they left me where I was and strolled back inside the charge office. I could see them drinking cooldrinks and laughing and I banged on the side of the van to get their attention. My captor came out by himself and stood smiling at me. It wasn't a pleasant smile.

Can I have some water, I said. Please, man. I knew better than to get angry, not yet anyway. I knew these guys. These guys would shoot for *nothing*.

He wrinkled up his nose. You stink, he said, and made childish retching noises, before strolling away again, chuckling.

For another hour I sat baking in the sun, just about crawling up the sides of the van, nauseous and shivering and trying not to black out. Finally the same cops came back again to stare at the animal in the cage.

Just some water, I said. Come on, guys. It's hot out here. IT'S HOT OUT HERE. I lunged at the doors and they stepped back in perfect formation. Must have been all that training.

Water, said my guy reflectively. Oh, you want *water*? Well, why didn't you say so?

ARE YOU FUCKING DEAF? I was ready to kill someone, anyone, myself if necessary. Give me WATER, for fucksake.

So they did. They brought me water. In the police station's fire hose. A huge jet of it hit me squarely in the chest and sent me slamming up against the back of the van. I tried to fend it off with my hands up, protecting my face, but it was like a live thing, whipping about like an anaconda in a frenzy, solid as steel and twice as cold. I didn't know something so cold could sting and burn like that water did. It had me pinned down on all fours on the corrugated floor, choking and gagging and practically drowning. Then it flipped me over like a puppet and I slipped and slid around on my bum while the cops all clutched their sides and slapped their thighs like the assholes they were, swearing at me and calling me every degrading name their small brains could invent.

Soaked through, my bruised chest heaving, I swore back at them.

Maliciously, I hoped that I was selling drugs to their children.

A Day in the Life …

I live – not on purpose – close by to a rehab centre in a beautiful area in the Cape. I have the mountain outside my back door and the wild cold sea at the front. Thick ropes of deep red-brown seaweed churn in the foam and when the wind is blowing in a certain direction a mixture of kelp and fynbos hits your nostrils with a strong, sour smell. I love it. I stride along the beach as often as I can, taking big gulps of air and feeling the wind throw handfuls of salt-spray at my shirt that will make it stiff and crusty when I take it off before I go to bed.

When I go walking on the beach with my dog and my son our path takes us past the rehab centre. Before we get there, though, we stop at our local café on the corner where I buy my cigarettes and newspaper.

On a late summer's evening while I'm watching Claydon standing on tiptoe waiting to pay for his sweets at the counter, I feel a tap on my shoulder.

Jesus, Steve – it is you. I thought it was you.

I know him only as Graham, the guy who OD'd on epilepsy tablets in Phoenix one time. He's just come out of the rehab centre and he's at the café trying to score. He has his suitcase on the floor between his feet.

I look at him. He changes expression. He looks over his shoulder, both ways, and lowers his voice.

Steve, he says, you've got to help me.

I helped you in '92 at Phoenix, I remind him. And

in '94 at Riverfield. I can't help you, man.

Steve –

Claydon is ripping open his roll of sweets, holding them out to me, at least three sweets already crammed into his mouth. My all or nothing kid, just like his dad.

Dadda? He looks up at me. The dog is pulling at the leash in my hand. Claydon looks at Graham and then backs into my leg, holding onto my jeans with sticky fingers.

Steve, Graham says again. Please.

I put my hand on my child's head. His floppy dark hair is silky to my touch, and his face is warm from running.

Steve –

Let's go, Claydon.

The wind has picked up and it's freezing on the beach. There's dirty foam in the rock pools and it smells horrible. We don't stay out long.

SEVENTEEN

When I got back from one of my three-month army camps a friend drew me aside in a pub one evening.

It's Tracey, he said. You got a problem, hey.

I don't understand, I said.

As far as I knew, Tracey and I were cool. For various reasons we'd spent a lot of time apart, but somehow we always drifted back together again. Although our relationship had gone from close and loving to greedy and codependent without us even realising it, we were still a couple and we'd be in and out of each other's lives for a long time to come, or so I believed. Tracey was still a major part of my life and I cared about her, even when, like now, she was drugging so hectically that I didn't know where she was a lot of the time. We hadn't managed to hook up since I'd got back from camp.

I don't know how to tell you this, bru, so I'm just going to say it. Tracey's been sleeping with your buddies while you've been away. She's sleeping with Mlungu. Some of the other dealers too.

Nobody is ever ready for news like that. I completely lost it. I went crazy. Whatever substances I pumped into my body that night, it wasn't enough. I poured alcohol down my throat, trying to pass out, just to get the hell away from the graphic vision I had in my head of my girlfriend offering her body to god knows who for drug money. What happened the rest of that night is patchy. I remember taking a cap of LSD and I remember running onto a highway intent on killing myself.

Apparently, when my friends came looking for me they found me lying unconscious at the side of the road, bleeding from the nose and stomach. They picked me up, threw me into the back of a car – my car, as it happened – and drove me to Addington Hospital. There they paused only long enough to push me out at the entrance like you see in the movies before they drove off in a squeal of retreads. If they hadn't, I'd have been dead for sure. As it was, by then I had gone into a coma, and I remember nothing of the days that followed when it seemed that this time I would not make it. I do remember my mother sitting beside my bed, massaging my raw wrists, chafed and angry from where I pulled constantly against the restraints that held me down, my terrified, desperate attempts when I woke up to fight off everyone who approached me, flinging myself violently, impotently against the walls, howling in anguish like a trapped animal, and vomiting until my throat bled.

And I remembered Tracey, my girlfriend, the captain of the netball team, with the laugh so full of joy I could have watched her all day. Where was Tracey when I was fighting for my life in Addington? Where were my buddies, for that matter? I pictured Tracey giving some dealer a hasty blow job so that she'd be back on the street and able to score before her withdrawal could begin to bite, and I could feel hot tears prickling the inside of my eyelids. With Tracey it was pinks and I knew better than anyone that when you're coming down off pinks you have *got* to make a plan. Withdrawal from pinks is terrible. You suffer awful physical pain, cramps in your stomach, cramps in your legs that are so painful you can barely stand, let alone walk. You *have* to make a plan. Well, Tracey had that under control all right.

I dreamed about her and all of my dreams were ugly and bitter and coated in betrayal. What I dream about now, when I think of Tracey, is a day long ago when she and I had this conversation.

You don't want to go messing with that stuff.

You do it.

Yes, but only now and then. It's no big deal. It doesn't even affect me.

Well, if it's no big deal, let me try it. Just once. I just want to see what it's like. Please? Just for the experience.

I don't know . . .
What's the worst that can happen?
Well, OK. Just once though.

✳

I got moved from Addington intensive care into the psych ward, and then on to a rehab clinic. Was it Lulama, that time? Yes, I think so. I was in a bad way and I knew it. I couldn't stop thinking about Tracey and it was driving me crazy. Most of the time what I still really wanted to do was end it all, but I had neither the energy nor the opportunity for suicide. The psych ward nurses made sure of that. On better days I grasped at the slim possibility of a life without street drugs. It had become clear to me that I if I continued on my self-destructive path I was going to run out of second chances. I was already pushing my luck. I wouldn't make it again, not at the level of abuse I'd got myself up to.

Somehow, I dug deep and found a small handful of courage that must have got stuck in the lining of my pocket or something and I went into rehab intent on turning my life around. This time it was going to be different. I'd get clean. I'd get a job. Find new friends. Maybe in time even a girlfriend who wouldn't cheat on me. Maybe we could go to a movie. People still went to movies, didn't they?

By the time I'd worked through the first and most difficult phase of the recovery programme, I'd converted all of the maybe's into definites. This time it was for real. I *knew* I could beat this thing. I was going to get myself right and turn my back on drugs once and for all.

Spot the error? Never, ever turn your back. Not for a second.

✻

I came out of Lulama shaky and ill, but determined to keep clean. I knew I was at risk, though, I wasn't entirely stupid, and I wished that I had someone to talk to who would understand where I was without my having to explain myself. I told my mother that I thought it was deeply unfair that alcoholics had AA and drug addicts had nothing. The support that AA gave their members was tailor made and effective. They had someone they could call up at three in the morning if they needed to, when the pull of the nearest shebeen was becoming overwhelmingly powerful.

There should be an AA for addicts, I said, don't you think?

My mother looked at me steadily for a couple of minutes, as if she was weighing something up. Then she said a surprising thing.

Why don't you start one?

Out of that brief conversation Narcotics Anonymous was born. I talked to the manager at Lulama and he also thought it was a good idea.

In fact, he told me, someone else is thinking along

the same lines as you. I'll introduce you, if you like. He's over there. In the garden.

His name was Kenneth and he was a crack cocaine addict. We were on the same wavelength from the outset. We agreed that we couldn't do it on our own, though, two addicts still in recovery. That wouldn't have inspired a whole lot of confidence, and we didn't really know what we were getting into anyway. To kickstart us, we needed a gram of credibility and a shot of experience. First we had to get someone else on board who had some serious clean time. The manager suggested a mate he knew, an AA guy who might be willing to help us. He had a lot of experience of the pitfalls and risks of setting up and maintaining a support network. We made contact. The guy was keen and he had some useful ideas. One of these was to put an ad in a local newspaper, announcing the formation of NA and inviting anyone who needed us to come along. Budget constraints, ie fuckall money, meant that you practically had to use a magnifying glass to see the ad it was so small, but we put it in anyway and sat back and waited. OK, so it wasn't exactly a crush of bodies beating their way to our door, but it was a start and the response we did get was gratifying nevertheless.

An unexpected spin-off, though, came from another direction.

At the same time as Kenneth and I were about to embark on our tiny venture, a woman in Durban who was connected, I think, to Lifeline, had identified the need for a support group for kids with drug problems. She was in the process of setting up a group called Teenagers Against Drug Abuse when she saw our ad. She called me up and asked if Kenneth or I might be willing to go along to a school in Durban and talk about our experiences. She was looking for a real live drug addict, she said.

Not a chance, said Kenneth. No way. I'm not a specimen to be held up for inspection in front of a lot of rich kids.

My thoughts exactly, but Kenneth had got in first. I said I'd think about it and call her back. I did think about it and after a while I rather liked the idea. After all, I *was* something of an expert in the field and no one had ever asked me before to talk about what addiction was like for me. Maybe I could even help someone.

I was still in that 'pink cloud' phase of recovery where optimism rules. Not altogether clean, but handling it. I'd started smoking the odd joint now and again, mostly just to stave off the boredom that follows a spell in rehab when you definitely don't want to look up old friends and there isn't anything else to do.

I was in control though.

It was just one, every now and then, nothing hectic.

My mother subscribed to the idea of the devil finding work for idle hands and she wanted me to try and find a job right away. I think she was scared that if I got *too* bored staying and home and watching TV, and if I lost interest in the NA idea, as I lost interest in most things, I might go looking for something else to do. She was right to be scared. My mother knew all about patterns. I wasn't worried at all. I was clean.

While I was still thinking about the school thing and not calling the Lifeline woman back, someone my mother knew through her work had put feelers out for me about a construction site on the Wild Coast. A new casino and hotel complex or something that was nearing completion. She said she'd heard they might be looking for unskilled people and just might be able to swing it for me if it sounded like something I'd like to try?

In a moment of bravery and confidence, I said yes to the Lifeline woman and yes to the job.

✳

The last time I'd stood on a stage in a school hall I'd been wearing handcuffs and had come fresh from a magistrate's court with a shiny new four year suspended sentence for the possession of an illegal substance as a warning. It hadn't had much effect on me, had it? Nor on Brian and James and Tracey. I was a real live drug addict even then, so what advice could I possibly give to a group of kids who were probably going to be a bunch of bravado filled fifteen year old Steves? Don't do drugs? Yeah, right. That worked.

I didn't know what I was going to say but I guessed that something would come to me on the way in to Durban. I smoked a joint with John before the Lifeline woman came to fetch me, so I was quite relaxed by the time we hit the city. Something would come. Perhaps me and the guys would just have a sort of formal discussion.

We pulled up outside Durban Girls' High. I felt a faint fluttering in my stomach.

Are we here, I asked.

Yes, said my companion, who was already half-way out of the driver's seat. Why?

This is an all girls school.

Yes, she said again, patiently. Why? Is that a problem, Steve?

Someone had put glue on the seat. I couldn't move my legs.

Um, how many girls am I speaking to, I asked.

Gosh, I don't know exactly. She looked thoughtful for a minute as she walked round to my side of the car and held the door open for me. Anyway, we're lucky. They've given us the whole high school this afternoon. I'd say somewhere in the region of – she smiled – twelve hundred?

Now I *definitely* couldn't get out of the car. Twelve hundred *kids*? And *girls*? She had to be kidding.

Come along, Steve, she said briskly. She reached into the car and prised my fingers loose from the dash-board. Let's go.

I saw them filing into the hall as we walked across from the teachers' parking area. They were all in uniform, neat hair, white ankle socks, rows of badges for one splendid achievement or another like insects pinned to their blazers. Some of them glanced at me with mild curiosity. I knew what I represented to them. An opportunity to get out of geography or maths. How could a real live drug addict have anything to do with their lives of netball and music and parties?

There was the stage all right, and a thousand attentive high school girls in front of it, all of them waiting to give me the once over. A single light bulb hung down from above the stage and it shone on a wooden chair that had been placed, supposedly for me, right in the middle. I walked in from the wings without looking out into the sea of faces. I walked up to the chair and I kicked it as hard as I could. It slammed off to the side of the stage and cracked against the wall. Then I strolled forward and began.

To this day I have no recollection whatsoever of what I said or how long I stood there. All I remember was at the end there was a roar like thunder and twelve hundred girls were on their feet. I didn't know what I'd done to deserve it, but I felt like a champion. I felt better than that. I felt like I belonged.

I went home and told Kenneth and my mother that we were on the right track. There was a need for recovered addicts like us to go out there and spread the word, while at the same time creating a safe space within the NA system where addicts could congregate on a regular basis and find support.

Oh, did I say *recovered* addicts? Sorry – just a slip of the tongue.

✳

I travelled down to the casino complex the next day and signed up as security manager on the construction site there and then. I was so pleased with myself. The coast down there was beautiful. I planned to go back and fetch my surfboard as soon as I could. I would spend quality time with the waves on my days off. I'd get fit and tanned and put on some weight. I'd put some of my earnings aside and buy something really special for my mother.

I took back every negative thing I'd said about rehab clinics. They were right. It *was* possible to beat drug addiction and turn your life around. I'd just done it, hadn't I?

In reality, I was already relapsing.

INSTITUTIONS

Tim plays a mean guitar. He tells me he has a whole little studio thing going at home that his dad built for him. His dad's an architect who has his own firm and apparently designed some award winning building somewhere. I get the idea that they're mega-wealthy. Anyway, the studio used to be servants' quarters but they had it soundproofed and they put in a skylight and an amazing sound system and everything. Tim has his own mixing desk and three guitars, an Ibanez, a really great bass guitar – I forget the make – and the acoustic guitar he has with him here in rehab.

He's teaching me to play and I love it. He tells me I've mastered the basic chords in a fraction of the time that most people manage to and that I have a very good ear. I know that's true. I think I get it from my father. He had perfect pitch and could sing a song right through without a single wrong note after he'd only heard it once.

Tim is addicted to pethidine and pinks and he's been in rehab three times. This is his fourth, but his first in this place. He's nineteen. He has long black hair that he wears in a ponytail and small granny glasses like John Lennon's. He also has a great sense of humour, one of those dry ones where you have to listen twice before you get it, if you know what I mean. He makes up songs about the staff here and puts a tune to them as quick as anything and when he starts to strum them and we know who the song's about and how rude the lyrics are we can all just piss ourselves laughing. We get along so well, Tim and me. I'm going to see his studio when we get out of here. He's going to start a band and who knows, maybe I could jam with them sometimes. He's almost completed his time here and he's feeling good about himself and confident about his chances out there in the big bad world this time. At least he's made a lot of promises to his dad and maybe that counts for something.

His parents come to visit him quite often, especially his father. He brings magazines and fudge from his aunt who owns a bakery. There's money there all right. It's Rolex watches, two different Mercs, and I tell you what – the sneakers don't come from Mr Price. His father has that distinctive private school accent that comes from privilege and snobbery. But we're all the same in here, whatever our backgrounds. Addiction might be the greatest leveller of all.

To give him credit, Tim's father is very friendly and he seems to have taken a shine to me, perhaps because Tim and I get on so well and we're both doing OK on the programme, supporting each other and that. We've got to the stage where we're allowed to go out in a supervised environment and for some reason, perhaps because I'm a few years older and am wearing my responsible inmate mask a lot lately, his father invites me out to lunch. I gather quite quickly that I'm not there just because I'm a pretty face. I'm to keep an eye on his son. He doesn't altogether trust this new, clean Tim.

I'm cool with it. I can do lunch with the best of the larnies, and I'm not bothered that I'm Tim's minder. We're going to a restaurant way out of the sort of Colonel Saunders price range that is more my style, but I'm not complaining. I have fillet steak in my head, with little potatoes and mixed veg, and maybe a small chocolate mousse at the end of it. At least it will make a change from the steamed fish a person could easily OD on in this joint. I suppose rehabs are not renowned for their cuisine but the one we're in, I reckon, is at the bottom of the culinary scale. But hey, addicts aren't there to be pampered and a treat is a treat.

It's a nice restaurant. We sit at a table near the open French windows that lead out to a wooden balcony. There are fresh flowers on the tables and the serviettes are crisp and white. Some laidback jazz is coming from the speakers and I feel so relaxed I almost begin to believe I'm a normal person like everyone else in the place. Tim's dad is interesting to talk to and, what's more, he seems to be genuinely interested in what I have to say. It's been a long time since I engaged in a conversation that didn't have drugs as its focus. We talk about politics and music but I'm a little at sea when it comes to sport. I used to love rugby and my mother tells me I had promise when I was about eight, but I can't even remember the rules anymore.

Tim is quiet and a bit pale. He doesn't contribute much to the conversation but taps his fingers to the music and closes his eyes with a small smile that tilts up the corners of his mouth. He's cool. Tim's cool.

Coke all right for you guys?

Now *there's* a sudden sharp reminder of who we really are, just when we were beginning to feel like civilised grownups. The waitress gives me a raised eyebrow look and hesitates for just a fraction of a second before she removes the wine glasses. She brings a Coke each for me and Tim and a Castle for Tim's father. She gives us plastic straws and I feel stupid and irritable, as if I'm wearing a sign on my forehead that tells everyone I come from the place with the men in white coats on the other side of town and I'm out on a special good behaviour pass. I can sense that the mood has shifted, just a little, and I struggle to get back to the subject that had so engrossed me moments before. I sip at my Coke and it tastes too sweet. Tim downs his in seconds and orders another. He downs that too and then excuses himself.

Take a leak, he murmurs.

The waitress is back with warm bread rolls covered over in a basket. She clears a space and the smell of freshly baked bread makes me think of when we were kids Brian and me would be despatched to the café at exactly the time the last delivery of the day was due in. Sometimes the bread would be so warm that the plastic bags it came in were all steamed up. There's salad too – baby tomatoes and a weird kind of frilly lettuce and some big hunks of crumbly cheese. I heap salad onto my side plate and wait for Tim's father to finish with the marge. I can hear bashing sounds coming from the kitchen. My steak maybe.

We're talking about sailing. I'm not sure whether it's their own yacht or whether they hired it for the summer but Tim's family used to go to Greece every other year, and sail from one sun-drenched island to the next. I can't imagine anything that exotic. Brian and I co-owned a second-hand rubber duck once which we used to take out into the ocean as far as we dared until it got so many punctures from the rocks it was beyond fixing. So the Greek islands, hey . . . I can only dream.

The steak is every bit what I fantasised about. The baby potatoes are there and the veg. Tim's having duck, the house speciality. His plate has rounds of purple beetroot on it and some more of the frilly lettuce.

Where *is* Tim, his father asks, looking round.

He went to the bathroom.

We look at each other. It's been, what, ten minutes, fifteen?

I nearly knock the waitress over as well as the whole tray of drinks she's carrying. The bathroom, where's the damn bathroom, I shout at her. Her eyes widen in fright and she points to the back of the restaurant. Tim's father is right behind me. My heart is pounding.

Tim!

There are two toilet doors closed. Both have the engaged flag showing.

Tim?

A toilet flushes and one of the doors opens and a short man with a crewcut walks past us, looking curiously over his shoulder. There's no sound from the other toilet.

Tim – are you in there? Tim's father has a beaded line of perspiration on his upper lip. He bangs with his fist on the door, but there's just silence and I don't like the sound of that silence at all. I'm about to hoist myself up and over the partition from the toilet next door when I hear another sound so familiar to me that my blood runs cold. It's a sort of bubbling, gurgling sound and it's coming from behind the locked door. I tell Tim's father to stand back and I lift my foot and smash the lock.

Tim is half-sitting on the floor, wedged back between the partition and the toilet bowl. His fly is open and his hands lie slackly on either side of his body, palms upward, almost as if he's been meditating. While his father tries to push past me to see what's going on, my eyes go immediately to the empty syringe in my friend's groin. I kneel down beside him and feel for a pulse. There is none. His eyes gaze sightlessly past my head. I cannot turn round to look at his father's face.

I won't ever see Tim's father again and our sailing conversation will never be completed. After the ambulance has been and gone, with his dad following behind in the silver blue Merc, the waitress calls a taxi for me and that's how I get back to the clinic. All the way there I curse myself for my stupidity and especially for my stupidity in making the fundamental mistake of thinking that I am a normal person who can go out to lunch and do normal things.

You didn't have to be a brain surgeon to work out the sequence of events. Tim had somehow managed to phone a buddy who got to the restaurant ahead of us and left some Wellconal tabs for him in toilet number two from the left on the small ledge inside the cistern. Basic addict behaviour. Elementary. Just one shot, that's all Tim wanted. Just one. He knew exactly what he needed but he forgot one crucial thing, and you're almost guaranteed to overdose if you don't take it into account. Before you go into rehab you know what level of drugs your system needs in order to reach the high you're craving. That same level is way too potent when you've been clean for a month and it can be lethal.

I would have thought Tim would have known that. He's probably kicking himself now, wherever he is.

EIGHTEEN

Jake in surveillance and Steve in security. What was wrong with this picture? Nothing that we could see, nothing at all. We were as happy as pigs in shit.

Once you looked drugs were everywhere. We got trashed most nights and partied every weekend. Our Wild Coast parties became legendary. Soon I had my buddies driving all the way down from Durban on a Friday afternoon and staying over till Sunday. I never went to sleep and I worked eighteen hours a day. You can do that when you're high, like we were, almost all of the time. It was hectic.

I saw Tracey again. She came down to the casino one night with friends but she kept her distance that first time. Soon she was coming down regularly and I actually found I was cool with it. I had all the coping skills I needed in a bottle of Russian Bear or a line of coke. We even danced together sometimes, like we used to do in the old days, but up close her face was drawn and her makeup too thick. There were deep shadows under her eyes and when she threw her head back and laughed in that way that she had, it didn't sound like it used to. There was a coarseness to it, more of a Let's fuck the world than Let's celebrate life kind of laugh. She'd got hard and closed in on herself.

One weekend Tracey came down with three buddies. She was shooting up pinks again and she was driving, not the greatest of combinations. On the way back to the city on Saturday night she OD'd at the wheel of the car, crashed into a bridge and wiped out all three of her friends in one hit. They lay spread across the tarmac in a bloody tangle of legs, arms and bright party clothes. Tracey herself wasn't so lucky. She had some bad head injuries but she was still alive when they got her to the hospital. There was little anyone could do for her. By the time her parents were located, she had slipped away and was already in a deep coma when they reached her bedside. That's where Tracey stayed – deep in her coma for eight long years.

I went to see her once when I was in between rehabs, but I couldn't bear it. I wasn't prepared. No one had told me that her eyes were open and it completely freaked me out. I had imagined a sort of Snow White in the forest kind of scene, my beautiful Tracey sleeping peacefully, but it wasn't like that at all. Her feet and hands were already curving inwards, stiff as a doll's. That means irreversible brain damage. A nurse would come in every so often and massage them. I hated that and I hated how guilty I felt for wanting to leave almost as soon as I got there. I'd taken her some flowers and when I moved across to the basin in her room to fill a container with water, I could swear that her eyes followed me. It was eerie. I couldn't stand going to see her, but I forced myself to visit a few more times. Then I stopped going altogether and justified my absence with anger. She must have been brain dead. Why didn't her family call it a day and switch off the machines, for fucksake? It was plain cruel.

I don't know why they didn't do it then and I don't know if they actually did in the end either. I didn't ask and I stayed away from Tracey's mom. Perhaps they had their reasons or perhaps there was some faint medical hope they didn't want to extinguish, just in case. Either way, it must have been painful for them. When she was drugging and selling her body, they never got to see their daughter. Now they could see her every day and never talk to her.

Anyway. Tracey died in the end. Somebody phoned from the hospital to tell me.

I was in Joburg doing my show, telling kids at schools to stay away from drugs.

※

On Thursdays the dancers at the casino had a night off. They worked double shows at the weekends and needed to let their hair down. They were a great bunch of women, wild and crazy, into everything that was going – and all of them were gorgeous. They became our buddies and we partied with them till the sun came up, then went straight to work on Friday morning, did a full shift, and got back into party mode as soon as we knocked off and the weekenders arrived. You can do that when you're on speed. Cocaine was the fashionable drug at the time and there was plenty of it, but Jake and I supplemented our coke intake with our old stand-bys: alcohol, dagga, mandrax, acid and pinks.

On one particular Thursday night me and Jake were in the surveillance room, shooting up Wellconal. I had one tab left, which made half a tab for each of us. At the last moment I changed my mind and gave Jake only a quarter. We used to use these little 5 ml syringes, the ones for diabetics. They were perfect for our purposes. I watched Jake inject himself in his groin, then I rolled up my jeans and injected myself in the back of my leg.

I woke up in Port Shepstone hospital three days later.

God knows how I did it, but in a panic I checked myself out and got a ride back down to the casino where I managed to convince my boss that I was a diabetic – he'd found needles in my bungalow – and that because I'd forgotten to have my shot one evening I'd gone into a diabetic coma in the middle of the night. Jake had had the presence of mind, thank goodness, to get me to hospital. His granny was a diabetic so he knew the signs. My boss looked sceptical but he took the days as sick leave. I took them as a reprieve and made a feeble promise to myself to go carefully from then on, cut back a bit. Maybe give Thursday nights a miss.

Exactly one week later I overdosed again and this time no one was buying the diabetic story. I had to be helicoptered out and was taken to yet another institution where the whole by now bitterly familiar pattern groaned into gear once more.

I knew the drill. First I was pumped full of psychiatric drugs, then it was sleep therapy, then shock treatment, then sessions with psychiatrists, and sessions with therapists.

The aftermath of shock treatment is the worst, and it's the most difficult to explain. It's like they've burned your soul. Afterwards they put you in a chair and you just sit there. You can't do anything. You can't even take a shower. The whole world looks like it's moving in slow motion and you're slower than everyone – a fucking zombie, the living dead. Your mouth goes slack and you can't control your saliva. You sit there drooling, like an insane person, the ones you read about in loonybin stories.

All around you there are scenes of terrifying madness – psychotic patients rocking and pacing, creeping along the walls, and talking to themselves. I watched an alcoholic who kept tearing off his clothes as he went through his withdrawal, and another who leapt from bed to bed in huge unsteady strides. One woman, another alcoholic in withdrawal, clung to the railing of her bed and wailed pitifully at the nurse attending to her. She told me that afterwards, with a shaky laugh, that it looked to her like the nurse had fallen into a fire. Her burnt up face was blackened to a crisp and her skin kept flaking and peeling off and flying about the ward like soot. It explained why I'd seen her batting at the air in front of her with frantic hands.

Then slowly, slowly, things start to come back into focus and the high dosages of Valium and other drugs are reduced and you begin on the treatment and recovery programmes.

I was too far gone to care much that time. I just wanted to get the hell out of there. I went through the motions on automatic pilot but binged and nearly OD'd again as soon as I was released. I got a job in a tyre factory but that was an experience so shortlived and so coloured in a haze of drugs and alcohol that even now I couldn't tell you what my job actually was. There was an incident with a lathe that I do have a sort of flash memory of. I was pissed and drugged up to the eyeballs and something snapped inside me. I went crazy with this lathe until I heard a voice coming at me from a foggy distance – Steve! What the fuck are you doing? – and then I was back in an institution, raving, strapped down and bleeding from the eyeballs.

When they spat me out again, prescription in my pocket, I went back to the factory and, strangely enough, was given my job back. It didn't go any better second time around and there was another incident, also involving dangerous tools and a couple of close calls, and I was committed once again.

My mother pulled some contacts with her sister up north and when I came out I was sent to live near my aunt in Pretoria. I hated it there. I had a flat that looked onto the back of the Transvaal museum. It was gloomy and sad and I was close to suicidal. That was the time I worked the assembly line with Reuben in our space suits at Pelindaba. Reuben cheered me up, though, and we drugged together in the evenings. We went to Hillbrow in Joburg at the weekends and I met a girl, Samantha, who was the daughter of a millionaire but whose not inconsiderable monthly allowance still didn't stretch far enough to cover her habit. She was temping as a prostitute. For a short while we formed a little team, Sam and me and a guy called Bobby the Comic. Bobby was covered head to toe in tattoos. He told me he got a new one each time he went to prison. You couldn't see any skin in between the artwork so I figured he must have done some *serious* time.

Anyway, Sam would pull a guy who was cruising the streets and lead him to a deserted parking lot with the promise of sex. Bobby and I would be waiting there, and we'd beat up the guy and take his wallet and stuff. We did that quite a lot. It was easy money. Sometimes we timed ourselves and played Let's see if we can break our record games from the time Samantha got someone interested up on the main Hillbrow drag to the time we'd score.

When we got bored with that we used to break into pharmacies together. Security systems weren't so good in the eighties and there was often a small window at the back of the store, facing onto an alley, where you could get in if you were skinny enough and desperate enough. I was both, and we got a lot of pills that way.

In the end I gave up the Pelindaba job or, more accurately, the job gave up on me, and I drifted back down to Durban.

Then came a very bad time and again a lot of the details are sketchy. I got involved with Mlungu's operation again and there were a couple of busts in quick succession. There was this one time, around two in the morning, when we were staying at a really ghastly flat down near Point Road. We were expecting a delivery of forty thousand mandrax tablets coming in from Joburg in convoys of stolen cars and nobody was about to go to bed. I was in the front room with some other guys, among them a buddy of mine called Blackie. He was the closest to the *spoeg* bucket – the spit bucket. You had to have one of those in a mandrax circle. It has about a half inch of water in the bottom and its use is self-explanatory. It was there for spitting in, for vomiting, for cigarette butts, for all the disgusting end products, I suppose you could call them, that are part and parcel of putting drugs into your body and not always being in total control of what might come out.

We had just lit a pipe when there was a knock on the front door. No one had heard a thing. In seconds we knew it was a full on raid and the house was swarming with drug squad cops and sniffer dogs. Mlungu and his bodyguard disappeared into the back bedroom and hid beneath a blanket, lying together as close as lovers. The rest of us stayed where we were. The cops began a noisy search, starting with us, turning things over and shoving us about. They flung open the door of the bedroom where Mlungu and his bodyguard were hiding.

Who's that? One of the cops indicated the bulky shapes under the blanket on the bed.

It's the maid, I said. They sleeping, man. Leave them. It's the maid and her boyfriend.

Why are they sleeping here in the house and not in the servants' quarters, the cop asked suspiciously, sidetracked for a second from his real purpose here. He had to ask that, I suppose. You couldn't just have a simple drug raid without bringing politics into it, could you, not in South Africa anyway in the eighties.

There's a witchdoctor out the back, I replied and Blackie nodded vigorously. He's got the servant's room.

They hesitated over the sleeping maid and her boyfriend for a minute longer. I think Mlungu actually gave a little snore. Then they closed the door and turned back to us. What they were really looking for was the consignment we were waiting for too. Fortunately, there must have been some delay on the road and there was not much that they could find other than the remains of the mandrax pipe at the bottom of the spoeg bucket. One young cop, super keen to leave no stone unturned in what was obviously his first bust, had pulled back his sleeve and was swishing around in the bucket with his hand. *Obviously* his first bust. He had a peculiar expression on his face. Warm spit

320

and dribble and some of the sandwich Blackie had brought up earlier with his seventh beer must have made the liquid quite soupy.

I knew there was one mandrax tab left. I could see it clearly. It was scrunched up in the plastic from a Chesterfield pack and was tucked down the side of the couch I was sitting on. Just as the cops were about to leave, *vloeking* us and giving me a *klap* on the side of the head for the smirk on my face, the keen young cop spotted it. He pounced on it and held it up triumphantly.

Search them again, said the guy in charge. See who's smoking what.

I was a Stuyvesant man myself, and my packet of cigarettes still had its plastic snugly round it. Another guy, Marty, smoked Rothmans and Blackie just spread his hands innocently and said, Who me? I'm a non-smoker, man. *I* don't want lung cancer.

Poor Blackie. He'd forgotten the Chesterfield he'd stuck behind his ear.

Busted!

He spat in the bucket as he passed me on his way to the door, and gave me the finger from the handcuffs behind his back.

❋

I got into pimping. Down near Point Road there were a lot of prostitutes. All of them were on drugs and a lot of them were really young, runaways mostly, from

Joburg and Pretoria. They came from foster care, from abusive or broken homes, or from places of safety where the care was casual and the safety doubtful. We fed off each other. They supplied us with sex. We supplied them with drugs. It was functional. It worked. We shared the money they got from the rich business-men who came cruising from uptown late at night, and sometimes we cut short the transaction and did what Samantha and I had done up in Joburg. There was a particular block of flats where we had a couple of rooms. The rooms were on the second floor. The girls would take the men up in the lift and we'd run up the stairs and get there before them. Before the guys knew what was happening, me and my buddies would jump them from behind and beat them to a pulp. We'd strip them of whatever valuables they had and be gone before they could stagger to their knees or think about calling for help. Not that there would have been any help in that area. They were only too happy by then to get into their BMWs and go home to their wives.

We also protected each other after a fashion. I suppose because the girls were pretty much at the bottom of the prostitution ladder, if you can imagine such a thing, and they were often craving and desperate, they were open to all sorts of abuse at the hands of the kind of man who is looking for some perverted sex with children and knows where to come looking for it. These girls didn't want to be found and wouldn't be in a hurry to report a rapist or a paedophile. We never got too close to them, but we watched out for each other.

I was a heartbeat away from the gutter. Emaciated and sick, I had a sore in my groin that wouldn't heal and most of my veins had collapsed. I was shooting up in the back of my neck or under my nails. I hardly knew whether it was day or night and I didn't care either. My body ached when I moved and ached when I didn't. I hadn't been near my mother for months.

I hung out with Blackie a lot, and with Phil and another guy called Charlie. We'd smoke together almost every day, sitting in a mandrax circle watching greedily, eyes narrowed, as the pipe went round, waiting, hoping for someone to OD or drop so that you could get your turn quicker.

One day Charlie OD'd on us. We were shooting up heroin. We left him where he collapsed, the needle still in his arm, shit and urine staining his pants and his eyes black and staring. We were out of the door in minutes, falling over each other to leave before someone came and found us with a corpse. He wasn't breathing. I knew that because I went back. Not to check if he was alive, but to go through his pockets and take his drugs. I almost took the needle too – I'd seen someone do that once – in case there was any heroin left in it.

There was a drug called PCP. It was used as an animal tranquilliser, or so I was told, when they dart buffalo or elephants or something to move them around. We used to sprinkle it on dagga. It had two immediate effects and you never knew which one it was going to be. It made you either incredibly euphoric or incredibly violent. It also gave you so much energy you could believe you could fly to the moon or run to the ends of the earth and back again. Or stay on the dance floor all night long. That's what I did one night. I was also high on acid and I danced like a maniac. Everyone stood back in awe to watch me. Kiss my ass, Travolta. In fact, it so happened that the club I found myself in had a dance competition going that very night. I entered and came third and won a bottle of champagne. I popped the cork on the spot with my buddies and we passed it around without leaving the floor or missing a beat. I was going *wild*. Like Audrey Hepburn, I could have danced all night and I would have, too, if the bouncers hadn't decided that enough was enough and it was time for me to go home and leave some space for the other patrons.

Go home? They had to be kidding. I *was* home. I *lived* to dance, couldn't they see that? I'd just won the fucking *championship*, hadn't I? *Get outta my face, china.*

I smashed the champagne bottle and danced on, punching the jagged edge in the air in time to the music, and jabbing it viciously at anyone who dared to encroach. There was a wide circle of admirers around me by now, watching my performance. I was on top form.

Suddenly, a blow on the back of my head sent me sprawling and three two-ton gorillas with no necks and T-shirts too small for them picked me up by my shirt and jeans and threw me out into the road like a sack of potatoes. Someone had already called the cops and I didn't even have time to get to my feet. Minutes later I found myself a reluctant passenger in an un-marked cop car, riding up front with a grim-faced rookie who had a pump-action shotgun resting between his knees. The safety catch was off.

When you get busted like that strange things can happen. Trigger happy cops don't always do things by the book and trouble making junkies like me were easily expendable. No one would miss me and one less dope-head on the street causing shit on their watch would make their lives easier. When you got to the freeway, there were two ways the cop car might turn. Right would mean you'd be cooling your heels in the cells in Toti. Left meant you'd be going to 'back bush' and might never be seen alive again.

I'd known people who'd been taken to back bush and had returned, broken beyond recognition, unable to speak. Others had simply disappeared. It wasn't talked about. It never got to the press. All you knew was that you didn't want to turn left off that freeway, not at three in the morning, or any other time.

I was still wired, but beginning to come down. As we got closer to the T-junction, I got more and more nervous with my silent companion. This guy had a jaw like a comic book hero but he didn't seem like the hero type. He had very thin lips and he hummed to himself in a way that was disturbing. I eyed the shotgun between his knees and measured the distance between it and my hand. As he changed down, still humming, still not saying anything at all, I decided that if we took a left I was going to make a swift grab for the shotgun and blow his head off. Rather his than mine. I could think of better ways to kill myself, thank you, than subject myself to the tender mercies of a psychopathic cop giving me the silent treatment until we reached the desolate outskirts of town.

I flexed my hand, preparing myself. Then we turned right and headed for Toti and I realised that I had been holding my breath for about five solid minutes and had given myself a massive headache.

✳

Fuck you, John. I need a blow, bru. I need a *pill*. What you mean you haven't got? What the fuck you saying to me, bru?

It was late, about one in the morning, and I'd been drinking all night with a guy called Zollie. Now I was craving and I had to make a plan. My reliable source of supply was letting me down and I was getting angry.

Wait, wait. Let's go. Where's your car?

John could see that nothing he could say or do would help. I couldn't wait. I was pacing up and down. I was fighting off waves of nausea. My bones ached and my head was thick from the alcohol I'd consumed. He could see he would have to make a plan for me or there'd be big trouble.

We went into the township, me, John and Zollie, and woke up a guy John knew. He couldn't help us either, he said, and he turned to shut the door in our faces. I was quicker than he was though. I put my foot in the door and had him up against the wall, one arm twisted behind his back and his nose bleeding.

Fuck you, I hissed viciously in his ear. You give me something and you give me something *quick*, you know what I'm saying? I pulled on his arm and he winced.

Wait here, he told us.

Zollie was jumpy now too. He was drunk but not as tense as I was. I was like a bloody grasshopper, walking up and down, kicking at walls with the toe of my boot. John's friend came back in a couple of minutes. He had something in his hand but he looked nervous.

I don't know – he began, looking at John.

John made a movement with his head. Make a pipe, he told the guy.

What is this stuff, Zollie asked. He'd never seen a white pipe before. He was strictly a dagga man, hence his name. What are we doing?

I didn't care what it was, frankly, or what they were doing, just as long as they got me to where I needed to be, and *soon*. Nobody took any notice of Zollie. I was aware of the strange looks that passed between John and his friend but I didn't care about that either. I was getting really edgy. Get *on* with it, I told them.

They got busy. I saw some brown powder – it looked like Bisto – and some tinfoil and some weed. They started crushing, getting the mix right for a pipe.

I stepped closer. I hadn't seen that stuff before

either, and I thought I'd seen everything. What is it, I asked. What's that?

From the amaGents, John replied shortly. It comes from the Indians in town. They call it brown sugar.

My first experience of unrefined heroin.

Make like you going to smoke mandrax, John coaxed Zollie. It was Zollie's first pipe and he followed my lead.

The rush was indescribable. Straight to the brain and then we were vomiting, our bodies jerking spasmodically. Then we went higher, and higher, and higher, until our entire bodies were numb. I thought it was incredible. Zollie was in shock.

Later, driving home along the freeway just before sunrise, still high, Zollie grabbed at my arm.

Slow down, he said. *Fuck.*

Sorry. I eased my foot off the accelerator pedal. We were flying.

Jesus, Steve, Zollie said again a few minutes later. I said Slow *down.*

I hadn't even realised how fast I was going, but I eased up again. Then, in the rearview mirror, I saw the blue light of a freeway patrol car.

Ah, *shit*, I said.

Oh, nooo, Zollie groaned. He slid down in his seat.

The car passed us, and the cop in the passenger seat indicated to me to pull over onto the shoulder of the road. I rolled down my window and resigned myself to a speeding ticket.

Everything all right, the cop asked, leaning his head right in.

Yes, officer, I said. Everything's cool.

I've been watching you from a couple of k's back, he said. You been drinking?

No, officer, I said truthfully. It had in fact been several hours since my last drink.

It's just that you were creeping along so slowly, the cop said. It's usually a sure sign when someone's hugging the edge of the road like that. Get on home now, hey.

He banged the roof of my car with the flat of his hand and sent us on our way. Zollie looked at me and I looked back at Zollie. We drove in total silence the rest of the way.

Finally, I drew up outside Zollie's house. Check you, bru, I said.

Zollie clutched at my arm, looking over his shoulder fearfully. Steve, he said urgently. Don't leave me. Don't leave me *here*, bru.

Isn't this your house, though, Zol?

No. It isn't. You can't leave me here in the middle of nowhere. Please, man.

So I put the car in gear and did a couple of circuits around the neighbourhood before I pulled up again outside the same house.

Thanks, man, said Zollie, climbing out happily. Check you, bru.

Check you, Zol, I said, and I drove away.

A Day in the Life ...

The older I get the more heavily this path I've chosen weighs on me. I can feel it taking its toll. I get sick a lot. My immune system struggles to fight off infections. I don't sleep well. I drink too much coffee and I smoke a ridiculous number of cigarettes. My life is full of ironies. I realise all too well that the oh so innocent drag on a cigarette that started me off in my career as a drug addict is the very thing that may finish me. My family has a history of heart disease and my lung function is that of a much older man than me. I avoid the word emphysema but god knows I can feel the physical damage – bigtime – and I'm reminded of it constantly.

When I'm working I may do several shows a day – a primary school, two high schools, a corporate presentation or perhaps a talk to the workers in a factory where the use of mandrax is getting out of hand. I don't know which is worse sometimes: the physically demanding side or the way it all leaves me emotionally drained. When you think about it, I lead a very weird life. I am constantly reliving my worst times, exposing my weaknesses, my failures, the awful things I've done, the choices that I'm least proud of. My show is my life. Every working day I pound home the DON'T BE LIKE STEVE message. I am the role model you don't need, the one your parents warned you about. Even now I know that my family and Candy's see what I'm doing as a temporary thing. Even my patient mother hopes that I will get a 'real' job one day, a respectable job (saving lives not respectable enough for you, mom?) and put the drugging behind me.

How long will it take Steve to get this out of his system, is the unspoken question. (The answer, by the way, is Never.) They look at my health (not good), my age (pushing forty), Candy, in the prime of her life, the fact that we have a little boy who's going to need to be educated, fed and clothed for many years to come, and they look at our lifestyle.

It's not rocket science to see where their concern is coming from. I'm sympathetic even. But has everyone who watched me go to hell and back several times suddenly got amnesia? It's not like I'm enjoying where I am.

I don't have a salary or even a fixed income. I don't have insurance policies – can you imagine what the premiums would be for someone in my position? I don't have a nest egg, offshore funds or a bunch of unit trusts, whatever they are. I don't own a car or a house. So I know what they're thinking and I know they can't quite bring themselves to say it.

I'll say it for them, then, in the imaginary conversations I have with my father-in-law, with my uncles, with my mother.

I'm sorry, I tell them in my head. I have to do this work. People are dying out there.

Sure, we know that, they say vaguely, but you've done your bit, haven't you? Think of what you've been through, what we've been through. It's time to stop now.

Surely?

Time to stop? Why? Here's a small statistic to chew on. Since Claydon was born the number of intravenous heroin users in his country has increased by forty per cent. And that's only the reported cases. This scourge is not going away anytime soon and I have to do something about it, what little I can, whatever is in my power.

Well, exactly. That's our point. It's too big. It's too big for one person. Let someone else take a turn. Why does it have to be you?

Because I've been there. And if I can save one person, just one, that's good enough for me.

Yes, but this dressing up, this travelling all over the country, shooting food colouring into an audience of twelve year olds. Yeah, it's great but it's kids' stuff. You're not a child anymore.

No. I'm not a child. And you know what the really tragic part of it is? I never really was.

Ah, come on – enough is enough. Leave this work to someone else now. Look to the future. Things are different for you now. Isn't it time to get a real job? You have a family, a child of your own. It's time for you to be a responsible provider and father.

Hmm. A responsible provider and father. Now there's an interesting concept. Cast your minds back and think carefully – who exactly was my role model in that particular department?

We're just trying to give you some advice . . .

Advice? From you? Now?

Yes, but – well, anyway, just think about it: a

respectable job with security, annual paid leave and a thirteenth cheque at Christmas. You could go to rugby matches and buy a caravan. Join the PTA. Why not? The drugs are over now, aren't they? You've done fantastic work, we all acknowledge that, but it's time to stop. The past is the past. You might not have had the easiest childhood, we'll admit, but what's done is done. You've got to be a role model for your son. Why can't you do something else now?

Why? You just don't get it, do you?

What? Why?

I'll tell you why, and make sure you watch my lips.

I'm not qualified to do anything else.

I have a criminal record, remember?

I don't have an education.

I can't get a respectable job.

Get it?

✳

Why do I do it and what happens when I can't do this work anymore are two questions I do in fact ask myself, aggressive imaginary conversations with my family aside. I review them constantly. I don't have any answers yet. Maybe I'm a masochist at heart, or maybe I'm like the dry drunk who seeks out work as a barman. Stay close to the booze and you won't go looking for it. I think I have to stay close to drugs, to keep them in my sights, so that I can't get too comfortable or distance myself too much and think they're no longer part of my life.

I do believe, though, that something else is driving me. I have my own deeply personal name for it, but you can call it what you like. It doesn't matter. What does matter to me is that I have to believe that the stuff I went through for so many years had its own purpose. I had to have been there in order to understand. Looking at those couple of sentences they sound so glib, as if I both understand and accept the clichéd notion of *The only way out is through*. Well, I don't. I don't understand a lot of the time and a lot of the time I don't accept it either.

I don't want to do this work. I wish I didn't have to. I deal in pain every waking day, not just mine, and sometimes I don't even know why I try. All I have to hang onto is the hope that I'm making a difference to someone's life – yours maybe, or your brother's, or your little sister's who's eight and watches TV in the living room while you're blazing with your friends. It could be that my show hit her school last week and something got through. Perhaps she was the shy little girl in the ponytail who came to me afterwards and struggled to put this question into words: *if you knew that someone was smoking weed while that someone's mother was at work, what would you do?* I know, perhaps better than anyone, that one wrong word can kill a kid so I try to find the right words, the ones that make sense and offer a little direction. That's the hope I'm talking about when I'm on the road away from my own family and fighting day by day for my survival in this world.

We live in a time of uncertainty and stress, where the pressures to succeed and to excel have never been stronger. Competition is tough, unemployment is a very harsh reality and, at least in the circles I move in, we're confronted on a daily basis with fear, prejudice, crime and squalor in a very real, in your face way. We need something to grab onto, something to tell us that life can be good, that we do have a place in the world and something special to contribute to the universe.

In the major cities the lucrative lure of the public speaking circuit is proof of this need. The circuit is crammed with role models who all have inspiring stories to tell of triumph over terrible odds. The good ones are in high demand and they can command some awesome 'performance' fees. These people have agents and a budget for their stage clothes and everything.

You'd think I'd be able to tap into that, wouldn't you? Well, you'd be wrong. Why? I'll tell you why.

I was approached by a high-powered agent a while back who'd seen my show and whose own child had gone off the rails once or twice. I suppose she saw an opportunity in me but I'd like to give her the benefit of the doubt. She said she wanted to manage me. I was thrilled. The relief of having someone else take care of the bookings, the money and the timetable was enormously attractive. Candy and I were really tired and our telephone bill was frightening.

We had a meeting. The moment the agent started talking I knew it was never going to work. I began to realise what performing on the mainstream circuit meant. She wanted me to tell it like it was – no problem with that – but my show needed 'tweaking'. She wanted it to culminate in one triumphant, Steve Hamilton has beaten drug addiction and turned his life around, glorious Hollywood moment. She had it all worked out. She'd get me a stylist, some decent clothes, a haircut, even a brochure. I'd need to put on a bit of weight and lose the bags beneath my eyes.

I'd have laughed if I didn't want overwhelmingly to cry. She just didn't get it either. I haven't beaten drug addiction. You never do. That's the whole point. That one day at a time thing isn't just a catchphrase. It's reality. It's my only way to survive. Give me a trendy haircut and a pair of designer jeans and who's going to believe me when I tell them addiction is a life sentence? The worst danger in believing the image of reformed junkie is the danger of buying into it myself and I can't risk that. If I can't believe in my truth now, after all that I've been through, what good can I hope to be to anyone?

This isn't a game, you silly woman, I wanted to tell this agent. If my performance has impressed you, that's great, but if it hasn't shown you the abyss beyond the dollar signs too then either I have failed (again) or you haven't been paying attention. Drugs are real and they're dangerous and people are dying out there. That's reality.

So we're on our own, me and Candy, and with a little help from the core people in my life who do get it, and whose practical, no nonsense assistance is invalu-

336

able to me, we make our own circuit and do our own bookings and hope like hell that we get paid at the end of the day.

Another irony. I never had a proper childhood, yet I 'play' being a child when I'm talking to twelve year olds. I was chucked out of school with only a Grade 9 Technical and I never went back, yet I spend most of my year hanging about in school halls telling kids to get an education and not be like me. Corporates – that's pretty funny too. My working clothes aren't high budget, that's for sure: no Armani suit for me, just a blood-stained sleeveless T-shirt, a bandana and a pair of old jeans. My briefcase holds the tools of my trade – a broken bottleneck, food colouring, firecrackers, a couple of syringes – and my closest business colleague is my stage manager, a tattooed addict from Cape Flats gangland.

Hey, Candy. I'm going to work. How do I look?

You look fine, Steve, a bit tired maybe.

No, I mean, do I look bad enough?

Oh. Let me see. Turn to the light. Perhaps you've overdone the dark rings under your eyes a little?

I haven't put any makeup on yet, Candy . . .

NINETEEN

Perhaps I should have called this book Things You Won't Learn in Rehab or Ten Things Rehabs Won't Tell You, but hopefully I've got at least *some* of them across somewhere in all of these pages (and there are probably more than ten, by the way). But if you're drugging and you're reading this and you want to stop – drugging, that is – there's just one thing I *do* want you to take away with you, and it *is* something the rehabs won't tell you. It's a hard truth, so be ready. This is what it is.

Life does not offer anything to compare with the high that drugs can give you.

It's the one truth you've got to get into your head, process and deal with, OK? Drugs are cool – they are. But they'll kill you.

In rehab you learn to become a professional

patient. I've had a lot of practice in one sort of institution or another. Eleven altogether, actually, one more than Candy, although she was only nineteen when I met her, so you could say I'd had a head start.

In most professions there is a certain amount of routine. Patterns are started, habits formed. From around the time I finished my basic army training and landed up on the city streets, my life, too, fell into a pattern of sorts.

Drugging-dealing-overdose-hospital-psychiatric institution-rehab-relapse-drugging-dealing-prison-rehab-relapse-drugging-pimping-dealing – BUSTED – prison . . .

Sometimes I ended up in rehab clinics when my mother didn't know what else to do with me and pushed me in that direction, alternately pleading and threatening. Sometimes I admitted myself because I knew I was going to die if I didn't. Sometimes it was a condition of my parole. And each time, each and every time I believed that this time, *this time* it was going to be different. I was going to try. I was going to get clean and stay clean. Each new clinic, each new therapist or doctor was going to be the one to guide me out of the whirlpool of self-abuse that had me flailing and floundering and sliding back down again.

Why, you might ask, each time I went into rehab, if my intentions were really to stop doing drugs, to get clean and lead a different kind of life, why did I start drugging again as soon as I came out? And it's not just me. Most addicts do exactly the same, nine times out of ten, no matter how sincere the will to change. So what is it then – a kind of collective amnesia or something? Knowing everything that I did, having experienced the agony of withdrawal and coming as close to death as I came so many times, why on earth did I keep doing it if I knew what was going to happen? *Why*?

I'll tell you why.

It's that small, quiet, repetitive phrase again, coming from far back inside your head, seductive as any siren song.

Just one. Just one. Just one more . . .

When you check into a clinic or rehab facility, it's usually because you have reached a crisis point. It could be an overdose. It could be a family intervention. Doctors. Prison. Whatever. The day I met Candy we had both, independently, hit a crisis point in our lives. I was trying desperately to stay clean but was losing my grip. Temporary refuge until I felt safer, rather than treatment, was what I was looking for.

Candy was a mess. The first time I saw her she was sitting in a corner in the lounge. There had been a rumour going round the clinic earlier that a model had been brought in but anyone looking less like a model right then would have been hard to find. Her hair was unwashed and matted and her pale face was noticeable only for the heavy shadows beneath her eyes. She wasn't interested in talking to anyone. She sat scowling in a chair, her arms folded tightly across her chest, looking ill and pissed off.

Most addicts in crisis check themselves in in the

morning. Breaking point usually hits you the night before or in the early hours. That's when you realise that you need help, and fast. As the day wears on and you begin to feel the nibble of withdrawal, you're already forgetting what brought you in. The crisis, whatever it was, doesn't seem so important now. The urgency's gone away. You begin to feel edgy, fidgety, nauseous. You need to make a plan. You need to score, that's all you need – just once – and you'll be OK. In fact the last thing you need is a bunch of asshole sisters in white uniforms and white shoes, sauntering casually up and down the passages, going about their business and ignoring you. It's the other people in here who need help and good for them. You don't, however. It's all been a huge mistake. All you need is to get out of the damn place and –

But you can't. You're stuck. And *Jesus* but that pisses you off!

I could see all of those stages at once passing over Candy's furious face that evening as she stalked past me on the way to her room. I watched her go. She opened the door, walked inside, and closed it firmly but quietly behind her. That was unusual. By bedtime you're craving, no two ways about it, and you're angry and agitated, often violent by that time too. Trust me – that door gets SLAMMED.

I followed Candy and knocked. There was no sound from inside so I opened the door and asked if I could come in. She was a tightly curled ball on her bed.

Hi, I said. I'm Steve.

I'm a coke addict, I've lost my boyfriend and I want to die, said Candy.

For four hours that night I sat with Candy, talking to her, talking her down, taking her mind away from the agony of her withdrawal. For four hours we were refugees together. Neither one of us would ever have imagined, then, that we'd still be refugees together today.

✳

Once you've committed yourself to rehab, life takes on another pattern and rhythm, quite unlike the ricocheting extremes of your existence outside. It is ordered, organised and predictable. After a while it can bore you silly and it will.

One significant thing that happens when you reach this point is that you surrender control. In crisis you might do this willingly at first, but you might resist it right from the minute you enter the snakepit and discover suddenly that it's not where you want to be at all. I resisted, many times, with violence and aggression, but it didn't help.

Sometimes that moment of surrender is not a conscious thing. It's more of a transition, a handing over of the burden. There's relief in that, comfort too. In rehab, ghastly though you know your withdrawal is going to be, you also know – especially if you've been through it before – that there is light and hope and purpose in the treatment and recovery process that comes next.

In rehab you feel safe. That's good.

OK, you're given psychiatric drugs that make you feel like a zombie, or they knock you out with drugs to make you sleep for days and days, or they fry your soul under the guise of shocking some portion of your brain to its senses, but still, at the end of all that, you aren't out on the street worrying about how you're going to score or where your next high is coming from. You *know* where it's coming from – the night nurse who pushes the trolley with the squeaky wheels.

Your days slip into a pattern. There's a lot of talking, a lot of sharing and caring. Group sessions. One on ones. Telling your life story, passing 'hope' notes of encouragement, and spilling your guts in an environment where you're not judged and other people have similar stories to tell. That's good too, especially as this time you really *are* going to come right and so is the buddy you're rooming with. You're going to beat this thing together. You can do it. That's what they're telling you, isn't it, that you can do it? You can be drug free if you just pay attention, listen to what they say and follow the instructions.

It's what they're *not* telling you that's the problem, and it's what was and continues to be my biggest issue with rehab programmes. In that Joburg clinic, where I realised that Candy was dying and I could either watch the process impotently from the sidelines or nag, cajole and argue with her doctors and therapists until they let me work with her, I discovered that I could make a difference.

How? By sitting with an addict, taking his lies and giving him back his truth.

Why? Not because I'd been there and back again, but because I was *still* there, wobbling on the edge, and that edge for a drug addict is a permanent address.

Most rehabs are reluctant to say the R word so they don't, not often anyway, and not right up front at the beginning of your treatment, where you can stare it down.

Relapse. They don't talk about the very high probability of relapsing once you've completed their programme.

Why not? I don't know, actually. I suppose it's a bit like a teacher who prides himself on the excellence of his teaching telling his brightest and most conscientious students that they have a three per cent chance of passing even if he goes through the exam paper with them in advance. Imagine if they took that negative message home to their parents? Chances are, their parents would ask for their money back, wouldn't you say?

So maybe talking about relapsing is too negative a thought and too hopeless a word when the priorities are, firstly, to find a chemical combination that will keep you calm and balanced and more or less functioning and, secondly, to try to build up your self-esteem and restore your confidence. The motivation is not misguided or unsound. They are trying to equip you with what you need, mentally, physically and emotionally, to cope in a normal environment among normal people. They try to make you see that you, too, can be like everyone else.

Normal. Now, you see, that's another fundamental error. Once you're an addict a 'normal' environment is not OK, it's not safe. It's dangerous for you, and they need to tell you that. It's dangerous to lose sight of that and it's doubly dangerous to try to disprove it.

I was once getting a lift to AA meetings regularly with a guy who'd had twenty-five years of clean time. He was an alcoholic and a company director. He travelled a lot but when he was in town he never missed his weekly meeting. One night I waited outside for him as usual and he didn't pitch or call so I got to the meeting on my own. The next week he wasn't there either. I wasn't really worried. I thought he was probably away on a business trip and had forgotten to let me know. The third week, I was sitting on my wooden chair towards the back of the hall when I smelt whisky and was aware of my friend slipping onto a chair behind me. He looked pretty bad. He was unshaven and his eyes were puffy and bloodshot. Later I asked him where he'd been, what had happened.

I made a crucial mistake, he told me with a wry little smile. I forgot I was an alcoholic.

So what happens in rehab once you buy into the programme is you enter a sort of second phase, the one I call the 'pink cloud' phase. It's surreal and optimistic and full of hope. You feel good. You're clean.

You're not craving. You're not even thinking about scoring. You're rehabilitated, cured.

Big mistake. Perhaps the biggest mistake of all.

You'd be foolish to believe that addiction can be cured. It can't. There *is* no cure. It's that simple.

Think of it this way. If you knew you were one of those people who has a deadly allergic reaction to oysters or something, you'd steer clear of them, wouldn't you, even if they were your favourite food? For ever. You wouldn't just think Well, one mouthful's not going to kill me, is it? because you know it will. An addict has to think like that too. Me and Candy, we have a deadly allergic reaction to drugs.

You might be one of the lucky ones who steps out of rehab and never does drugs again. You might stay clean for the rest of your life, and I hope you do, but don't believe for a minute that you've 'beaten' your addiction or that your drugging life is 'behind' you. You haven't and it's not. It's round the corner just up ahead, waiting for that split second when you let your guard down and say Well, one mouthful's not going to kill me, is it?

An addict's body will never stop wanting chemical substances. It looks for them in everything and it finds them in the clinics and hospitals it goes to for help.

In rehab they treat drugs with drugs and I'm telling you now it will never work.

Once, when Candy was still quite a distance into my future, I was in rehab in a group of twenty-four people. We went through the whole programme to-gether. All of us graduated. Only two are alive today and I'm one of them. The others all died drug-related deaths, some only weeks, some just *days* after they completed the programme and took the pink cloud express out of there.

Tim. Andrea. Miriam. Pete. There's a whole roll call I could do. Pete, who was a pethidine junkie, cut an artery in his groin the day after I left and he died. Two weeks out of the clinic Andrea OD'd on pinks in a toilet somewhere, forgetting, as Tim did, that going for the same level of drugs to reach the last high you remembered is now lethal to your system. I heard from a friend of a friend that Miriam had been found dead in a filthy apartment somewhere with a needle in her neck.

I'll just do it once . . .

I left that clinic the same day Andrea did, and got on a bus to go home to the coast. This time, not only was I going to stay clean, but I was also a man with a mission. I knew how serious the drug problem was getting and I knew that not everyone was going to make it to rehab. People were dying out there. I'd watched them. I'd helped them do it. I'd almost joined the thousands of dead junkies myself. Someone was going to have to do something and I knew, with a deep inner conviction, that that someone was going to be me.

How I was going to achieve this goal wasn't clear. Maybe it was just the drugs they'd been feeding me, but I believed that some force was guiding me and although the track seemed to be leading straight into the eye of the storm, as far as I could see, there was no doubt in my mind that I should follow it.

Was I crazy? Well, if you don't know the answer to that by now, you haven't been paying attention.

I sat at the back of the bus next to a window, watching the scenery change. There weren't a great many passengers and the seat beside me was free. I put my small bag on it and tapped a cigarette from a fresh pack I had in the pocket of my denim jacket. In the other pocket I had packets of pills from the clinic's well-stocked dispensary, and a whole wad of prescriptions to be filled at my neighbourhood pharmacy when I got home.

My mother would be there to welcome me, and I could already picture the expression on her face when she opened the front door – a sort of nervous, hesitant, you aren't in any trouble yet, are you? kind of expression. This time, I could have told her, she didn't have to worry. I was going to be OK this time. I'd been down to depths even *I'd* never imagined before and I wasn't planning a return visit.

The damage I had done my brain through drugging, I'd been told, meant that I needed to be medicated to help balance the areas most affected. These areas were the ones responsible for the control of emotions. Anger, particularly, was going to be an issue for me and it already was. I had demonstrated that quite dramatically on several memorable occasions. There were a couple of orderlies walking around the psychiatric wards of the country's hospitals with the scars to prove it. Drugging might not have been the root of the level of anger I kept in a box inside my head but drugging was what lifted the lid on it. I couldn't keep that lid on and it was drugs that were responsible for my inability to channel those feelings into something other than brute aggression.

But it was OK. The doctors had come up with a solution for me.

Different drugs. The feel good kind.

For the rest of my life 75mg of Tryptanol a day would maintain the balance I would need to keep me from flipping out.

Ironic really, when you think about it. It might not have been crack cocaine or Malawi gold they'd given me, but they'd sent me on my way with a pocket of dynamite all the same. And it was legal. I had the papers to prove it. No one was getting busted this time.

By the time I reached home, my career as an anti-drugs crusader was showing signs of coming apart before it had got off the ground and I didn't feel so guided anymore. On the six-hour journey home, I'd got slightly sidetracked, to be honest. It was boredom partly, and I was also beginning to feel a little anxious and vulnerable without my support network.

I popped one of my pills, then another. I felt a bit better. A third tablet made me feel pleasantly buzzy and a fourth allowed me to drift into a sleep of sorts. By the time I got home there wasn't a lot left in my party pack, but I had enough tabs left to see me to opening time at the pharmacy in the morning.

My mother's face was as anxious as I had anticipated. I reassured her. I was home and I was fine.

I went up to my room and rolled a joint.

PS Don't say the R word.

THE MANAGEMENT

DEAR ALL

A RUMOUR EXISTS THAT STEVE HAMILTON
WILL BE INSTRUCTED NOT TO MINGLE WITH
THE PATIENTS.

AS PATIENTS WHO HAVE BEEN HERE FOR
SOME TIME, AND PARTICIPATED IN LECTURES
AND ACTIVITIES, AS WELL AS TREATMENT
PROGRAMMES [WE] FEEL THAT THIS IS
TOTALLY UNJUSTIFIED AND WRONG!!!!

WE HAVE GLEANED VAST KNOWLEDGE ON
ADDICTION THROUGH OUR ASSOCIATION
WITH STEVE, WHO FROM PERSONAL EXPERI-
ENCE HAS BEEN ABLE TO GIVE US INVALU-
ABLE ADVICE FOR THE FUTURE, INSTEAD OF
SPENDING OUR FREE TIME IN MINDLESS
PURSUITS (VIDEOS ETC).

WE HAD FRUITFUL DISCUSSIONS REGARD-
ING THE PROBLEMS TO BE FACED IN REHAB-
ILITATION.

OUR WHOLEHEARTED SUPPORT STANDS
BEHIND STEVE HAMILTON.

SIGNED ....

INSTITUTIONS

That has got to be the worst tattoo I've ever seen. It's obviously home drawn, has to be. Any tattoo artist would have been run out of town for that sort of *kak* job. I think it's supposed to be an eagle majestically spreading its wings. Anyway, it's *huge*. The stuff of nightmares. It stretches right across his chest and looks more like a pigeon trying to *be* an eagle and besides it's all out of proportion. The wingspan on one side is way broader than on the other. It's so horrible it's mesmerising.

Christopher, this guy's name is, and he's just moved in with me. I'm in one of the two-bed wards this time. I prefer them, mostly, and he seems like a cool enough guy if only he'd keep his shirt on. I've noticed (and I'm not the only one) that he likes to walk around topless so that the dopey looking bird is on permanent full mating display or something. You can tell he wants everyone to comment on it and compliment him on his artwork. Hell, I can't bring myself to do it. Did he stand in front of a mirror and copy the thing from a jigsaw puzzle, I wonder? Maybe I'll ask him.

At least we're out of the snakepit, so the detox period is over, and they're gradually reducing the dosage of Valium they shove into us in the first week. I wonder what drugs they'll use to experiment on me this time, what combinations and dosages they'll think up to get me buzzing?

All I know is that I'm not buzzing now and it's Friday night and both Christopher and I are bored. Bored out of our minds. Neither of us can sleep. He's wearing a T-shirt with his tracksuit pants tonight and he's lying on top of his bed with his arms behind his head.

I can't sleep, I say.

Me either.

I sit up and lie down again.

I need something, I tell Christopher. I need a shot.

You'll be lucky. Have you seen who's on duty tonight?

Shit. What time is it? I can't sleep. I can't fucking sleep.

Me either.

We lie in silence for a while. I can hear a familiar theme tune coming from the TV in the lounge down the passage, but I can't place it. I lie there thinking for a bit. Dallas? No. That other one, with Ted whatsisname, the bartender oke who's an alcoholic? Can't get it.

I look across at Christopher, who looks like he might just be dropping off.

I knew this guy once, I tell him – Jeremy. He used to watch TV a lot. A *lot*. Like the minute supper was

353

over he'd be in the TV lounge and always in the same chair. I think it was here actually. Have you been in this rehab before?

Christopher's eyes fly open and he looks disorientated for a moment.

No, he says. Others, but not this one.

Well, anyway, I continue, having got his full attention, this guy Jeremy. We always wondered why he could sit in one spot and stare at the box for hours on end, and it wasn't even as if he was really *watching*. More like looking. You know what I mean?

Mm. Christopher's changed position. He's lying on his side now, watching me, with his hands folded neatly beneath his head. I can see a blue feather sticking out of the neck of his T-shirt. Do eagles really have a wonky crest like that on the top of their heads?

I carry on. Jeremy was so relaxed, I tell him. We all thought it was peculiar. He would just sit there, staring away, and gradually he would sink lower and lower in his chair until his eyes were practically closed.

I chuckle, remembering.

Well, asks Christopher. What was he on?

Whisky, I tell him.

Whisky?

Yeah. Through a drip he'd got all rigged up behind the speaker on the floor behind the door. Straight into the back of his knee.

Christopher whistles amazement. Fuuuck, he says. Fuuuck.

I think Jeremy was a doctor, I add, irrelevantly.

What happened to him, Christopher asks after a couple of minutes.

I heard he OD'd a week after he got out. I think it was pinks. Maybe pethidine. I forget.

We lie in silence a while longer. I have no idea what the time is. It could be seven o'clock or midnight.

I'm going to get something, I say suddenly, swinging my legs off the bed. I really can't sleep. I'm going crazy here. What time is it?

I don't know why I ask that. Neither of us has a watch and there are no clocks in our room. How would Christopher know?

I go shuffling along to the duty sister at the nurses' station. She eyes me suspiciously.

Sister, I say in a low, urgent voice. You gotta help me. I need something, man. I can't sleep. Please, hey?

Her eyes narrow a bit. Have you tried doing your breathing exercises, she asks.

Yes, I lie. I have, sister, and they're not working for me tonight. I just need a shot. Just a shot. You can give me one, can't you?

Have a mug of Milo, Steve, she suggests. You know I can't give you a shot. You know the rules here.

I'm getting agitated. A wave of aggression sweeps through me at her bland, expressionless face. Hasn't she heard me? I lean across the counter until my face is inches from hers.

I'm telling you, sister, I say. I'm *telling* you. I need a shot. You better give me one.

I start bunching and unbunching my hands and

I pace up and down in front of her like what I think an animal in a cage would do. Then I lunge at her across the counter area, stopping short just before our foreheads bump.

Just one, I say desperately. Nobody has to know. I wouldn't ask you if I wasn't –

She looks at me for another long minute. I think maybe I've blown it. Maybe the pacing was too much. Then abruptly she turns and disappears into the dispensary. She comes back with a syringe.

When I get back to my ward I'm eager to share the news with Christopher, but Christopher is fast asleep.

I stand beside his bed for a second, looking down at his chest, rising and falling evenly. He has a small smile turning up the corners of his mouth, like a child dreaming of nice things. This won't do. He'll miss a great opportunity.

I bend down and shake him vigorously by the shoulder. Christopher! Hey, Christopher! I got my shot! I got my shot, hey. Go get yours. Now! She'll give you a shot if you go now.

Christopher isn't having any. He is dead to the world. I grab his shoulder and shake him again. I keep doing this until he wakes up and stares blearily up at me with unfocused eyes.

I got my shot, I tell him again. I'm getting impatient now and the shot's beginning to take effect. Go get yours, bru.

So Christopher gets tiredly off the bed. Fuuuck,

he says. He stretches and yawns. He stumbles off to the nurses' station mumbling to himself, Got to get my shot, got to get my shot, and I vaguely hear voices coming from down there, but now I'm tripping, lying on my bed looking at the ceiling and smiling. It isn't long before I feel myself drifting off to sleep. How long it is before Christopher comes back to bed I don't know.

I catch up with him the next day before our first session (we're having a talk on time management today – *you* work it out).

Christopher looks awful.

What happened, I ask. Are you all right?

He doesn't look impressed by my fresh faced interest in his wellbeing but he tells me, in between yawns and stretching, that his quest had been less successful than mine. He has his shirt off again and each time he stretches the pigeon-eagle leers at me.

First of all, he says, the cow takes one look at me and asks if I'm sharing with you.

Uh-oh.

Yeah, well, I tell her yes but I can't sleep either, but I can scarcely keep my eyes open and I'm rubbing them and just about falling over and she's just looking at me like Yeah, right, I've been played once tonight and it's not going to happen again. Anyway, she takes me behind the counter right into the nurses' station and I think I'm going to get my shot but instead she shows me a chair. I'm like What the fuck –? and she just gives me this tight little smile and says *Have a seat* in this really menacing tone. But, sister, I insist,

I'm battling, hey. If you could just give me a – Have a seat, she says. I'm just heating up some Milo. That should do the trick.

Poor Christopher. She had him sitting with her at the nurses' station until six in the morning, pressing cup after cup of Milo into his hands. Finally, she let him go when the sun was coming up and he had to go and pee.

It's not funny, hey, Steve, he says. I pissed chocolate. I'm *still* pissing chocolate.

TWENTY

My mother was into spiritual things, especially after her husband died and her son continued his downward spiral into the underworld of drugs at a velocity that was nothing short of spectacular. She needed answers and she needed hope and, realising that she wasn't about to get either of those two things from me, she went looking for them elsewhere. She clung to conventional religion, taking comfort from Sunday service in the church down the road, but she consulted spiritualists, too, and occasionally accompanied my aunt to slightly off the wall church gatherings where women in cloaks brought consoling messages to the lonely from 'the other side'.

My mother had always taken a great deal of comfort from groups and she continued going to Al Anon, the AA support group for the families of alcoholics, long after my father got sober and even after his death.

Most of the time after my father died and I came out of the army she didn't know where I was. Months went by where I hardly knew where I was myself. Then I'd turn up out of the blue, broke, sick and wasted, and she'd take me in or march me off to rehab. When she didn't hear from me she would wait by the phone for the call she knew (and still believes) would come one day. It would be a dispassionate voice from a hospital or a police morgue, talking to her in letters. DOA or OD, and she didn't need an interpreter.

During the periods between institutions and prison, she tried to get me jobs, but the only one I really liked was the one at the casino – and look how that turned out. I think, before he died, she and my dad had hoped that the army would straighten me out. I'm afraid it was a vain hope. After two grim years in basics, interrupted at irregular intervals by my frequent internment in hospitals and clinics, and an awful time as a psych patient in One Mil Hospital, I think she gave up on that one. I still signed up for three month camps though and when these came up my mother would look cheerful and wave me off at the bus station, glad to have me removed for a while from my unsavoury friends who persisted in giving me drugs. If she'd had any hopes at all of me salvaging my career in the military, these were dashed forever when I was dishonourably discharged after about my fourth camp, facing twenty-five charges, from attempted murder to desertion.

At the court martial hearing I pleaded temporary insanity while under the influence of alcohol and dagga and got myself a two-year suspended sentence. It was a long and rather silly story and I never did tell my mother the details of it. It all started, if I remember rightly, over a sandwich that the cook refused to make for me and my buddy Brett because the kitchen was closed. Things kind of deteriorated from there really, but they probably wouldn't have if we hadn't been high at the time.

Anyway, there was a small issue of a rifle held at a one-liner's head and a carving knife at the cook's throat. After that the snowball effect kicked in and suddenly what we believed had been a reasonable request from two hungry soldiers had turned into a mini hostage situation that, unfortunately by then, included a sergeant major. When I realised that the situation was getting way out of control, I did what I do best. I left the hostages in Brett's care on the pretext of going to the toilet, squeezed through the bathroom window and hit the road, taking a stolen rifle with me for protection. I was picked up the next day by the military police and hauled back to face the music before being sent back to face my mother.

After my breakup with Tracey, when I'd come out of Lulama and was moping around at home waiting for my life to begin again and making an attempt to start Narcotics Anonymous, my mother made contact with a famous clairvoyant and medium. This was a woman who had been the catalyst for a book written by a man who had lost his son in a car accident. She had contacted him out of the blue with a message from his dead son. They had never met. They had never heard of each other. But what she told this boy's father, apparently, in detail, both about the accident and 'life on the other side', was extraordinary.

The medium lived in Natal and my mother persuaded her to come and see me. I'm not sure what she thought she could do for me, perhaps tell me that she saw a future for me without drugs in it. I wouldn't have put it past my mother to have *paid* her to say that, just to encourage me. Anyway, she didn't and she didn't say anything about drugs at all. She was big on reincarnation, though. I didn't even know how to spell the word, but she told me I had been a Chinese mandarin in a past life, that I had been shot twice, once in World War Two when a bullet went right through the palm of my hand – yes, that's right, and she turned over my hand and touched my accident scar. You died, she said, in that war, but you came back and lived to fight again.

She also told me that I would drive a funny car one day and make a lot of money, that I would meet someone very beautiful, a girl with long hair, much younger than me, who would change my life forever. She told me to be careful driving. There was something wrong with the front of my car. And if I had a friend with a foreign name who had a motorbike, I should tell him to be careful too, especially with the back of his bike.

Then, as she was leaving she turned. Oh, and I have a message for you from your father, she smiled. He says he can go fishing with you now.

A couple of days later I drove my Beetle into that stiff diagonal part of a telephone wire, the one that's anchored to the ground. I drove straight into it without seeing it and it split my car in two, like a knife slicing through paper.

My friend Blackie had a foreign name – Hungarian, or something – but nobody could pronounce it and somehow he just got called Blackie along the way. I didn't know this at the time. It was only after the chain on his motorcycle snapped and he lost a chunk of the back of his foot that it occurred to me to ask him.

Whether I believe in such things or not, I don't know now and I didn't know then, but I choose not to discount anything that appears to be out of the ordinary and not to scoff at what others put their faith in. Up until my last stay in rehab, at Phoenix House, I hadn't found a whole hell of a lot in my life to put faith in and even what happened to me there, when I was dying, I'm completely aware can be open to any number of interpretations. On the subject of near death experiences scientists will go into rapturous detail about chemical reactions in the brain that create the white light at the end of a tunnel effect and I've no doubt there's something in that. I'd be the first to admit that when you're close to death in a rehab clinic, ten to one there's some serious chemical clashing going on in your head.

Anyway, I'll tell you about my near death experience and you can make up your own mind. If you're that way inclined, you will have no doubt that it was God or some other supreme being talking directly to me, perhaps not in so many *words*, aside from the lying to my children part, but in images, certainly. If you're a non-believer you may choose to side with the scientists. The truth is, it doesn't actually matter. Maybe God is a frustrated scientist and it was him all the time, manipulating the scientists to manipulate the chemicals to cause my powerful dream that day.

Whatever.

See for yourself.

I had had enough of drugs and, in equal measure, I had had enough of drug programmes. I decided to die. It was a very conscious decision, made when I was sitting quietly at the back of yet another group session. I finally accepted as fact what I had already known subconsciously for a long time. Nothing the rehabs could do for me was ever going to work. That was it, plain and simple. I closed my eyes.

I remember being carried to my ward and being put into bed. I was very weak. I lay with my eyes closed, vaguely aware of people around me and one of the sisters sitting beside the bed, holding my hand and praying aloud. People came and went, in and out of my room, and stood looking down at me, talking in hushed voices. I couldn't hear what they were saying. I couldn't see them properly either. Their voices came from far away and when I opened my eyes their shapes were not clear either. There was a time when I had the illusion of being somewhere high up, looking down at the room and the people in it and the figure on the bed that was me, lying there so still and quiet. I tried but I couldn't get to them. I called out but they couldn't hear me.

This illusion of floating and looking down at yourself from a height is also well documented, by the way, and there are convincing scientific explanations for it too.

Then suddenly everything speeded up and I found myself propelled forward into a whirling kaleidoscopic vortex. I was falling, flying, tumbling, and waiting for the crash that would inevitably come. (I'm a drug addict, remember. I know how it works.) It didn't and I found myself being forced to look down at a scene that was taking place somewhere below me.

I saw a coke addict sitting among a mountain of white powder. He was shoving the powder up his nose and rubbing it on his gums, grabbing frantic handful after frantic handful. No matter how hard he tried, he couldn't get high. Then I saw an alcoholic surrounded by acres of booze. He poured bottle after bottle down his throat but he couldn't get drunk. Then a body-builder, a man with powerful shoulders and a stomach as flat as a board. Before my eyes I watched his flesh rot and fall from his bones until all that remained was a grinning skeleton. Next came a man who was sitting on a pile of money, a cascade of golden coins. He picked up a handful and let it fall through his fingers, then another, and another, and all the while his face was the saddest face I'd ever seen.

Then the images faded and I felt myself melting into what I can only describe as a warmth, a light-force that was so comforting that I wanted to stay wrapped in it for ever. I heard myself say, I'm tired. I'm so tired. I want to go home, and another voice in my head say No, you can't go home, Steve. Not yet. You can't go home. But I'm *tired*, I said. *Why* can't I go home? Because, said the voice, *they are lying to my children.*

I opened my eyes and looked around me. I wasn't confused. I knew exactly where I was – Phoenix House – but I also knew exactly what I had to do. I'd been in bed, more or less in a coma, for more than a week. I was as weak as a kitten. Even before I had decided to let go of my life, I hadn't been able to walk unaided. Now I sat up. I ripped the drip out of my arm. I swung my legs over the side of my bed like an athlete ready to go out for a training run, and I walked to the door.

I strode straight past the nurses' station without pausing and the two sisters on duty there gaped at me. After a second, one of them, the one who had prayed for my soul as I lay dying, came running after me.

Steve! What are you doing out of bed? What –? How –? But you can't –

I ignored her.

I walked down to the lounge where a few people were sitting about, smoking and watching TV. Andrea was there, and Miriam, and they stared at me just like the sisters had done. There was a white board at the far end of the lounge on the wall. Sometimes group sessions were held in there and the board was used in those. Sometimes people left messages on it for each other.

I rubbed the messages off with a swipe of my sleeve and began to draw. I stopped when I'd completed five sketches. It seemed like the right number. Then I threw down the marking pen and stood back and studied my curious artwork. A small crowd had gathered round me, inching forward without my noticing while I was drawing. I wasn't sure what I'd drawn myself actually and we stood there together, frowning in concentration and turning our heads sideways to follow the arrows and lines.

Some of the sketches were clearly my own visual interpretations of what I thought were the messages I needed to take from my dream, like the one of a syringe with an angel above it and three people bowing down before it. I'd also drawn a series of three dustbins, the last one full of overflowing, rotting garbage. What was that about – the need to get rid of your shit and not try to keep the lid on it because it would overflow in the end and turn nasty? Is that what we do, I wondered? Is that what *I* do?

My sketches stayed there for the rest of the time I was in Phoenix. Everyone gravitated towards them. No one erased them. They were endlessly discussed and dissected. The head of the clinic, Dr M, got to hear about them and he stopped by and, I learnt later, stood staring at them for a long time. Then he turned to the scattering of patients in the lounge.

Who did you say did these drawings, he asked.

Steve did, someone told him.

Steve did?

He came to my room the day I was packing my bag to leave, waiting only for my prescription to be filled at the dispensary.

You did those drawings, he asked me.

I nodded.

I've never seen anything like them, he said. They're very powerful. What made you draw them? What was your motivation, do you think?

I was guarded. I told him I wasn't sure. I didn't tell him about my dream, nor about the voice that had reverberated in my head, nor the growing conviction inside me that I had been chosen, picked out, selected from among a cast of thousands for a special mission. Can you *imagine* what that would sound like to a shrink? He'd have been out with the electrodes before you could say paranoid schizophrenia, for a start. Next thing I'd be telling him I was Charles Manson and had some business to finish off in Hollywood.

Drug-induced madness or just plain delusional – whatever spin you want to put on Steve the Amazing Anti-drug Crusader's great moment of truth, go ahead. I don't have the time or the education for a debate on theology versus science – I only have a Grade 9 Technical, don't forget. I don't have proof that a 'supreme being' exists or whether heaven is a place or a state of mind. I *do* know about hell, though. Hell exists. I've been there. I could draw you a map.

Anyway. If my mind was playing tricks on me, that was one thing. My body, however, was surely less easy to fool. I had been dying, no doubt about it, too weak to stand unaided or to totter so much as a few steps on my own. Then I lay in a coma for more than a week, while my body slowly but surely relinquished its grip on life. From a dying, crippled wraith of a man to someone who could stride down the corridor bursting with purpose and vigour – well, you tell me.

As I've said before: the mind is a powerful thing. And if that's all there is to it, you know what, hey? That's a good thing. That's a very good thing for an addict to know.

∗

What will you do now, Dr M asked me. You're leaving us today, I believe?

Yes, I said. I'm going out there to tell the truth.

And the truth is –?

I looked at him steadily. I liked Dr M. He was a good person, doing his best to help people in trouble.

That there's no cure, I told him. That there's no cure for addiction.

He turned away from me then and stopped half-way down the passage. I heard his footsteps returning.

You'll never make it, he told me. You know that, Steve, don't you?

＊

That was the day I got on the bus and worked my way through half a packet of Tryptanol before we reached Durban. Not exactly a good start, I agree, but no one said it was going to be easy.

After a few days at home I went to look up Kenneth and see how Narcotics Anonymous was shaping. I was amazed. In the months that I'd been gone it had grown into a respectable organisation. We hadn't been wrong about the need for this group and that was gratifying.

As a founder member, I was invited along to a meeting one evening as a guest speaker. There were two types of NA meetings, an open one, that the public could attend, and a closed one, that was addicts only. The one I was due to attend was a closed meeting and I was looking forward to it in an odd kind of way, although, as had happened before at the girls' school, I wasn't sure just what I was going to say yet.

A few minutes into my talk I began to feel uneasy. My addict's sensors were picking up something that didn't quite fit. Drug squad? This might have been a private, closed meeting, but the chances of a deal going down here or at least one member of the audience having a bankie of weed in a pocket were fairly high. I had one myself. I shrugged the feeling off and carried on for a couple more minutes but I still wasn't happy. Then I got it. There were four people sitting together near the back who weren't addicts. They weren't drug squad either, but they weren't addicts.

I didn't say anything then but I cut the meeting short. As the group broke up into smaller groups, some guys heading for the trestle table and tea, others putting on their jackets and getting ready to go home, I accosted the group. They looked startled that I'd called their bluff so quickly and confessed that they were students doing research for a play about drugs which they hoped to perform in schools. Two of the students were actors and they played characters called Tracey – good choice! – and Johan, who were junkies on their way out. They had a narrator and a stage manager.

After we had chatted for a while, one of the girls, Amanda, asked rather shyly if I would like to come along to a rehearsal and see what they were doing. Perhaps, if I didn't mind, I could even offer a bit of advice. From the horse's mouth, so to speak.

So I did. I went to more than one rehearsal and I gave my opinion on this and that. I also suggested, hoping that they wouldn't regard it as an intrusion from someone who didn't know the first thing about acting, that they think about bringing a real addict on stage at the end of the show, after the curtains had closed, who would say something along the lines of What you've just seen is true.

A real live addict. Where had I heard that before? What was I getting myself into?

I could do it, if you like, I suggested. Just to see, I mean. It may not work, of course. It's probably a stupid idea. I'm sorry I suggested it. I'll just –

Yes, said Amanda/Tracey. I think it's a great idea.

Let's give it a try.

I had nothing better to do. I didn't have a job and while I still wasn't exactly a model citizen and was smoking some weed every other day, I was determined to find some kind of work for the idle hands my mother worried so much about. I might not have been an actor, but I was damn well more qualified than anyone else I knew to play the part of Johan. Not that the actor himself wasn't convincing – he was, but I was becoming conscious, after the first few times we tried it and it worked, that the biggest applause for *Drug!* came at the very end, after the curtains had closed. That was when I came on and said my single line.

Still, I had no ambition to be an actor. My instincts, I discovered to my surprise, leant more towards directing. In my wildest dreams I would never have thought I had an aptitude for something like that. I didn't even know it *was* directing, in fact. I was just happy sitting on the sidelines and making the odd suggestion. They listened to me when I told them stories, really listened, and when they used my suggestions, sometimes to great dramatic effect, I was amazed at how good it made me feel. Not as good as a line of coke, you understand, but good enough in the circumstances.

After about three months of hanging around with the group as their unofficial adviser, they asked me to join them on a semi-permanent basis. They didn't plan for the play to run quite as long as *Cats*, they explained to me, so I shouldn't get my hopes up that this was a real job or anything, and there wasn't too much money to be shared among us – they charged R200 a show at schools – but what the hell? Would I at least think about it? The response they'd been getting so far had been so positive that they were even thinking seriously about taking the play to the Grahamstown Festival and seeing how it measured up against some other fringe productions. And who knew what might happen after that? They were drama students, keen to make their mark and do some work that was both worthwhile as well as challenging to them as artists.

By this time Amanda and I were involved. She was a good actress but she'd never done drugs and I had never had a relationship with someone who was a straight. Perhaps that was part of the attraction at first, for both of us. While for me, being with her might help to keep me focused and drug free, for her I think I represented the dark and the dangerous. Remember what I said about addicts being relationship time bombs? Right from the start ours was ticking. Anyway, I like to think it worked in its own way, on a number of unexpected levels. When we hit difficult patches, though, it wasn't easy to get past them and there were huge gaping holes in the way we communicated. Sometimes we just couldn't relate to each other at all. One of my problems, I think, was that I didn't understand the *giving* part of a relationship. Giving, emotionally, I mean, was a completely foreign concept for me. All of my experiences up till then, with women too, had been using ones. They were all transactions of one sort or another, with drugs at their centre. I didn't know there was another way to be.

I overheard the tail end of a conversation one day that Amanda was having with her father. He had viewed me with distrust from the start. I don't think I was what he had in mind for his only daughter and in hindsight I can't really blame him. He had never been comfortable with me living, as I was by then, in their basement and being free to come and go in their house. They had a lot of valuable stuff.

The sooner you break up with Steve, the better, is what I overheard. He's nothing but a burnt-out drug addict.

That wasn't the part that hurt, though. I knew what I was, no surprise there. What hurt was Amanda's response.

I'm trying, dad, she said. I'm trying . . .

The whole group was showing signs of breaking up. We'd been on the road together a while but, to tell the truth, I had never felt unconditionally accepted. I was different from them. Grahamstown had been a success and my 'performance' (I'd graduated to playing Johan by then, after 'Johan' had gone off to do something else for a while and hadn't come back) had been the one the critics had liked the most. I think by then I was the one most passionately involved in *Drug!* and I still gave it everything I had.

We moved it up north and started doing schools around Joburg and Pretoria.

Then Amanda went overseas. The excuse was a

family wedding, but I don't think that was the real reason she went. I detected her father's prints all over the plan. I tried not to let it bother me and Amanda called every few days. What puzzled me was that she didn't seem to have a clear idea of when she'd be returning and when I pressed her she became vague. Eventually, the old cliché happened. I got a letter in the post and the time bomb went off.

For a week I closeted myself with my old friends, the ones in bottles, and I found myself staring into the abyss once more. This time its appeal was more mesmerising than ever, way more seductive than anything else anyone could have offered me right then. What had I been thinking? I was nothing but a burnt-out drug addict, after all, and who gave a fuck anyway? Well, my poor long-suffering mother did, for one – the only one, I might add. She got on a plane and came and stayed with me. She wiped up the puke and took my abuse until gradually, painfully, I dragged myself to my unsteady feet.

I didn't feel good though. I knew I wasn't coping well at all. We had bookings for the play and schools were phoning constantly. I was the only one there to fend off the calls. The stress of not knowing what to tell them made me frantic. What could I say? That my lead actress had absconded with my heart and the real live addict was hell bent on changing that description into a real *dead* one? I began to realise that I had relied more on this job and this small group of people than was healthy. Joining up and touring with them was supposed to have been an interim thing while I was getting my act together to go out and spread the word, just as soon as I discovered what the word was. I'd allowed myself to get distracted and emotionally involved when I was supposed to be finding my focus. Now, with chaos threatening, I felt adrift and at risk and there wasn't a bloody boat in sight. I dug deep to try and find the remnants of that conviction that had carried me out of Phoenix but I came up empty. Maybe I'd imagined the whole thing.

Crisis point.

I called a rehab clinic in Joburg and asked if I could come in. I knew I would feel safer there. In rehab I wouldn't have to pretend I was normal. I wouldn't have to *act* a drug addict. I could *be* one. I could just be me.

They said I should come through right away.

I didn't though. I sat in an old, sagging armchair and I rolled a joint.

Just one.

Tomorrow, I told myself. I'll go through tomorrow.

It was quiet in the house. I'd been staying there on my own after the others left. We'd paid a month's rent in advance and I still had three days to go. I sat and smoked and watched the evening spread softly over the hills I could see from the windows of the front room. I could hear music coming from somewhere, faintly, but I couldn't place the tune. Across the valley lay a squatter camp and the smell of cooking fires made me feel homesick and depressed. I thought about John and wondered how he was. I thought about Tracey in her silent world, and Brian and James. I thought about my father.

Then the telephone rang and it made me jump. I realised that it had grown almost dark while I'd been sitting there and it took a moment for my eyes to adjust.

I reached out a hand and picked up the receiver.

It was the headmaster of the high school on the East Rand that had been leaving endless messages on the machine, none of which I'd been in any condition to return. It didn't matter anymore now. It was over.

Is that Steve, the headmaster asked. He sounded anxious.

Yes, I said.

Oh, thank goodness. *At last.* I'd almost given up *hope.* He laughed nervously. Steve, look –

I'm afraid we're not –

We both talked over each other at the same time and I didn't have a chance to finish my sentence, to tell him that I was sorry but I couldn't help him, that this was one show that wasn't going to go on.

Steve, he interrupted. Look. We need you. We *really* need you here.

I didn't know what to say so I didn't say anything.

Steve, he said. Are you there? Is this a bad time for you?

I almost laughed out loud. *Is this a bad time for you?* I still couldn't speak.

Look, he said again. May I call back tomorrow? On this number?

Then, Yes, I said quietly. Call tomorrow. But no, not on this number.

And I gave him the number of the clinic.

EPILOGUE

At the airport in Windhoek I'm waiting to catch a plane home. It has been a gruelling fortnight of difficult schools with huge drug problems. Namibia is one of the most notorious drug trafficking routes into South Africa and no one seems to care terribly much about it.

Today I am feeling particularly disheartened. I am close to packing it all in. When I get home, I decide, I'll talk to Candy about it. She will understand. I can't carry on fighting this war all by myself and sometimes it feels exactly like that's what I'm doing. It's just too much. I remember a vision I had once of this enormous tidal wave building to a peak before it comes crashing down. I'm the guy on the boogie board at the bottom and I can see that no amount of frantic paddling will get me out of the way in time.

Today has been the worst day of a dreadful week.

Big twenty year old boys in matric laughed all the way through my show. They'd sat in the middle rows flirting with the girls and passing loud remarks. No matter what I did I couldn't get their attention. My tragic life story was one big joke to them. Their gelled hair and smartass attitude irritated me beyond anything. I even caught the principal smirking out of the corner of my eye.

I hear my flight being called and I drag myself to my feet. As I am making my way through the crowd to get to the right gate, laden with bags and equipment, my boarding pass in my mouth, a sturdy boy of about seventeen plants himself squarely in my path. Shit. I don't need any more crap today. He has a cheeky face, black, black eyes, dreds and a rasta bracelet.

Hey, Steve, he challenges me.

That's me.

He grins, bright white teeth in a black face.

Keep doing what you're doing, man, he says.

Why, I ask him. I really want to know.

Because it's working.

He touches me on the arm, a light punch with his fist, and disappears in the crowd behind me. When I turn to look for him, he is gone.

Acknowledgements

There are so many people I need to thank – individuals who have touched my life by their words of encouragement and their thank you's; the thousands of children who have allowed me to bare my soul and listened to my message; teachers and headmasters who have welcomed me into their schools, trusting me with the lives with which they in turn have been entrusted. Many times, when I have felt I can't go on, I have been approached by a child who has motivated me to do one more school . . . Thank you.

In addition certain people, companies and organisations have given generously in many different ways to help me do what I do, and I acknowledge them here: Pam and Harry Wertheim, for so much; Theo and Louise Moolman; Chow Bissel; Mike Kingaby; Spur Steak Ranches; Protea Hotels; Bulldog Technologies;

Printomatic; Pick 'n Pay; Marcus Brewster Publicity; Nashua; Telkom ; Westbank; Clarins; St Elmo's Trading; Usabco; Automac Motors; Hertz; Omnigraphics; Market Toyota; Budget Car Hire; 702 Radio; Cape Talk Radio; Lions International; Rotary; Round Table.

Arthur Gillis, of course: thank you for believing in me.

And Alison – I could never have told my story to anyone else. Her compassion and her special talent made this book possible.

Lastly, to the future of our country, the youth: may you forever remain drug free! Don't be like me.

Steve

POEM FOR MY MOTHER

Dear mom
When you gave birth to me, you had dreams for me.
You wanted me to be something special.
I turned out to be your worst nightmare.
We call it a drug addict and alcoholic.

I'm sorry for stealing your wedding ring, and giving it
to the dealers.
They will never return it.
Forgive me for saying I hate you a million times.
I never meant it once.
It was the drugs in my head.
Thank you for standing in the rain waiting to see me
while I was in prison.
Where were my friends? Too scared, remember?
Thank you for wiping the vomit from my mouth when
I was strapped down in so many mental institutions,
because of the drugs, trips in my head.
Again – where were my friends? Too scared, remember?

Mom, if I die, do not cry.
Maybe I will be free, but not because of E.
OCTC will split my brain from my skull.
My liver my kidneys my heart will fail . . .
And when I do the dance of death,
When I die,

The DJs will never cry . . .
Because there are thousands of Steves waiting to take
my place.
The dealers, my friends, are dead and dying.
They will never send flowers to my funeral,
So I will send you three – for that precious son I could
never be.
You see, mom, my first time was free.
My second, my third, my fourth times were free.
And then the dealers said Steve – it is time
That you owe me.

Your precious child
Steve

Hazelden Publishing and Educational Services is a division of the Hazelden Foundation, a not-for-profit organization. Since 1949, Hazelden has been a leader in promoting the dignity and treatment of people afflicted with the disease of chemical dependency.

The mission of the foundation is to improve the quality of life for individuals, families, and communities by providing a national continuum of information, education, and recovery services that are widely accessible; to advance the field through research and training; and to improve our quality and effectiveness through continuous improvement and innovation.

Stemming from that, the mission of this division is to provide quality information and support to people wherever they may be in their personal journey—from education and early intervention, through treatment and recovery, to personal and spiritual growth.

Although our treatment programs do not necessarily use everything Hazelden publishes, our bibliotherapeutic materials support our mission and the Twelve Step philosophy upon which it is based. We encourage your comments and feedback.

The headquarters of the Hazelden Foundation are in Center City, Minnesota. Additional treatment facilities are located in Chicago, Illinois; Newberg, Oregon; New York, New York; Plymouth, Minnesota; St. Paul, Minnesota; and West Palm Beach, Florida. At these sites, we provide a continuum of care for men and women of all ages. Our Plymouth facility is designed specifically for youth and families.

For more information on Hazelden, please call **1-800-257-7800**. Or you may access our World Wide Web site on the Internet at **www.hazelden.org**.